American
Women
Writing
Fiction

American Women Writing Fiction

Memory, Identity, Family, Space

Mickey Pearlman, Editor

THE UNIVERSITY PRESS OF KENTUCKY

Copyright © 1989 by The University Press of Kentucky

Scholarly publisher for the Commonwealth,
serving Bellarmine College, Berea College, Centre
College of Kentucky, Eastern Kentucky University,
The Filson Club, Georgetown College, Kentucky
Historical Society, Kentucky State University,
Morehead State University, Murray State University,
Northern Kentucky University, Transylvania University,
University of Kentucky, University of Louisville,
and Western Kentucky University.

Editorial and Sales Offices: Lexington, Kentucky 40506-0336

Library of Congress Cataloging-in-Publication Data

American women writing fiction : memory, identity, family, space /
    Mickey Pearlman, editor.

    p. cm.
    ISBN 0-8131-1657-0; 0-8131-0182-4
    1. American fiction—Women authors—History and criticism.
2. American fiction—20th century—History and criticism.
3. American fiction—Women authors—Bibliography. 4. American
fiction—20th century—Bibliography. 5. Women and literature
—United States—History—20th century. 6. Women in literature.
I. Pearlman, Mickey, 1938-
PS374.W6A46 1988
813'.54'099287—dc19   88-18667

CONTENTS

Introduction   I
MICKEY PEARLMAN

JOYCE CAROL OATES / The Enclosure of Identity
in the Earlier Stories   9
FRANK R. CUNNINGHAM
A Bibliography of Writings by Joyce Carol Oates   28
A Bibliography of Writings about Joyce Carol Oates   35
ANNE HIEMSTRA

MARY GORDON / The Struggle with Love   47
A Bibliography of Writings by Mary Gordon   60
A Bibliography of Writings about Mary Gordon   63
JOHN W. MAHON

JOAN DIDION / The Bond between Narrator and
Heroine in *Democracy*   69
A Bibliography of Writings by Joan Didion   86
A Bibliography of Writings about Joan Didion   89
KATHERINE USHER HENDERSON

LOUISE ERDRICH / Of Cars, Time, and the
River   95
MARVIN MAGALANER
A Bibliography of Writings by Louise Erdrich   108
A Bibliography of Writings about Louise Erdrich   110
MICKEY PEARLMAN

ALISON LURIE / The Uses of Adultery   115
KATHARINE M. ROGERS
A Bibliography of Writings by Alison Lurie   128
A Bibliography of Writings about Alison Lurie   130
MICKEY PEARLMAN

SUSAN FROMBERG SCHAEFFER / The Power of Memory, Family, and Space   137
A Bibliography of Writings by Susan Fromberg Schaeffer   147
A Bibliography of Writings about Susan Fromberg
    Schaeffer   150
MICKEY PEARLMAN

TONI CADE BAMBARA / The Dance of Character and Community   155
A Bibliography of Writings by Toni Cade Bambara   166
A Bibliography of Writings about Toni Cade Bambara   168
MARTHA M. VERTREACE

GAIL GODWIN / The Odd Woman and Literary Feminism   173
RACHEL M. BROWNSTEIN
A Bibliography of Writings by Gail Godwin   184
A Bibliography of Writings about Gail Godwin   187
MICKEY PEARLMAN

JAYNE ANNE PHILLIPS / Women's Narrative and the Recreation of History   193
A Bibliography of Writings by Jayne Anne Phillips   206
A Bibliography of Writings about Jayne Anne Phillips   207
PHYLLIS LASSNER

MARY LEE SETTLE / "Ambiguity of Steel"   213
JANE GENTRY VANCE
A Selected Bibliography of Writings by Mary Lee Settle   225
A Selected Bibliography of Writings about Mary Lee
    Settle   227
JANE GENTRY VANCE and MICKEY PEARLMAN

Notes on the Writers   231

Notes on the Contributors   235

I will try
to fasten into order enlarging grasps of disorder, widening
scope, but enjoying the freedom that
Scope eludes my grasp, that there is no finality of vision,
that I have perceived nothing completely,
that tomorrow a new walk is a new walk.

—A.R. Ammons

Introduction

Mickey Pearlman

It is a commonplace in criticism to define American literature, in short story or novel form, as the chronicle of the solitary hero, of man alone, man against society, man as individual, endlessly testing his strength and durability against his own resources on a mythic, adventurous journey to epiphany and knowledge.

American literature, we are taught, is about space, open space, and the ways in which hearty or hesitant, defiant or defensive, American heroes experience both its potential and its limitations. American heroes live beyond society, and they are both freed by, and victimized by, the lack of entrenched behavior patterns. Walter Allen, for instance, says that "American literature is less interested in redemption than in the eternal struggle of good and evil; it is less interested in reconciliation than it is in disorder,"[1] and he suggests that the interior dramas of the great characters of the American Renaissance are expressed in symbolic terms encased in stories of initiation, isolation, transformation, and vindication.

American literature, we are taught, is about escape, escape from perceived or real evil (Hawthorne), from intellectual anguish (Bellow), from the debilitating effects of social, political, and religious forces (Dreiser, Mailer, Malamud), from the castrating parental figure (Washington Irving, Roth), or from psychological disorder (Melville), from materialism and the masses (Whitman), from the drudgery of the commonplace (Hemingway), from time that either entraps you (Faulkner) or that is amorphous and free-flowing (Twain).

American literature is about escaping from our propensity to become grotesques (Fitzgerald) and about the self-serving safety of life as a grotesque (Anderson). As Leslie Fiedler says, the "figure of Rip Van Winkle presides over the birth of the American imagination,"[2] the ancestor of Natty Bumppo and Rabbit Angstrom, of Ahab and Gatsby, of Yossarian and Jake Barnes, of Billy Budd and Miss Lonelyhearts, of Henderson the Rain King and "The Invisible Man" and scores of masculine and maverick heroes, most of them running from supposed shrews and bitches to symbolic women in mythical milieus. And, of course, all the while dreaming, sleeping, preferring (before and since Melville's Bartleby) "not to," opting out of society and still "lighting out for the territory" in a search for identity without the intertwining anchors of memory and family.

These, of course, are works written by American men, and they are, despite the engrossing portraits of Hester and the Daisys, Dilsey and Isabel Archer, among others, about men. Moreover, these are novels and stories that Adrienne Rich tells the reader to see with new eyes, and to know in a different way, because "once we pay attention to the crucial role the protagonist's sex plays in shaping the plot, its place in literary tradition irrevocably shifts."[3]

What happens, then, when American literature is written by women: by the fifth-generation native Californian Joan Didion in the West; by Mary Gordon and Susan Fromberg Schaeffer in the ethnic, urban Northeast; by Alison Lurie at Cornell, where bumper stickers read "Ithaca, New York: Centrally Isolated"; by women *from* the South (Jayne Anne Phillips and Gail Godwin) and women *in* the South (Mary Lee Settle), where a "strong sense of place continues to shape the Southern characters' view of themselves"[4] even though "today's South is more typically urban than rural . . . more mobile and transient than rooted in the southern past"[5]? What changes are produced by the Native American Louise Erdrich, member of the Chippewa nation, who was raised near the Turtle Mountain Reservation in North Dakota and now lives and writes near Dartmouth in Cornish, New Hampshire? What changes are wrought by Toni Cade Bambara, since historically "the problems and pleasures of Black [female] life have been defined, ill-defined, and redefined, explained and re-explained, sawed and chewed and twisted, more often than not."[6] What changes occur when American literature is not only written by American women but uses women as narrators? Diane Johnson notes the "problem that comes from having as your central character a female person. The male narrative voice is still accorded more authority. The female narrative voice is always questioned—is she crazy? Are the things she's saying a delusion, or reality?"[7]

What happens to the concept of open space, the notion that escape is a viable, even an enviable, option as it is for American heroes, or to the enigmatic problem of identity: how you acquire it and how you protect it? All women, as has been repeatedly documented, gain identity, personhood, voice, by association—somebody's daughter, mother, sister, wife. They are caught, repeatedly, in the double bind of the female, responsible for both the trivia and the significant emotional memorabilia that link the experience of family members, thereby providing an environment for identity, and, at the same time, denied both the opportunity and the initiative for identity independent of those very links or the means to escape from the memories they helped to create. And these ten authors write about identity, whether it is Gail Godwin struggling with the "time-honored roles for [southern] women: the Southern lady, the belle, the sheltered white woman on a pedestal, the pious matriarch, the naive black girl, the enduring black mother"[8] or Joan Didion, whose women share "a sense of living one's deepest life underwater." (Mary Gordon chronicles the often thwarted Irish-American women suffocating above water.) Joyce Carol Oates and Louise Erdrich, who seem at first glance to have little more in common than gender, create fictional families marked both by interior or exterior violence and by pain. Susan Fromberg Schaeffer, who writes in her recent novels of verbal, neurotic Brooklynites, and Mary Lee Settle, whose West Virginia characters are obsessed by mystery and hatred, both acknowledge the labyrinth of family and the often negative and imprisoning power of memory. To quote Nina Auerbach, there is no "common female experience that makes sense of all women and of the books they write."[9] That is not to say, however, that different experiences have not had similar and resounding effects on these ten authors since all of these authors write in the long and glorious tradition of various foremothers and godmothers and the time-honored struggle represented in Muriel Rukeyser's poem "Myth."

> Long afterward, Oedipus, old and blinded, walked the
> roads.   He smelled a familiar smell. It was
> the Sphinx.   Oedipus said, "I want to ask one question.
> Why didn't I recognize my mother?"   "You gave the
> wrong answer," said the Sphinx.   "But that was what
> made everything possible," said Oedipus.   "No," she said.
> "When I asked, What walks on four legs in the morning,
> two at noon, and three in the evening, you answered,
> Man.   You didn't say anything about woman."

"When you say Man," said Oedipus, "you include women
too. Everyone knows that."   She said, "That's what
you think."

Sandra Gilbert and Susan Gubar in *The Norton Anthology of
Literature by Women* suggest that in the last forty years "women
writers . . . [developed] a newly intense awareness of their role as
female artists . . . [with] a great [inherited female] tradition, and a
newly protective sense of their vulnerability as women who inhab-
ited a culture hostile to female ambition and haunted by eroticized
images of women,"[10] an explanation more social than biological. In
Literary Women Ellen Moers suggests that what women writers have
in common are "women's bodies, which affect their senses and their
imagery," a "girl"-centered upbringing that gives women "a special
perception of the cultural imprinting of childhood. They are assigned
roles in the family and in courtship, . . . given or denied access to
education and employment, [and to] . . . property and political representation, [all means of differentiating] women from men. [Con-
sequently, Moers adds,] if they denied their bodies, denied whatever
was special about being a woman, they would be only narrowly
human and could hardly be much good as writers,"[11] an explanation
more biological than social. Patricia Meyer Spacks adds that "the
note of pessimism is pervasive in women's writing when it focuses on
women's fate: true amelioration rarely seems conceivable."[12] And in
1986 Elizabeth Janeway said that what influences writing by women
is not their biological sameness, or their socially determined roles,
but the commonality of their audience. It is, she says, "the continuing difficulty that the rest of the human race has in imagining
that the experience of women could be pertinent to their own
lives. . . . Our lives are still regarded as irrelevant and even as abnormal. . . . In the past women's lives were disregarded or undervalued
because everyone thought they were less important than those of
men. At present, yes, we have come a short way—society is willing to
agree that women's lives may often be important to women, but they
are never accepted as being equally important to men's."[13]

The ten writers represented here do not share identical insights
about the experience of women (or of men), and their content ranges
from Phillips's machine dreams to Didion's recent musings on democracy. What, then, if anything, does unite them, considering their
widely divergent regional, ethnic, and generational perspectives? It is
still possible to suggest that some common preoccupations do exist,
but it would be facile and superficial to suggest that American wo-

men write about memory, identity, family, and space and that men do not. It is not inconsistent to suggest that these ten writers are, to varying degrees, aware of the changes in the lives of contemporary American women and of the tension that change inevitably provokes. That tension is recorded and explicated from multiple angles of vision here, and it leads to a refocusing on thematic ideas like family and memory and identity.

Most American women do not write of open spaces and open roads, rife with potential and possibilities, or of successful escapes from multiple and various enemies. They write, from Edith Wharton to Sue Miller, of the usually imprisoning psychological and actual spaces of American women, of being trapped, submerged, overwhelmed, of the "suffocation of family life,"[14] and of the "suffering of living."[15] American women write about "caged birds," as Maya Angelou put it, who "sing" as a plaintive wail against confinement and emotional inundation at the hands of the family. In the southern gothic stories of Carson McCullers, Flannery O'Connor, and Eudora Welty, literary foremothers for women writers nationwide, generations of women age and atrophy in lonely houses and sad cafes; in Eudra Welty's story, "Why I Live at the P.O.," the unloved daughter moves only from the suffocating fiefdom of family squabbles to the equally enclosed space of the local post office. Flannery O'Connor's Hulga/Joy character, who dominates "Good Country People," becomes a symbolic female figure—trapped not so much by her wooden leg as by the internalized inertia of a woman burdened by her mother's familial myths, her own emptiness, and the actual spaces of a country house and barn in a bleak and vapid environment that mirrors her own emotional decay. Hulga is surrounded by spiritual and intellectual ugliness, and she chooses that ugliness as a way of life. Tillie Olsen, worlds away in the urban blue-collar world of the Midwest, wrote about the silences that for women are both the safehouses and the penitentiaries of the powerless, and she has noted repeatedly that society finds it convenient and expedient to silence writing women. Women also lapse into silence as a defense against the world, a protective space that demoralizes the silenced. Olsen evokes this in her famous story, "I Stand Here Ironing," where a tired and enervated mother, dreaming of recovery and reconciliation, hopes her daughter will be more "than this dress on the ironing board, helpless before the iron." Silence is an emotional space that evokes a sense of imprisonment, of enclosure and entrapment. Louise Erdrich, for instance, who writes about "the insistent tug of memory," evokes in Love Medicine the stolid, grudging silences of her North Dakotan plainswomen whose sense of helplessness and quiet desperation transcends their native American experience. In her second novel, *The Beet Queen*, a work curiously marked by images of flight and fantasy, the white women are no less immured in the impossible. And in Phillips the characters "strive mightily to protect themselves, though usually they can't. They are hard and smart and heroic and they suffer anyway. There is a sense of intrusion . . . obligation intruding on solitude, death intruding on life, chaos ever seeping in through the cracks."[16]

The ten critics represented in this book were asked to recognize the reoccurrence of these themes but to go beyond them in ways they found most appropriate. Consequently, all of the essays published here were written specifically for this collection and are being published here for the first time. A conscious effort has been made by both the editor and the critics to avoid vocabulary that would make these essays inaccessible to readers unfamiliar with the terms of literary theory. Finally, the choice of Oates, Gordon, Didion, Erdrich, Lurie, Schaeffer, Bambara, Godwin, Phillips, and Settle was made by the editor and could easily have been doubled in number. Fortunately, there is an abundance of energetic, evocative, and original American women who are writing in our time. None of these voices should be silenced, and we can only hope they will be analyzed in future volumes. It should be noted that these are working writers; without exception they will have more to say, and nothing published here can represent a final assessment of a career in progress.

The bibliographies of works by the authors are also original and have been included to make it easier for readers, critics, and teachers to explore, experience, and teach more deeply the work of these authors, who are a part of the plot of America's literature and not a subplot variously labeled women's literature, for, by, or about women. In addition, this collection includes a selected bibliography of works about each author; this is the editor's acknowledgment of that criticism that has preceded ours, much of which is both useful and important.

American literature is no longer the refuge of the solitary hero. Like the society that it mirrors, it is, in 1988, a far richer, many-faceted explication of a complicated and diverse group of people—racially, culturally, and ethnically comingled and interwoven and, at the same time, fractured, fractious, and dichotomous. The authors represented here reflect that diversity, and by writing in America today, they have changed the pages of American literature into a broader, wider reflection of the people we are.

NOTES

1. Walter Allen, *The Modern Novel in Britain and the United States* (New York: E.P. Dutton, 1964), xvi.

2. Leslie Fiedler, *Love and Death in the American Novel* (New York: Stein and Day, 1966), 26.

3. Joseph A. Boone, "Point of View." *Chronicle of Higher Education*, July 8, 1987, 76.

4. Peggy W. Prenshaw, "Introduction," in *Women Writers of the Contemporary South*, ed. Peggy W. Prenshaw (Jackson: Univ. Press of Mississippi, 1984), viii.

5. Ibid.

6. Roseann Bell, Bettye S. Parker, and Beverly Guy-Sheftall, eds., *Sturdy Black Bridges* (Garden City, N.Y.: Anchor Press/ Doubleday, 1979), 235.

7. Marilyn Yalom, ed., *Women Writers of the West Coast* (Santa Barbara: Capra Press, 1983), 127.

8. Prenshaw, "Introduction," viii.

9. Nina Auerbach, *Romantic Imprisonment* (New York: Columbia Univ. Press, 1986), xxiv.

10. Sandra Gilbert and Susan Gubar, *The Norton Anthology of Literature by Women* (New York: W.W. Norton & Co., 1985), 1677.

11. Ellen Moers, *Literary Women* (New York: Oxford Univ. Press, 1985), xi.

12. Patricia Meyer Spacks, "Introduction," in *Contemporary Women Novelists*, ed. P.M. Spacks (Englewood Cliffs, N.J.: Prentice-Hall, 1977), 8.

13. Elizabeth Janeway, "Prioritizing the World," *Chronicle of Higher Education*, Dec. 17, 1986.

14 Mary F. Robertson, "Medusa Points and Contact Points," in *Contemporary American Women Writers*, ed. Catherine Rainwater and William J. Scheick (Lexington: Univ. Press of Kentucky, 1985), 136.

15. Ronald Schleifer, "Chaste Compactness," in *Contemporary American Women Writers*, ed. Catherine Rainwater and William J. Scheick (Lexington: Univ. Press of Kentucky, 1985), 37.

16. Peter Nelson, *Vis a Vis*, May 1987, 80.

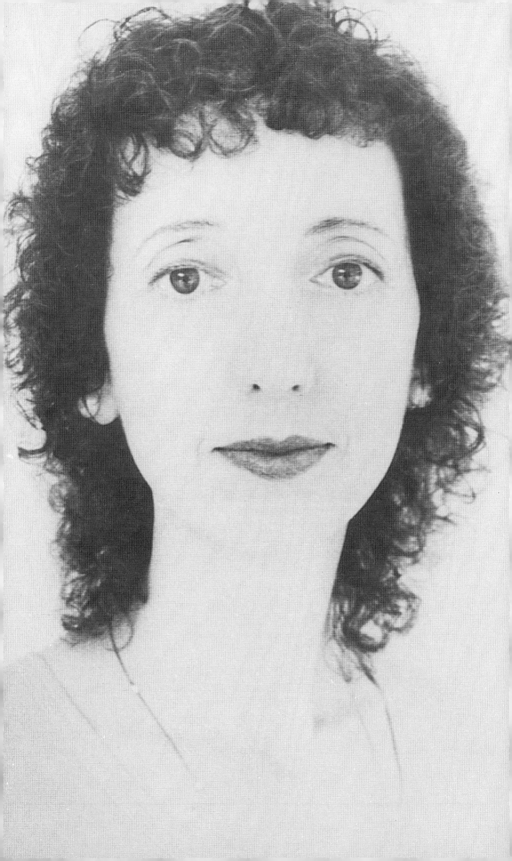

JOYCE CAROL OATES

The Enclosure of Identity in the Earlier Stories

Frank R. Cunningham

"Halfway through the decade, something went terribly wrong. The most useful image I have today is of a man in a quagmire, looking into a tear in the sky."

John Cheever[1]

Joyce Carol Oates was in her late teenage years in upper New York State in the mid-fifties when John Cheever sensed the onset of the postwar dissolution of value and coherence since noted by so many men and women writing in America. Perhaps it was this sense of almost overwhelming social and international forces that seemed to minimize our human stature, to displace and diminish us in relation to the vast organizational structures brought about by the war effort and the postwar institutionalization of the corporate way of living, that contributed to Oates's fascination over nearly the last three decades with the encirclement and twisting of human identity that is so prevalent in her fiction. Many critical observers have commented upon the almost pervasive pessimism and bleakness throughout her stories and novels,[2] a vision sometimes approaching morbidity. From the psychotic who consumes broiled female human sexual organs in *Wonderland* (1971) to the suicidal violence in *You Must Remember This* (1987), from the emotionally dead brother smoking out the remains of his life in "A Legacy" (1961; collected in *By the North*

Gate, 1963)[3] to the raped suburban housewife of "The Double-edged Knife" (1987),[4] Oates's characters are unique in contemporary American fiction in the frequency and severity of their destructive behavior, as Oates has created—and continues prolifically to create—a panoramic vision of an America in which, indeed, something has gone "terribly wrong." Particularly in her realistic stories and novels, Oates seems intent to show us that forces both societal and natural have led to the crippling of a sense of willed, formed identity, a constructed selfhood, among large numbers of people of the middle and working classes in America who can (sometimes, we like to think) deal effectively with the pressures and even the horrors of contemporary life. Perhaps the greatest terror in confronting Oates's work lies in the critic's admission that, unlike most writers in the great humanistic European and American traditions, we are faced with a contemporary woman writing in America with formidable dedication who seems seldom to believe in human capacities for learning and for emotional growth and awareness, in the ego's connection to anything beyond its temporary sensory gratifications. Oates is engaged in writing a circumscribed moral history of what she appears to observe as a failed, decadent time in our national history.

Not all critics agree, despite Oates's considerable national reputation as a writer, teacher, and essayist, that she has so far been consistently successful aesthetically in her representation of retrenched contemporary life on native grounds. The scope of her attempt to portray the diminishment of self across a wide sweep of representative Americans is an impressive one. Oates has, as of autumn 1987, published nineteen novels and thirteen volumes of collected stories since 1963, many highly acclaimed, including a National Book Award for *them* in 1969 and several O. Henry citations for outstanding achievement in the short story.[5] Indeed, some previous commentators on her work have judged her finest artistic achievement to have come in the short story. Despite considerable critical examination of such frequently anthologized stories as "Where Are You Going, Where Have You Been?" little scholarly attention has been devoted to Oates's considerable achievement in some of the predominantly realistic stories comprising roughly the first half of her short fictional career—including those to which I will devote focal attention in this essay—from *By the North Gate* in 1963 to *The Goddess and Other Women* in 1974, prior to Oates's shifts both in subject and in technique, in her next two collections of the mid-seventies, *The Hungry Ghosts: Seven Allusive Comedies* and *The Poisoned Kiss and Other Stories from the Portuguese*. And given Oates's return to realism in her most recent novel and in *Marya: A Life* (1986), it may be valuable at this point in her career to examine more closely her ideas and concerns in the first five collections of stories.

Oates's career-long preoccupation with the self-enclosure and externally induced stifling of the development of mature and independent identity in men and women is a prominent concern in these five volumes of short stories.[6] While her strong reputation as a psychological explorer of the stories of women of all ages is evident in these ninety-five fictions, Oates also writes with penetration and insight of men's situations; twenty-five of the stories are concerned either centrally or significantly with explorations of male personality and identity. Oates is less concerned in these stories with the formative stages of personality than with the full-fledged dilemmas of young and middle-aged men. Just two stories, "Wild Saturday" and "Boy and Girl," trace the numbing of normal personality in children and young boys. In the former the boredom and purposelessness of a father and his current girlfriend, who take out a ten-year-old boy each week for a supposedly memorable celebration, begin to close down the boy's identity. By the story's end, he can only sit in the middle of a small, white room where "watchful and suspicious" he stares about him, beginning to be aware "how blank and open everything is, how much empty space surrounds him" (WL, 169). "Boy and Girl" tells the story of two early adolescents, trapped by ritualized suburban lives and boring teenage parties, who take a wild drive in a borrowed car. The girl, Doris, also "borrows" her brother's baby and halfway through the ride suggests to Alex that they kill it for a thrill. As will often happen to Oates's older characters, these teenagers, stunted by a lifeless culture that allows limited opportunities for the expression of sane, organic emotions, must fill in their desert spaces with crazed ventures to try to make something happen.

In her earlier stories centering upon youths and young men, Oates reveals, particularly in *By the North Gate* and *Upon the Sweeping Flood*, the enclosing influence an unforgiving, culturally sterile background can exercise upon the postadolescent personality. In "Boys at a Picnic," three youths go on a Gothic spree of robbery and murder, until late at night as their car speeds across the countryside, the leader hallucinates the only death image he can comprehend, the biblical white horse, galloping along beside the car, and then begins to scream out the coming of his own inevitable death "at the jumbled, empty land . . . until the wind tore his words away" (NG, 91). As Vale and Mae, in "What Death with Love Should Have to Do," deepen their hopeless cycle of life through the image of their ceaseless and unrewarding motorcycle rides, Oates's narrator makes wise observations on the ignorance and indifference of the working-class poor. "Once begun, all races were alike: they were perhaps the same race: their noises dispelled all mornings, all previous nights, fused them into a sameness that seemed a broad, thick, muddy stream to which everyone had to return" (SF, 211). When Mae dies as a result of their mindless racing, Vale can only cry out at the end, "There's so much of it I don't know" (SF, 229), hurling his half-finished can of beer against the side of a house, yet another violent act of whose cause the youth possesses the dimmest understanding. And in "Archways," the college instructor, Klein, is condemned by a working-class background that, despite his acquisition of a doctorate in literature, allows only for the technical assimilation of intellectual facts. He ends as lifeless as his doomed students in remedial composition, themselves from remote parts of the state, whose failure reminds Klein of the wild look of endangered animals as they find the university forbidden ground despite their high school diplomas, "its great machinery even now working, perhaps, to process cards, grades, symbols that would send them back to their families and the lives they supposed they had escaped" (SF, 168). Stunned out of lifelessness himself by an intelligent female student whose personal sufferings reflect his own, Klein enters and then withdraws from an affair with her, fearing, like Sister Irene of Oates's famous story "In the Region of Ice," to risk an ultimate human commitment with another person who dares to need him. In the most cruel and impersonal way, he ends the affair, his mind already on his next essay on medieval poetry as he writes her a final note she will find taped to the door. Klein has used her to aggrandize his own faltering self-image; as he fails her in the class, he realizes only that her love for him has made him seem to himself more grand, more endowed with prestige. Buoyed by this illusion, Klein settles into another death-in-life upon completing his doctorate, leaving graduate school for a comfortable little college, marrying a wife of whom he is proud "for her chic competent womanly look," accepting the values of his cultural group without examination, to the end of his days "grateful for and humble to the great academic tradition in which he would live out his life" (SF, 185).

The narrator's insistent irony in the story's final passage reminds us that Klein begins to die psychologically when he is still a very young man, never allowing for the completion of his being. As so often happens in Oates's group of stories about young men, an abdication of willed choice, combined with unfortunate external circumstances, manages to circumscribe very early on the individual's capacity for giving to others, for making future choices that could potentially enrich his life. Perhaps of all the stories concerning the development of identity in young men, Oates's "Edge of the World" is the most artistically and thematically convincing. Shell, the eighteen-year-old whose impoverished rural life is, again, defined by machines, is taught by an older farmer, Jan, the universality of bitterness, disappointment, and boredom. The youth has developed no identity except his fascination with his motorcycle, with the competition it allows him with his peers. Even earlier in his youth he has enjoyed the mechanical impression he makes on his boyhood friends. "His eyes were hidden by the merciless gleam of sunglasses, so that he looked impersonal, secret, and vaguely threatening" (NG, 148). Throughout the story the narrator ascribes to his friends two phrases, "you drew blood" or "he's got blood," to characterize Shell's self-estimate of his strength and power. As with many of Oates's men, Shell's cultural values center on competitiveness and aggression and define his identity in ways he pathetically cannot begin to understand. On his way to the older farmer's junkyard, however, the boy begins to feel a sensation that he is falling; as he gets closer to the junkyard, the parts of machines seem to assume human shape, and Jan himself appears to Shell like a machine, his body and clothes matted together, stiff with grease. As he arrives at the farm and begins the "ritual" by combing his hair in a manner that will enhance his self-image and contempt for the older man, he feels a momentary anxiousness. "Shell shivered with excitement; he did not know why" (NG, 151). Among the primal feelings the youth cannot comprehend is his antipathy for the older man, his wish to set fire to his yard and all its machines. As he brags to Jan and his own motorcycle gang about his wish to escape the deserted farmland and get out to the world's edge, he senses with trepidation Jan's "ponderous, indifferent strength" as the narrator reminds us of the older man's "edge of humor that threatened them more surely than his anger" (NG, 150). Shell taunts the older man about the enclosure of his life and its rural sameness; Jan gradually goads the boy into a motorcycle exercise that is not really to be a race but an exhibition designed to reveal to Shell the old man's vision of the essential changelessness of things, that Shell's identity is fixed forever, just as Jan's is, and can never develop out to the edge of their world. He forces a dim recognition in Shell that he is nothing more than his machine. "It might be you just don't know enough about the world and what it does to you," the old man says early in the story, and in one of Oates's most pessimistic passages, he adds: "But anywhere you go ain't no different than here.

Don't you know that? . . . That's how this-here world was put together. It ain't no different, one side or another; an' there ain't no edge to it, neither, but only one side that keeps on goin' around. . . . Yet it's all the same, it never changes, it keeps the same in spite of you" (NG, 158). Inevitably, Shell succumbs to Jan's "lesson in drivin' " (NG, 159) and to his veiled suggestion of some harm to Shell, even though the youth is even stronger and, of course, decades younger than Jan. Suddenly, Shell senses dimly the real threat, in Jan's very existence, "a man who had always looked as he did . . . a man who had waited for Shell, standing just so, for years" (NG, 161–62). Shell is correct that the old man poses no physical danger to him, yet in the bloodstain he imagines on the track as the two prepare their slow cycle around it, Shell senses again that in thirty years he himself will occupy the center of this world, ready to impart the same mythic message of closure and defeat to another younger shell of a man.

Oates widens her focus beyond the mechanism and stasis of the rural scene in her group of stories concerning atrophied identity among middle-aged and aging men. Included in this contingent are such previously explored fictions as "The Census Taker," "Swamps," and "By the North Gate."[7] From old men like Walt Turner's dying father in "Stigmata" to men still in their physical prime, such as Norman in "Norman and the Killer" and Helen's father in "By the River," Oates's older men are marked by a sense of lost opportunities, careers and families blunted and stifled by dimly perceived earlier choices in their lives. Norman's life, which "had attached itself" (SF, 126) to his family, is an ordinary one as manager of a clothing store. Essentially passive, Norman is wracked with guilt—as are so many men in Oates's stories. For he has not died when a nameless killer murdered his brother years ago during their boyhood. Suddenly and accidentally discovering a man upon whom he probably projects all of the frustrations of his life and the emptiness of his marriage, Norman decides that he is his brother's killer and sets out at least to destroy the man's peace of mind by confronting him with his past "crime." Helpless like so many men drifting upon Oates's sweeping flood, Norman's game gets beyond his control, and he kills the man, as the narrator meditates upon the flaccid "airless routine" of the remainder of his life, "the numbed, beatific emptiness of one who no longer doubts that he possesses the truth, and for whom life will have forever lost its joy" (SF, 150). An overzealous certitude in possessing the "truth" frequently traps Oates's male characters; in her ironic "Stigmata," both Walt Turner and his father foreclose their human development by a rigid adherence to faith or to an opposing cynicism.

As Walt decides that his father's alleged miraculous hand markings are in reality a punishment and vengefully reviles with his bitter doctrines the dying man, his family, and the Catholic adherents at the hospital, Walt acts out his hatred of his father's rejection of the family in favor of what Walt considers his sanctimonious life. He does not realize that his own identity has become as static as his father's, his cruelty as hardened as his father's hypocrisy. "Walt understood what had happened to his father. Safe in his old age, before that safe in his tranquility, he had refined himself out of life—he had had, so easily, six children; he had given them nothing, not his own identity, not identities of their own, he had not distinguished one from the other . . . and, now, an old man, he had never been a man" (SF, 33). Walt fails to recognize that his father's emotional legacy has been well effected and will have far-reaching, never-ending consequences in the sterility of Walt's future life. Similarly, the young priest in "Shame," Father Rollins, is so caught up in what he considers the "magical name" (WL, 103) conferred upon him by his church that he dissolves his personality in a word and cannot respond to the organic charity offered him by the young widow of his dead boyhood friend. As she gives him a symbolic robin's egg at the end of their meeting, he can only stereotype it within the ironclad canons of his faith as a "miracle achieved by some forlorn, enslaved robin" (WL, 126), exclaiming, "What the hell is this?" as he crushes it in his hand. In more secular worlds, the fathers in "Ruth," "By the River," "Extraordinary Popular Delusions," "Upon the Sweeping Flood," and "Wednesday's Child" all lack the flexibility to extend their full identities to their children, really to love them. Instead they foreclose their lives, stunting them either physically or spiritually and, in the case of Brenda's father in "Wednesday's Child," serving as a symbolic correlative of the child's autism, "disliking silence because of its emptiness . . . he distrusted shapelessness" (MI, 260). Such fathers, like those in "Delusions" and "Stray Children," sometimes estranged from their own fathers, frequently seal off development of their personalities in professional specialisms of the sort the poet Snodgrass warns against in "April Inventory," either never knowing who they are and what they feel or else never allowing themselves to feel what it is they truly feel.

Among the most thematically and aesthetically compelling in this group of stories is "An Encounter with the Blind." Bethlehem Arnold Hollis, aged 42,—"whom folks would turn to look at" (NG, 114)—is one of Snodgrass's pathetic men defined only by his professional certainties, possessing little sense of personal identity beyond his position of power as a farmer and town "senator." He is secure in his skills and even in his charity as he assures the blind boy who he meets in the town saloon, Robin, that he will help him on his way by giving him a ride in the same boastful tones that he conceives of his "thousand-acre spread that gave to the world potatoes and wheat and beans" (NG, 115). Driving out into the country, the senator hears the boy play one song on his harmonica, over and over again like Mr. Olaf Helton in Katherine Anne Porter's *Noon Wine*. As they talk, the senator's blustering bonhomie begins to fade as the boy talks of the man who seduced him at age fourteen because of his soft voice and delicate features and of his determination since to kill with his sharp-bladed knife all such men and, indeed, all sinners he encounters on his travels. Fearing for his life, Hollis promises the boy money, but Robin says that although he desires money for his mission, "that ain't half of what I want" (NG, 123). His knife pressed to Hollis's throat, seemingly crazed by his quasi-religious "duty," Robin echoes the obsessiveness of many of Oates's characters of all ages and from all classes in contemporary America as he comments on his peculiarly enjoyable specialization. "Listen, mister . . . I ain't partial to this life myself. I ain't. A blind boy with no pillow for his head, no home to live in, no fambly to love. Just my duty an' the road an' the different men trapped. . . . But I got to be true to myself. I got to be true to my duty. There's all of us men trapped in ourselves, in our duty, an' can't quit till we die. My life all strung out on roads an' in cars an' in them men's faces I never get to see" (NG, 124). Against the senator's protest that he is without evil, Robin ironically assures him that "You're goin' to have the privilege of sharin' the world's sin, then, since you got none of your own" (NG, 125). Suddenly, the boy's symbolic purpose is achieved as Hollis strikes out, both physically and verbally, knocking the knife from his attacker's hand, and the town's supposedly most prestigious citizen hears "his own mad voice" confessing his past sins of exploitation of the town's Negro boys and other citizens. "Let me alone! You know too much! You found out too much—somebody tole you" (NG, 125). As Hollis lets the boy out for his next ride, the omniscient narrator observes that while the boy is serene the senator's heart is still pounding. Hollis stuffs money into Robin's pocket and returns the boy's ostensive authority, the knife, to him, but the act is needless, for the knife but reflects the facade the town leader has attempted to erect all his life. Robin's slow smile makes him gradually realize this as Hollis continues down the dirt road of his life. "When he tried to forget it he could not. His heart was cold and tight within him, like the part of him that had died" (NG, 127). Like so many "mature" men in Oates's stories, however, this man ironically has died long before he is made to realize it by circumstance, by a boy who, like Porter's Mr. Olaf Helton, seems more obsessive than he really is. In "An Encounter with the Blind," the boy is the father of the man, leading him at last to areas of identity previously unrealized and unexplored.

While Oates's skill in depicting the diminishment of identity among her male characters is well exemplified in the stories just considered, her central fictional energies have, of course, been directed to the situations of female characters. In her first five short fiction collections, Oates focuses her main attention upon four groups of female characters: children or girls just on the edge of discovery of adulthood and sexuality; young women, generally in their twenties, as yet insecure of their position in career or marriage; and ostensibly more "mature," middle-aged women, usually married or more professionally established in the world, some of whom— rather a small group—are somewhat personally and emotionally independent, having established, however tenuously, some measure of freedom and identity. Included in the first group of stories about women are some, such as "How I Contemplated the World . . .," "At the Seminary," "In the Warehouse," and "Four Summers," which have received explicatory treatment by previous scholars.[8] Among the less well known and well studied stories in this group are some that deserve wider recognition, both because of their powerful treatment of the theme of confined and foreclosed identity during a crucial stage in women's development and because of their fine execution. In "The Daughter," Thalia resents the burden her mother has imposed upon her via an unusual, foreign-sounding name, given, she senses, more to fulfill perceived lacks in her mother's sexual identity than to endow Thalia with an individul identity of her own. Oates is seldom better on mother-daughter rivalry, real and imagined, for the attentions of the all-dominating male image by which so many Oatesian women judge themselves throughout their lives and on girl children's sharp sense of betrayal that may close off their developing potential at this stage more than any other source. Thalia thinks, as her mother strokes her daughter's hair and attempts to compliment her nascent beauty, "of weakness, of the ignobility of being weak, delicate, vulnerable to betrayal, loving rather than everlastingly loved" (G, 62). In "Images" Oates represents the development of a child's self-image based on memories from thirteen years ago to one year before the story opens; we are present at the formation of a frightened, insecure identity that fears to become anything definite, fears not conforming to expected social standards for a little girl of her class. In adolescence she is dominated by the roles and the images others have made for her, as she sees—and probably forever will see—"a little girl, a pale, thin-faced little girl with astonished, ashamed eyes." And she also sees her parents and grandfather staring at her, trying to claim her, crying, "This is not you! You are someone else!" (NG, 146). Thirteen-year-old Gretchen, in "Stalking," loosed by a pleasure-saturated society into the sterility of "Radio Wonderful" land and shopping malls as the sole source of support, aside from network TV, for her developing sense of self, must invent an "Invisible Adversary" to give her life any meaning, any identity at all. She can define herself only through a fiction upon which she can impose alternately masochistic and sadistic roles that will influence her life, one imagines, for many years to come.

One of the most evocative—and grisly—stories in this grouping is "Happy Onion." Teenager Maryliz is a slightly older, somewhat prettier version of Gretchen in "Stalking," whom Oates presents as deadened by the insulated, numbed world of the rock music in which she obsessively immerses herself, having already dropped out of high school to follow her lover, singer Ly Cooper, on his concert tour. Oates depicts well the insecurity underlying the exhibitionism of much in the rock world, its frequent preoccupation with external images rather than freely chosen values, the sense that Ly and Maryliz substitute showmanship for reality, while fearing the silences, self-restraint, and self-control, beneath which a deeper, though less showy, emotional range and fervor can often be found in people free enough to have gained personal maturity. Oates also sees the ironically close, parasitic relationship between free-enterprise culture, in this instance represented by Ly's doctor father, and the glitz and superficiality of rock culture that reflects it, as Ly sings at the "Megadome," his face suffused with the drug overdose that will kill him before he has reached even his legal maturity. Ironically, Ly's group has won fame for the song that has given them their name, "The Happy Onion," a lyric about the progressive peeling away of superficiality that must take place before authentic identity and personhood can be reached. But as they sing this, Maryliz primps and preens before the crowd, drawing her identity solely from her status as Ly's future wife. A showpiece, dressed all in white, enjoying the adulation of the less renowned members of her high school group, Maryliz is the conventional antithesis of the very values Ly preaches about on the stage each night. "Maryliz Tone, dressed in a white buckskin skirt . . . a violet shirt of the flimsiest see-through material . . . waving at him, hurrying down to the stage with her birdlike little walk. . . . So many little girls staring at her, *at her*, so many boys . . . her false eyelashes like tiny whisk brooms, maybe a little overdone when someone stares right into her face, but the hell with it. She knows she looks good" (MI, 204, 206). But even sad little Maryliz has some sense that all concerts finally end, and then there is the time that must somehow be filled up until the next series of electronic thrills begin again. In an Oatesian plot device that is too quick to gain verisimilitude, Ly dies very quickly of intestinal cancer caused by his habitual drug use; while this circumstance strains belief, particularly for such a young man, it is the results accruing to the adolescent girl's identity that seem to interest the author here. Worried as much that he recover from his illness in time to make the June wedding she stereotypically yearns for as about the severity of the illness, Maryliz becomes grotesquely sentimental after her lover's sudden death. Convinced that "it's my duty to be with you" (MI, 215), she requests to be admitted to Ly's autopsy, dressed now in yet another conventional outfit, that of the black, officially sanctioned widow's weeds. Oates now spares the reader no detail in the full presentation of Ly's autopsy, even to the drawing down of the scalp to obscure the face for removal of parts of the brain as Maryliz sees the once happy onion peeled back to reveal whatever reality their relationship seemed to possess during Ly's life. While the girl's motives are sincere insofar as she understands them, to be somehow closer to her lover, so sentimentally sensational are her ideas of attachment that the only way she can do this is through a procedure that leaves even the experienced pathologists and nurses shocked and speechless. Oates's satire is rich as she blends both the seeming unconventionality of this rock child's response to tragedy with the mundanity of her thoughts about the wedding gifts she might have enjoyed had the wedding taken place. The perhaps overly omnisicent narrator concludes the story with an indictment of the girl's absent identity, her complete absorption in her image of wedded bliss. "She walked in her rapid birdlike way, Ly's bride in black, his beautiful permanent darling" (MI, 219). As in "Stalking" and "Where Are You Going, Where Have You Been?" Oates's revolting narrative in "Happy Onion" serves, if too broadly, her frequent thesis that the death of the spirit begins very young in contemporary America.

In Oates's grim vision of the inevitable results for adult lives that are too early truncated, there is little happiness for the slightly older sisters of the girls we have just considered. The married young woman of "Four Summers," for example, is now more practiced than in her childhood at self-denial, in barring herself from her real feelings, at accepting the ceaseless struggle to inure herself to the forms that men expect of young women in her lower-class surroundings. In Oates's great early story, "Pastoral Blood,"[9] Grace, thwarted by the mold of success, marriage, family so neatly laid out for her by her fatherless family and her society, plans suicide both as a means of escape from conventional boredom and as a way of asserting an attempt at identity somehow separate from their plans for her. Trying in every conceivable way to destroy the image her environment provides for her, she degrades herself with drugs, petty theft, and itinerant men. Failing on her first suicide attempt, significantly on the anniversary of her father's death, Grace sits in bed at the end of the story, watching her mirror image, planning her next attempt at death after the passing of an appropriate interval. "The girl in bed will resume her role, Grace knows, give her but the words to do it with, the correct glances. Time can be nursed, there is all the time in the world; give her time to be freed, time to arrange for another escape, another flight" (NG, 112).

The young women in "Demons," "Bodies," and "I Was in Love" are almost as fragmented from any sense of integrated identity as Grace; the first-person narrator of the latter story begins her tale with the insane logic that "I was involved with a man I couldn't marry so one of us had to die" (WL, 388). Love is often seen by Oates's younger women as a containment; they seem little more than physical space that requires filling, little more than abortive identities capable only of possessing or being possessed. The girl in "The Maniac" frequently finds herself thinking, "*I Want . . . I Want . . .* Helplessly, she would have to think herself back into nothing: a droplet of fluid, a single tear-sized drop of fluid in which a universe swam" (G, 114). Paula, the girl who has nearly died of a drug overdose, confesses to the orderly who has helped to revive her, in "The Narcotic." "Jesus, I'm such a natural addict, it's in my blood . . . to need things . . . and I always needed people. . . . I can't control it" (G, 314-15). Paula has attempted suicide simply because her life is so vacant that "there was no reason not to." Like Grace in "Pastoral Blood," she is so cut off from her feelings, from any sense of a possibly integrated ego, that she was "curious to see what my hands would do; to see if I was serious or just bluffing" (G, 315).

Paula's instability will probably cause a more successful suicide attempt; so uncertain is she of her personal worth that, after sleeping with the orderly on an impulse, she immediately and again impulsively exiles him from her apartment. Such extreme manifestations of Adlerian insecurity and lack of personal integration abound among Oates's women who have managed to establish neither a satisfying work or professional commitment nor a sharing of somewhat developed personal identity with another relatively mature human being. A particularly horrifying example of this failure occurs in "Did You Ever Slip on Red Blood?" in which a stewardess, saved from a war-protesting airline hijacker by an FBI sharpshooter's two rifle shots that have made the hijacker's head explode, covering her with blood on the tarmac, begins an affair with the FBI agent that obsessively focuses upon the violent act that brought them together. In a rented room with blinds always closed, he reminds her, "Nobody knows what we know" (MI, 284). Their very words during lovemaking are filled with images of the violence that was the occasion for two personally incomplete people to establish contact. "When they were together in the room she was brought up close to him, as if centered in the telescopic sight of a rifle" (MI, 284). The energy that gives them life does not "belong to either of them" (MI, 291); it stems from a destructive fantasyland suggested by her lover's name— Oberon, who tells her in response to her obsessive questions that he has never killed an American before. His death force was, however, immediately recognized by her when, one day after the incident, he appeared at her apartment saying, as from the grave: "You know who I am. . . . You know why I'm here" (MI, 302).

A more profound and equally horrifying story is one of Oates's best, "By the River." Here, Helen, an unconventional free spirit, returned home after the failure of yet another relationship with a man to visit her parents, is picked up at the bus depot by her father, driven home by a river they both have loved for many years, and then savagely murdered at the story's conclusion. While the story has gained admiration for its gothic evocations, its psychological realism, especially the understated need of the young woman to sacrifice all to feeling and perhaps to find a love more fulfilling than she has experienced from her kind and supportive parents, also deserves recognition. Through Helen's chaotic memories, Oates imparts her unbridled desire for continual zeniths of feeling at the cost of all-balancing insight—the quality that ultimately, despite her kindness and charity, dooms her. As her father questions her about why she has run away from her husband and then come back to her father's home, she can only answer, "I don't know why I did it" (MI, 121). Slightly uneasy, yet mainly surprised that her father has taken her by the river and has not told the rest of the family that she is coming home, she can only wonder—"she was not used to thinking" (MI, 126)—that the relentless flow of the river's time is somehow apart from her relentless need for giving, for emotional love and sensation. (In fact, at her first appearance, at the bus station waiting for her father, her first thought is, "Am I in love again, some new kind of love? Is that why I'm here?" [MI, 112].) So disorganized and poorly integrated are her responses to the world, so lost is she in her beloved movies' way of presenting reality (in the city she has gone to weekday movies at eleven in the morning), that she cannot consciously understand her beloved father's long-repressed desire for her, mixed with his hope for her material rise in the world to compensate for his lifelong feelings of humiliation concerning his neighbors who "got money." Nor can she understand how her return has catalyzed his sense of doomed vulnerability, his need to lash out at a woman he can never possess, not even through materialistic fantasy. His needs are made clear by the narrator's graphic description of the murder. "He did not raise the knife but slammed it into her chest, up to the hilt, so that his whitened fist struck her body and her blood exploded out upon it" (MI, 128). His needs are also clarified by something he says to her just before his intimate touch on her shoulder before the thrust. "It wasn't never money I wanted" (MI, 127). But as she sees "in his hand a knife she had been seeing all her life," Helen may sense that she has been approaching this moment for many years. She needs more than she is aware her father's "rough hands," her childhood memory of giving her tired father the jug of water and watching him "lift it to his lips and it would seem to Helen, the sweet child standing in the dusty corn, that the water flowed into her magnificent father and enlivened him as if it were secret blood of her own she had given him" (MI, 123). Truly, she has come to her home to die.

A volume of Oates's poetry, published after the last volume of stories considered in this essay, features these closing lines to the title poem, "Women Whose Lives Are Food, Men Whose Lives Are Money."[10]

> it is raining out back
> or not raining
> the relief of emptiness rains
> simple, terrible, routine
> at peace.

There is a sense throughout most of Oates's work in various genres, and certainly in the earlier stories, that the perversion of identity in contemporary America is almost inescapable, that Cheever's quagmire and the tear in the sky—threatening always, but never ubiquitous throughout Cheever's work—is a constant in Oates's world. While some relief beyond emptiness occasionally occurs in *Do with Me What You Will* (1973) and *Childwold* (1976) and in some of the romances of the eighties, there is scarcely surcease from the sterility and the horror ascribed to all in contemporary America in the first half of her short fiction career. Indeed, Oates has confirmed this pessimism directly in an early essay on Katherine Anne Porter's *Noon Wine* (1937),[11] stating, as she has implied in interviews, that humankind cannot know itself. Yet her essay on Porter, another woman of rural background writing in America during difficult times, reveals a profound misunderstanding of Porter's great tragic novella, for though his sufferings would strain Job, Mr. Olaf Helton does understand himself. Though circumstances and Mr. Hatch bring him almost unendurable grief, Porter shows that the itinerant North Dakotan has not abdicated moral responsibility for his actions and that his pathetic life retains a hint of the tragic because he insists on a small portion of it remaining under his command. The one song he plays on his harmonica is expressive of his awareness of life's misery, and it is consciously played and replayed, just as the farmhand consciously works, earns his way in the world, and so brings some dignity and respect (and *self*-respect) into what has been a trying life.

If occasionally an Oatesian character in these stories does manage to gain, with considerable effort, a measure of self-respect and self-regard—as does Blind Boy Robin of "An Encounter with the Blind," playing his harmonica and also bringing increased awareness into Hollis's heretofore spiritually mundane existence—in most of the stories there is little evidence to support Grant's assertion that Oates "is committed in her fiction to the raising of consciousness of those who are being destroyed"[12] or that Oates's characters very often "work at defining themselves."[13] Oates's own views, expressed in an essay on modern tragedy, that tragedy should "deepen our own sense of the mystery and sanctity of the human predicament"[14] seem not to be reflected in the reality of human lives represented in these stories. Sanctity cannot be possible without awareness and self-realization, and there is precious little of either human quality in much of Oates's earlier fiction. Walter Sullivan reminds us: "Literature requires action that is morally significant, which means that the characters must be at least theoretically free to choose for themselves. . . . There can be no question that life as we live it, as Miss Oates describes it, is enough to drive us crazy, but does this mean that we must continue to write the same story over and over—a chronicle where violence is a prelude to total spiritual disintegration and the only freedom is the total loss of self?"[15] Sullivan probingly expresses the insufficient moral spaciousness in Oates's vision of the world in those fictions where the crucially significant function of human struggle is absent. In her stories concerning more mature and middle-aged women in these volumes, such as "Magna Mater" and "Assault," Oates can tentatively indicate the liberating struggle beyond self-confinement in family and memory that forecloses the development of identities in so many women and men in her fictions;[16] but more frequently in this group of stories—"You," "First Views of the Enemy," "The Goddess," "Blindfold"—there can be no psychological liberation because there is no struggle, no effort at self-definition or self-understanding. Oates has frequently indicated in interviews and essays[17] her hopes for a wide cultural transcendence of the egotistic isolation she considers endemic since the European Renaissance, but she confuses, both in these statements and in much of her fiction, the distinction between the destructive aspects of rampant egotism and the development, through the struggle toward consciousness, of the more imaginative and empathic use of reason that has been one of the most elevating aspects of our culture since the Enlightenment. Her dismissal of Freud's contributions to modern culture is not surprising;[18] she insistently ignores the possibility that self-recognition can help humankind to become more loving and more free and seems unaware of Trilling's remarks in "Freud and Literature" praising Freud's lack of cynicism, that his classic tragic realism "does not narrow and simplify the human world for the artist but on the contrary opens and complicates it."[19] In contrast, her statement in a 1972 interview is revealing as she speaks of the importance to a person's memory of a beloved close circle of parents and family. "And if something has gone wrong inside this small universe, then nothing can ever be made right."[20] Oates's greatest failure as a writer of fiction is this frequent moral enclosure in her attitude toward her characters, her abdication of the necessity of struggle that alone can lift us from the unconsciously animalistic toward some measure of the human. Her completely circumscribed characters can be liberated only through accident or random violence, and that is no true liberation at all.

Among her stories dealing with somewhat more mature and middle-aged women, Oates can at times rise beyond her fascination with the inevitably circumscribed situation, the inevitably determined character, that sometimes become monochromatic case studies in Naturalism rather than rounded, multifaceted representations of the complex human condition.[21] In "The Heavy Sorrow of the

Body," Nina develops a quiet strength through humor and a considered confrontation of the feelings engendered by her father's slow dying, as movingly demonstrated by her washing of her father's wasted body. Through suffering, admission of memory, and an ironic awareness rare in these stories, Nina builds an identity of her own, proud of the processes of her woman's body, but "at a distance from them, observing them as a man might observe them, without comment or shame" (WL, 332). In "Shame" the young widow reveals more awareness of human sympathies than the priest. Mrs. Taylor has struggled with the deaths of both her husband and her infant son. She refuses to sentimentalize her dead husband, frankly declaring that he was a drunk and a professional failure. Because she has not abdicated the personal responsibility to see feelingly her misfortunes, she gains a subtle, unspoken strength far more liberating than anything Father Rollins can conceive.

But it is perhaps in "Puzzle" that Oates succeeds best in representing uneducated working-class people capable of working toward some recognition, however dim, of the reasons why they suffer, why they are so frequently isolated from one another. Here life's truths are elusive and difficult to bear, but they are not evaded by the dead Jackie's parents, and so for them life is not a total trap, not a compulsive enclosure into hopelessness, because each parent shares some responsibility for all their failures that in part have contributed to the accidental death of their five-year-old son. Throughout the action the woman struggles against her enveloping sense of numbness, vacancy; she does not merely submit to the repeated refrain in her mind, "*I am not really here*" in her "boxlike house, a coop for people" (MI, 42, 46). When both husband and wife summon courage at the end to confess their belief to each other that each is responsible for the needless death, they gain a liberation that is rare in Oates, especially the woman, who thinks: "Now I will tell this man the things I must tell him. It is time. It is time for me to tell him of my hatred for him, and my love, and the terrible anger that has wanted to scream its way out of me for years, screaming into his face, into his body" (MI, 51). As both husband and wife begin to accept that their son's death was uncaused by anything but irrational accident, they press their bodies around each other, and she admits her lack of understanding of pain, of her marriage, of her suffering. If she does not grasp through to the heart's mystery, neither does she run from the attempt to grapple with it.

Alfred Kazin has written that Oates, more than most women writers in America, seems "entirely open to *social* turmoil, to the frighteningly undirected and misapplied force of the American powerhouse."[22] Perhaps her significant contribution thus far in her career is as a social fictionist, caught up, as Kazin says, in this avalanche of time, whatever the limits of her moral and psychological imagination and the reiterative style may be. Her exemplary energy and dedication, her successful attempts to move beyond her earlier Naturalistic realism in stories and novels after 1975 attest to the hope that she may one day achieve the national "struggle for consciousness" she spoke of with such apparent sincerity in her acceptance speech upon receiving the National Book Award.

NOTES

1. Herbert Gold, ed., *Fiction of the Fifties* (Garden City: Doubleday & Co., 1959), 22.

2. Alfred Kazin, *Bright Book of Life* (New York: Dell Publishing Co., 1973), 198–205; Marvin Mudrick, "Fiction and Truth," *Hudson Review* 25 (1972): 146; Mary Allen, *The Necessary Blankness: Women in Major American Fiction of the Sixties* (Urbana: Univ. of Illinois Press, 1976), 133-59.

3. In this essay the five volumes of Joyce Carol Oates's stories are identified in the following way, and page numbers are given in parentheses in the text. *By the North Gate* (NG); *Upon the Sweeping Flood* (SF); *The Wheel of Love* (WL); *Marriages and Infidelities* (MI); *The Goddess and Other Women* (G). Since I shall range across the volumes of stories, organizing my commentary by thematic groups and not by individual volumes, here follows a list of the ninety-five stories, by volume:

By the North Gate: "Swamps," "The Census Taker," "Ceremonies," "Sweet Love Remembered," "Boys at a Picnic," "Pastoral Blood," "An Encounter with the Blind," "Images," "Edge of the World," "A Legacy," "In the Old World," "The Fine White Mist of Winter," "The Expense of Spirit," "By the North Gate."

Upon the Sweeping Flood: "Stigmata," "The Survival of Childhood," "The Death of Mrs. Sheer," "First Views of the Enemy," "At the Seminary," "Norman and the Killer," " 'The Man That Turned into a Statue,' " "Archways," "Dying," "What Death with Love Should Have to Do," "Upon the Sweeping Flood."

The Wheel of Love: "In the Region of Ice," "Where Are You Going, Where Have You been," "Unmailed, Unwritten Letters," "Convalescing," "Shame," "Accomplished Desires," "Wild Saturday," "How I Contemplated the World from the Detroit House of Correction and Began My Life Over Again," "The Wheel of Love," "Four Summers," "Demons," "Bodies," "Boy and Girl," "The Assailant," "The Heavy Sorrow of the Body," "Matter and Energy," "You," "I Was in Love," "An Interior Monologue," "What Is the Connection between Men and Women?"

Marriages and Infidelities: "The Sacred Marriage," "Puzzle," "Love and

Death," "29 Inventions," "Problems of Adjustment in Survivors of Natural/ Unnatural Disasters," "By the River," "Extraordinary Popular Delusions," "Stalking," "Scenes of Passion and Despair," "Plot," "The Children," "Happy Onion," "Normal Love," "Stray Children," "Wednesday's Child," "Loving/Losing/Loving a Man," "Did you Ever Slip on Red Blood?" "The Metamorphosis," "Where I Lived, and What I Lived For?" "The Lady with the Pet Dog," "The Spiral," "The Turn of the Screw," "The Dead," "Nightmusic."

The Goddess and Other Women: "The Girl," "Concerning the Case of Bobby T.," "Blindfold," "The Daughter," "In the Warehouse," "Ruth," "The Maniac," "Free," ". . . & Answers," "I Must Have You," "Magna Mater," "Explorations," "Small Avalanches," "The Voyage to Rosewood," "Waiting," "The Dying Child," "Narcotic," "A Girl at the Edge of the Ocean," "Unpublished Fragments," "A Premature Autobiography," "Psychiatric Services," "The Goddess," "Honeybit," "Assault," "The Wheel."

4. Redbook, May 1987, 50–56, 66, 194–97.

5. Good discussions of the earlier novels are found in Joanne V. Creighton, Joyce Carol Oates (Boston: G.K. Hall, 1979); Diane Tolomeo, "Joyce Carol Oates," in American Writers, suppl. 2, pt. 2, ed. A. Walton Litz (New York: Scribner's, 1981), 503–27; Ellen Friedman, Joyce Carol Oates (New York: Ungar, 1980); G.F. Waller, Dreaming America: Obsession and Transcendence in the Fiction of Joyce Carol Oates (Baton Rouge: Louisiana State Univ. Press, 1979); and Mary Kathryn Grant, R.S.M., The Tragic Vision of Joyce Carol Oates (Durham, N.C.: Duke Univ. Press, 1978). The most comprehensive study of Oates's novelistic career is Eileen T. Bender, Artist in Residence: The Phenomenon of Joyce Carol Oates (Bloomington: Indiana Univ. Press, 1987). The stories are treated according to genre theory in Katherine Bastian, Joyce Carol Oates's Short Stories: Between Tradition and Innovation (New York: Peter Lang, 1983), and in relation to speech act theory by T. Norman, Isolation and Contact: A Study of Character Relationships in Joyce Carol Oates's Short Stories, (Sweden: Acta I Universitat, 1984); by far the most intelligent criticism of stories treated is in Creighton, Joyce Carol Oates, and Joseph Petite, " 'Out of the Machine': Joyce Carol Oates and the Liberation of Women," Kansas Quarterly 9 (Spring 1977): 75–79, and idem, "The Marriage Cycle of Joyce Carol Oates," Journal of Evolutionary Psychology 5 (Aug. 1984): 223–36.

6. In my discussion I will set aside the approximately fifteen stories that may be classified as experimental or nonrealistic, such as "An Interior Monologue," "29 Inventions," and "Explorations," as well as those stories clearly intended by their author as revisions of past masters' fictions, such as "The Turn of the Screw," "The Metamorphosis," and "The Dead." A good interpretation of the important latter story appears in Creighton, Joyce Carol Oates, 134–36.

7. Ellen Friedman, Joyce Carol Oates (New York: Frederick Ungar, 1980), 17–20, interprets the former story; Creighton, Joyce Carol Oates, 27–29, explicates "Swamps" and "By the North Gate."

8. See especially Keith Cushman, "A Reading of Joyce Carol Oates's 'Four Summers,'" *Studies in Short Fiction* 18 (Spring 1981): 137–46; Doreen A. Fowler, "Oates's 'At the Seminary.'" *Explicator* 41 (Fall 1982): 62–64; and Creighton, *Joyce Carol Oates*, especially 115, 122–23.

9. Creighton, *Joyce Carol Oates*, 31–32, offers a more detailed interpretation of this fine story.

10. Joyce Carol Oates, *Women Whose Lives Are Food, Men Whose Lives Are Money* (Baton Rouge: Louisiana State Univ. Press, 1978), 4.

11. *Renascence* 17 (Spring 1965): 157–62.

12. Grant, *Tragic Vision*, 125.

13. Ibid., 119.

14. Joyce Carol Oates, "An American Tragedy," *New York Times Book Review*, Jan. 24, 1971, 2.

15. Walter Sullivan, "The Artificial Demon: Joyce Carol Oates and the Dimensions of the Real," in *Critical Essays on Joyce Carol Oates*, ed. L.W. Wagner (Boston: G.K. Hall, 1979), 82, 86. For a perceptive discussion of the ironically detrimental cultural effects of Oates's position, see Benjamin De-Mott, "The Necessity in Art of a Reflective Intelligence," in Wagner, *Critical Essays*, 22.

16. For perceptive discussions of the ambiguities present in such struggles, see Creighton, *Joyce Carol Oates*, 125–27; and Bastian, *Oates's Short Stories*, 82–84, 92–97.

17. "Interview with Oates," in *The New Fiction: Interviews with Innovative American Writers*, ed. Joe David Bellamy (Urbana: Univ. of Illinois Press, 1974), 23; Creighton, *Joyce Carol Oates*, 19–23.

18. Joyce Carol Oates, *New Heaven, New Earth: The Visionary Experience in Literature* (New York: Vanguard, 1974), 72–73.

19. L.I. Lipking and A. W. Litz, eds., *Modern Literary Criticism* (New York: Atheneum, 1972), 298.

20. "Interview with Oates," 29.

21. Grant, *Tragic Vision*, 140–41; Creighton, *Joyce Carol Oates*, 142, 150.

22. Kazin, *Bright Book of Life*, 199.

A Bibliography of Writings by JOYCE CAROL OATES

Anne Hiemstra

NOVELS AND NOVELLA

With Shuddering Fall. New York: Vanguard Press, 1964; Fawcett, 1971.

A Garden of Earthly Delights. New York: Vanguard Press, 1967; Fawcett, 1969.

Expensive People. New York: Vanguard Press, 1968; Fawcett, 1968.

them. New York: Vanguard Press, 1969; Fawcett, 1970.

Wonderland. New York: Vanguard Press, 1971; Fawcett, 1973.

Do with Me What You Will. New York: Vanguard Press, 1973; Fawcett, 1974.

The Assassins. New York: Vanguard Press, 1975; Fawcett, 1976.

Childwold. New York: Vanguard Press, 1976.

The Triumph of the Spider Monkey: The First Person Confession of the Maniac Bobby Gotteson as Told to Joyce Carol Oates. Santa Barbara, Calif.: Black Sparrow Press, 1976.

The Son of the Morning. New York: Vanguard Press, 1978.

Cybele. Santa Barbara, Calif.: Black Sparrow Press, 1979.

Unholy Lives. New York: Vanguard Press, 1979.

Bellefleur. New York: E.P. Dutton, 1980.

Angel of Light. New York: E.P. Dutton, 1981; Warner, 1982.

A Bloodsmoor Romance. New York: E.P. Dutton, 1982.

Mysteries of Winterthurn. New York: E.P. Dutton, 1984.

Raven's Wing. New York: E.P. Dutton, 1985.

Solstice. New York: E.P. Dutton, 1985.

Marya: A Life. New York: E.P. Dutton, 1986.

You Must Remember This. New York: E.P. Dutton, 1987.

[Pseud. Rosamond Smith] *Lives of the Twins.* New York: Simon and Schuster, 1988.

COLLECTED SHORT STORIES

By the North Gate. New York: Vanguard Press, 1963; Fawcett, 1971.

Upon the Sweeping Flood and Other Stories. New York: Vanguard Press, 1966; Fawcett, 1971.

The Wheel of Love and Other Stories. New York: Vanguard Press, 1970; Fawcett, 1971.

Marriages and Infidelities. New York: Vanguard Press, 1972; Fawcett, 1973.

The Goddess and Other Women. New York: Vanguard Press, 1974; Fawcett, 1976.

The Hungry Ghosts: Seven Allusive Comedies. Los Angeles: Black Sparrow Press, 1974.

Where Are You Going? Where Have You Been? Stories of Young America. Greenwich, Conn.: Fawcett, 1974.

The Poisoned Kiss and Other Stories from the Portuguese, by "Fernandes." New York: Vanguard Press, 1975.

The Seduction and Other Stories. Los Angeles: Black Sparrow Press, 1975.

Crossing the Border. New York: Vanguard Press, 1976.

Night-Side: Eighteen Tales. New York: Vanguard Press, 1977.

All the Good People I've Left Behind. Santa Barbara, Calif.: Black Sparrow Press, 1979.

A Sentimental Education: Stories. New York: E.P. Dutton, 1980.

Last Days: Stories. New York: E.P. Dutton, 1984.
Wild Saturday. London, England: Dent, 1984.

POETRY BOOKS

Women in Love and Other Poems. New York: Albondacani Press, 1968.
Anonymous Sins and Other Poems. Baton Rouge: Louisiana State Univ. Press, 1969.
Love and Its Derangements. Baton Rouge: Louisiana State Univ. Press, 1970.
In Case of Accidental Death. Cambridge: Pomegranate Press, 1972.
Wooded Forms [single poem]. New York: Albondacani Press, 1972.
Angel Fire. Baton Rouge: Louisiana State Univ. Press, 1973.
Dreaming America and Other Poems. n.p.: Aloe Editions, 1973.
A Posthumous Sketch. Los Angeles: Black Sparrow Press, 1973.
The Fabulous Beasts. Baton Rouge: Louisiana State Univ. Press, 1975.
Seasons of Peril. Santa Barbara, Calif.: Black Sparrow Press, 1977.
Women Whose Lives Are Food, Men Whose Lives Are Money. Baton Rouge: Louisiana State Univ. Press, 1978.
Invisible Woman: New & Selected Poems, 1970–1982. Princeton, N.J.: Ontario Review Press, 1982.

COLLECTED ESSAYS

The Edge of Impossibility: Tragic Forms in Literature. New York: Vanguard Press, 1972.
The Hostile Sun: The Poetry of D.H. Lawrence. Los Angeles: Black Sparrow Press, 1973.
New Heaven, New Earth: The Visionary Experience in Literature. New York: Vanguard Press, 1974.
The Art of Literary Publishing: Editors on Their Craft. Edited by Joyce Carol Oates, Raymond J. Smith, and Bill Henderson. Wainscott, N.Y.: Pushcart, 1980.
Contraries: Essays. New York: Oxford Univ. Press, 1981.
Shandyism & Sentiment, Seventeen Sixty to Eighteen Hundred. New York: Telegraph Books, 1982.
First Person Singular: Writers on Their Craft. Edited by Joyce Carol Oates. Princeton, N.J.: Ontario Review Press, 1983.
The Profane Art: Essays and Reviews. New York: E.P. Dutton, 1983.
On Boxing. Garden City, N.Y.: Dolphin/Doubleday, 1987.
Reading the Fights. Edited by Joyce Carol Oates and Daniel Halpern. New York: Henry Holt, 1988.

MISCELLANY

Scenes from American Life: Contemporary Short Fiction. Edited by Joyce Carol Oates. New York: Random House, 1972.

Public Outcry. Pittsburgh: Slow Loris Press, 1976.
Best Stories of Nineteen Seventy-Nine. Edited by Joyce Carol Oates and Shannon Ravenel. New York: Houghton Mifflin, 1979.
Night Walks. Edited by Joyce Carol Oates. Princeton: Ontario Review Press, 1982.

PLAYS

The Sweet Enemy. New York: Actors Playhouse, 1965.
Sunday Dinner. New York: St. Clement's Church, 1970.
Ontological Proof of My Existence. New York: Cubiculo Theatre, 1972.
Miracle Play. New York: Playhouse 2 Theatre, 1974.
Three Plays. Princeton: Ontario Review Press, 1980.

POEMS

"Madness." *Saturday Review*, Feb. 7, 1970.
"Our Dead." *Mademoiselle*, April 1971, 166.
"Fear of Going Blind." *Esquire*, Dec. 1971, 280.
"Acceleration Near the Point of Impact." *Esquire*, Nov. 1972, 89.
"After Twelve Years of Travelling." *Mademoiselle*, March 1973, 56.
"Preventing the Death of the Brain." *Nation*, Nov. 16, 1974, 510.
"Psalm"; "Appetite, Terror"; "Sweetest Gloomsday"; "Giant Sunday Rats";
    "Fever Song." *Texas Quarterly* 21 (Spring 1978): 6–9.
"Present Tense." *Atlantic*, Nov. 1979, 81.
"Ebony Casket." *Harper's*, April 1980, 118–20.
"Things Run Down." *Nation*, Sept. 27, 1980, 292.
"The Miraculous Birth." *New York Times Magazine*, Dec. 23, 1984, 12–13.
"The Heir." *Massachusetts Review* 26 (Winter 1985): 605.
"Winter Aphorisms, Uncoded." *Georgia Review* 39 (Winter 1985): 823.
"Detroit Expressway, 1976"; "Upstairs." *Michigan Quarterly Review* 25
    (Spring 1986): 364–65.
"Winter Wrath"; "Winter Boredom"; "Winter Threnody"; Winter Love."
    Paris Review 28 (Spring 1986): 153–56.
"Fish." *New Republic*, June 30, 1986, 39.
"Heat." *Yale Review* 75 (Summer 1986): 588.
"Luxury of Sin." *Georgia Review* 40 (Fall 1986): 757.
"An Old Prayer"; "Father of Us All"; "The Riddle." *Sewanee Review* 94 (Fall
    1986): 576–78.
"Scab." *Partisan Review* 53 (1986): 101–2.
"Snapshot Album." *Nation*, Feb. 21, 1987, 231.
"Playground." *Hudson Review* 40 (Spring 1987): 90.
"Here, Nights Are Distinct from Days." *Southwest Review* 72 (Summer
    1987): 414.
"An Ordinary Morning in Las Vegas." *New Republic*, Feb. 22, 1988, 30.

ARTICLES, REVIEWS, STORIES

"The 'Fifth Act' and the Chorus in the English and Scottish Ballads." *Dalhousie Review* 42 (Autumn 1962): 119–29.

"The Comedy of Metamorphosis in the *Revenger's Tragedy.*" *Bucknell Review* 11 (Dec. 1962): 38–52.

"The Existential Comedy of Conrad's 'Youth.' " *Renascence* 26 (Fall 1963): 22–28.

"The Alchemy of *Antony and Cleopatra.*" *Bucknell Review* 12 (Spring 1964): 37–50.

"Porter's 'Noon Wine': A Stifled Tragedy." *Renascence* 27 (Spring 1965): 157–62.

"Ionesco's Dances of Death." *Thought* 40 (Autumn 1965): 415–31.

"Masquerade and Marriage: Fielding's Comedies of Identity." *Ball State University Forum* 6 (Autumn 1965): 10–21.

"The Ambiguity of *Troilus and Cressida.*" *Shakespeare Quarterly* 17 (Spring 1966): 141–50.

"Building Tension in the Short Story." *Writer* 79 (June 1966): 11–12, 44. Also in *The Writer's Handbook*, edited by A.S. Burack, 1968: 146–49.

"Background and Foreground in Fiction." *Writer* 80 (Aug. 1967): 11–13.

"Man under Sentence of Death: The Novels of James M. Cain." In *Tough Guy Writers of the Thirties*, edited by David Madden, 110–28. Carbondale: Southern Illinois Univ. Press, 1968.

"The Double Vision of *The Brothers Karamazov.*" *Journal of Aesthetics and Art Criticism* 27 (Winter 1968): 203–13.

"The Art of Eudora Welty." *Shenandoah* 20 (1969): 54–57.

"Art at the Edge of Impossibility: Mann's Dr. Faustus." *Southern Review* 5 (April 1969): 375–97.

"Article on Yeats." *New York Times Book Review*, Sept. 7, 1969, 2.

"Yeats: Violence, Tragedy, Mutability." *Bucknell Review* 17 (Dec. 1969): 1–17.

"Tragic Rites in Yeats' *A Full Moon in March.*" *Antioch Review* 29 (Winter 1969–70): 547–60.

"Ontological Proof of My Existence." *Partisan Review* 37 (1970): 471–97.

"What is the Connection between Men and Women?" (story). *Mademoiselle*, Feb. 1970, 244–45.

"Bodies" (story). *Harper's Bazaar* 103 (Feb. 1970): 122–25.

"What Herbert Breuer and I did to Each Other" (story). *McCalls*, April 1970, 102–3.

"Love and Death" (story). *Atlantic* 225 (June 1970): 57–66.

"Fact Is: We Like to Be Drugged." *McCalls*, June 1970, 69.

Review of *The Perfectionists*, by Gail Godwin. *New York Times Book Review.* June 7, 1970, 5.

"Wednesday" (story). *Esquire*, Aug. 1970, 80–81.

"Wild Saturday" (story). *Mademoiselle*, Sept. 1970, 136–37.

"Puzzle" (story). *Redbook*, Nov. 1970, 72–73.

"Normal Love" (story). *Atlantic*, Jan. 1971, 80–85.
"The Short Story." *Southern Humanities Review* 5 (Summer 1971): 213–14.
"With Norman Mailer at the Sex Circus: Out of the Machine" (story). *Atlantic*, July 1971, 42–45.
"Death of Dreams" (story). *McCall's*, July 1971, 70–71.
"Bloodstains" (story). *Harper's*, Aug. 1971, 82–88.
"How My Father Was Murdered" (story). *Atlantic*, Sept. 1971, 72–76.
"Obsession" (story). *Ladies Home Journal*, Oct. 1971, 96–97.
"6:27 p.m." (story). *Redbook*, Dec. 1971, 82–83.
"Did You Ever Slip on Red Blood?" *Harper's*, (April 1972) 80–88.
"Whose Side Are You On?" *New York Times Book Review*, June 4, 1972, 63.
"Narcotic" (story). *Mademoiselle*, Oct. 1972, 190–91.
"New Heaven and New Earth." *Saturday Review*, Nov. 4, 1972, 51–54. Reprinted in *Arts in Society*, 10 (1973): 36–43.
"A Personal View of Nabokov." *Saturday Review of the Arts*, Jan. 1973, 36–37.
"The Unique/Universal in Fiction." *Writer*, Jan. 1973, 9–12.
"Concerning the Case of Bobby G." *Atlantic*, Feb. 1973, 84 +.
"An Imperative to Escape the Prison of Gender." *New York Times Book Review*, April 15, 1973, 7, 10, 12.
"Joyce Carol Oates on Thoreau's *Walden*." *Mademoiselle*, April 1973, 96, 98.
"The Myth of the Isolated Artist." *Psychology Today*, May 1973, 74–75.
"The Death Throes of Romanticism: The Poems of Sylvia Plath." *Southern Review* 9 (July 1973): 501–22.
"Art: Therapy and Magic." *American Journal* 1 (July 3, 1973): 17–21.
"The Visionary Art of Flannery O'Connor." *Southern Humanities Review* 7 (Summer 1973): 235–46.
"A Visit with Doris Lessing." *Southern Review* 9 (Autumn 1973): 873–82.
"The Teleology of the Unconscious: The Art of Norman Mailer." *Critic* 32 (Nov.-Dec. 1973): 25–35.
"The Unique/Universal in Fiction." *Writer* 86 (Jan. 1974): 9–12.
"Disguised Fiction." *PMLA* 89 (May 1974): 580–81.
"Is This the Promised End?: The Tragedy of King Lear." *Journal of Aesthetics and Art Criticism* 33 (Fall 1974): 19–32.
"Snow Storm." *Mademoiselle*, Sept. 1974, 140–41.
"Will the Real Norman Mailer Please Stand Up?" In *Will the Real Norman Mailer Please Stand Up?*, 216–23, edited by L. Adams, Port Washington, N.Y.: Kennikat Press, 1974.
"Other Celebrity Voices: How Art Has Touched Our Lives." *Today's Health* 52 (May 1974): 31.
"Don Juan's Last Laugh." *Psychology Today*, Sept. 1974, 10 +.
"Crossing the Border." *New York Times Magazine*, Dec. 1, 1974, 127.
"The Immense Indifference of Things: The Tragedy of Conrad's *Nostromo*." *Novel: A Forum on Fiction* 9 (Fall 1975): 5–22.
"Updike's American Comedies." *Modern Fiction Studies* 21 (Autumn 1975): 549–72.

"Jocoserious Joyce." *Critical Inquiry* 2 (Summer 1976): 677–88.
"Tryst." *Atlantic*, Aug. 1976, 40–46.
"Famine Country." *Yale Review* 66 (June 1977): 534–50.
"Tattoo." *Mademoiselle*, July 1977, 144+.
Review of *The Simone Weil Reader. New Republic*, July 1977, 33–37.
"Voyeur." *Southwest Review* 63 (Winter 1978): 56–64.
"Lawrence's *Götterdämmerung*: The Tragic Vision of *Women in Love*." *Critical Inquiry* 4 (Spring 1978): 559–78.
"First Death." *Mademoiselle*, June 1978, 188+.
Review of *Silences*, by Tillie Olsen. *New Republic* 179 (July 29, 1978): 32–35.
"Washington Square." *Antioch Review* 36 (Summer 1978): 293–314.
"Novelists." *New Republic*, Nov. 18, 1978, 27–31.
"Joyce Carol Oates on Poetry." *New Republic*, Dec. 1978, 25–30.
"Excerpt from *Son of the Morning*," *Granta: New American Writing* 1 (1979): 51–63.
Review of *The Penguin Book of Women Poets. New Republic*, April 21, 1979, 28–30.
"Honey and Bill and Dan and Celia." Review of *Only Children*, by Alison Lurie. *New York Times Book Review.* April 22, 1979, 7+.
"The English and Scottish Traditional Ballads." *Southern Review* 15 (July 1979): 560–66.
"Outing." *Mademoiselle*, March 1980, 212+.
Review of *The Open Cage* and *Bread Givers*, by Anzia Yezierska. *Mademoiselle*, April 1980, 54.
"How Is Fiction Doing?" *New York Times Book Review*, Dec. 14, 1980, 3.
"Is There a Female Voice? Joyce Carol Oates Replies." In *Gender and Literary Voice*, edited by Janet Todd, 10–11. New York: Holmes and Meier, 1980.
"Why Is Your Writing So Violent?" *New York Times Book Review*, March 29, 1981, 15+.
"Imaginary Cities: America." In *Literature and the Urban Experience: Essays on the City and Literature*, edited by Michael Jaye and Ann Watts. New Brunswick, N.J.: Rutgers Univ. Press, 1981.
"Stories That Define Me." *New York Times Book Review*, July 11, 1982, 15–16.
"Frankenstein's Fallen Angel." Afterword to Mary Shelley's *Frankenstein*. Berkeley: Univ. of California Press, Pennyroyal Edition, 1984.
"Does the Writer Exist?" *New York Times Book Review*, April 22, 1984, 1, 17.
"Raven's Wing." *Esquire*, Aug. 1984, 94+.
"Man's Man? Woman Hater? Our Greatest Writer." *TV Guide*, Dec. 8, 1984, 5–6.
"A Terrible Beauty Is Born. How?" *New York Times Book Review*, Aug. 11, 1985, 1+.
"Ancient Airs, Voices" (story). *Antioch Review* 44 (Winter 1986): 17–39.
"Little Wife" (story). *Kenyon Review* 8 (Spring 1986): 42–61.
"Visions of Detroit" (memoir). *Michigan Quarterly Review* 25 (Spring 1986): 308–12.

"Ballerina" (story). *Georgia Review* 40 (Spring 1986): 234–49.
"Testimony" (story). *Southern Review* 22 (Summer 1986): 600–605.
Review of *The Progress of Love*, by Alice Munro. *New York Times Book Review*, Sept. 3, 1986, 1.
"Secrets." *Mademoiselle*, Nov. 1986, 156+.
"Surf City" (story). *Partisan Review* 53 (1986): 372–89.
"Double Solitaire" (story). *Michigan Quarterly Review* 25 (1986): 336–50.
"Barbara Pym's Novelist Genius." In *The Life and Work of Barbara Pym*, edited by D. Salwak, 43–44. Ames: Univ. of Iowa Press, 1987.
"Sundays in Summer." *Michigan Quarterly Review* 26 (Winter 1987): 218–27.
"The World's Worst Critics." *New York Times Book Review*, Jan. 18, 1987, 1.
"Kid Dynamite." *Life*, March 1987.
"Shopping." *Ms.*, March 1987, 50+.
"Killer Instinct" (excerpt from *On Boxing*). *Sports Magazine*, July 1987, 57.
"Soul at the White Heat: The Romance of Emily Dickinson's Poetry." *Critical Inquiry* 13 (Summer 1987): 806–24.
"The Abduction" (story). *Seventeen*, Nov. 1987, 176–77+.
"Success and the Pseudonymous Writer: Turning over a New Self." *New York Times Book Review*, Dec. 6, 1987, 12, 14.
"Intellectual Seduction: Meeting with Gorbachev." *New York Times Magazine*, Jan. 3, 1988, 16–19+.
"The Mysterious Mr. Thoreau." *New York Times Book Review*, May 1, 1988, 1+.

A Bibliography of Writings about
JOYCE CAROL OATES

Anne Hiemstra

Abbey, Marilyn R. "Private Lives Don't Beckon to Joyce Carol Oates." *Chicago Sun-Times*, Feb. 3, 1985, 24, 27.
Abrahams, W. "Stories of a Visionary." *Saturday Review*, Sept. 23, 1972, 76+.
Adams, R.M. "Joyce Carol Oates at Home." *New York Times Book Review*, Sept. 28, 1969, 4–5, 48.
Allen, Bruce. "Intrusions of Consciousness." *Hudson Review* 28 (Winter 1975–76): 611–15.
Allen, Mary I. "The Terrified Women of Joyce Carol Oates." In *The Necessary Blankness: Women in Major American Fiction of the Sixties*, 133–59. Urbana: Univ. of Illinois Press, 1976.

Anderson, Sally. "The Poetry of Joyce Carol Oates." *Spirit* 39 (Fall 1972): 22–29.

Applebaum, Judith. "PW Interviews Joyce Carol Oates." *Publishers Weekly* 213 (June 26, 1978): 12–13.

Avant, John Alfred. "An Interview with Joyce Carol Oates." *Library Journal*, Nov. 15, 1972: 3711–12.

———. "The Hungry Ghosts, by Joyce Carol Oates." In *Critical Essays on Joyce Carol Oates*, edited by L.W. Wagner, 36–41. Boston: G.K. Hall, 1979.

Balakian, Nina. "The Tragedy of Delusion: Criticism by Joyce Carol Oates." In *Critical Encounters*, edited by Nina Balakian, 139–42. New York: Bobbs-Merrill, 1978.

Barasch, Frances K. "Faculty Names in Recent American Fiction." *College Literature* 10 (Winter 1983): 28–37.

Barza, Steven. "Joyce Carol Oates: Naturalism and the Aberrant Response." *Studies in American Fiction* 7 (1979): 141–51.

Basney, L. "Joyce Carol Oates: Wit and Fear." *Christianity Today* 20 (June 18, 1976): 13–14; (July 2, 1976): 20–21.

Bastian, Katherine. *Joyce Carol Oates's Short Stories: Between Tradition and Innovation*. New York: Peter Lang, 1983.

Batterberry, Michael, and Batterberry, Adriane. "Focus on Joyce Carol Oates." *Harper's Bazaar* 106 (Sept. 1973): 159, 174, 176.

Bedient, Calvin. "Blind Mouths." *Partisan Review* 39 (Winter 1972): 124–27.

———. "Vivid and Dazzling." In *Critical Essays on Joyce Carol Oates*, edited by L.W. Wagner, 24–26. Boston: G.K. Hall, 1979.

Bellamy, Joe David. "The Dark Lady of American Letters: An Interview with Joyce Carol Oates." *Atlantic*, Feb. 1972, 63–67. Reprinted as "Joyce Carol Oates." In *The New Fiction: Interviews with Innovative American Writers*. Urbana: Univ. of Illinois Press, 1974.

Bender, Eileen T. "Autonomy and Influence: Joyce Carol Oates's *Marriages and Infidelities*." *Soundings* 58 (Fall 1975): 390–406.

———. " 'Paedomorphic' Art: Joyce Carol Oates's *Childwold*." In *Critical Essays on Joyce Carol Oates*, edited by L.W. Wagner, 117–22. Boston: G.K. Hall, 1979.

———. "Between the Categories: Recent Short Fiction by Joyce Carol Oates." *Studies in Short Fiction* 17 (1980): 415–23.

———. "The Woman Who Came to Dinner: Dining and Divining a Feminist 'Aesthetic.' " *Women's Studies* 12 (1986): 315–33.

———. *Artist in Residence: The Phenomenon of Joyce Carol Oates*. Bloomington: Indiana Univ. Press, 1987.

Bergonzi, Bernard. "Truants." *New York Review of Books*, Jan. 2, 1969, 40.

Birkerts, S. "*You Must Remember This*" (review). *New York Times Book Review*, Aug. 16, 1987, 3.

Bloom, Harold, ed. *Joyce Carol Oates: Modern Critical Views*. Edgemont, Pa.: Chelsea House, 1986.

Boesky, Dale. "Correspondence with Miss Joyce Carol Oates." *International Review of Psychoanalysis* 2 (1975): 481–86.

Bower, Warren. "Bliss in the First Person." *Saturday Review,* Oct. 26, 1968, 34–35.

Box, Patricia S. "Vision and Revision in *Wonderland.*" *Notes on Contemporary Literature* 9 (1979): 3–6.

Brown, Russell M. "Crossing Borders." *Essays in Canadian Writing* 22 (Summer 1981): 154–68.

Burwell, Rose Marie. "Joyce Carol Oates and an Old Master." *Critique* 15 (1973): 48–58.

———. "The Process of Individuation as Narrative Structure: Joyce Carol Oates's 'Do With Me What You Will.' " *Critique* 17 (Dec. 1975): 93–106.

———. "Joyce Carol Oates's First Novel." *Canadian Literature* 73 (Summer 1977): 54–57.

———. "*Wonderland*: Paradigm of the Psychohistorical Mode." *Mosaic* 14 (Summer 1981): 1–16.

Carrington, Ildiko de Papp. "The Emperor's New Clothes: Canadians through American Eyes." *Essays on Canadian Writing* 22 (Summer 1981): 136–53.

Catron, Douglas M. "A Contribution to a Bibliography of Works by and about Joyce Carol Oates." *American Literature* 49 (Nov. 1977): 300–414.

Chell, Cara. "Un-tricking the Eye: Joyce Carol Oates and the Feminist Ghost Story." *Arizona Quarterly* 41 (Spring 1985): 5–23.

Clemons, Walter. "Joyce Carol Oates at Home." *New York Times Book Review,* Sept. 28, 1969, 4 +.

———. "Joyce Carol Oates: Love and Violence." *Newsweek,* Dec. 11, 1972, 72–74, 77.

Coale, Samuel C. "Marriage in Contemporary American Literature: The Mismatched Marriages of Manichean Minds." *Thought: A Review of Culture and Ideas* 58 (March 1983): 11–21.

———. "Joyce Carol Oates: Contending Spirits." In Samuel Chase Coale, *In Hawthorne's Shadow,* 161–79. Lexington: Univ. Press of Kentucky, 1985.

Collins, A. Review of *Mysteries of Winterthurn. Macleans,* Feb. 20, 1984, 60.

Cooke, Michael G. "Recent Novels: Women Bearing Violence." *Yale Review* 66 (Oct. 1976): 148, 150.

Coulon, Michael J. *Isolation and Contact: A Study of Character Relationships in Joyce Carol Oates's Short Stories, 1963–1980.* Gothenburg: Acta Universitatis Gothoburgenis, 1984.

Craig, P. Review of *Mysteries of Winterthurn. New York Times Book Review,* Feb. 12, 1984, 7.

Creighton, Joanne V. "Unliberated Women in Joyce Carol Oates's Fiction." *World Literature Written in English* 17 (April 1978): 165–75. Also in *Critical Essays on Joyce Carol Oates,* edited by L.W. Wagner, 148–56. Boston: G.K. Hall, 1979.

———. "Joyce Carol Oates's Craftmanship in *The Wheel of Fortune.*" *Studies in Short Fiction* 15 (Fall 1978): 375–84.

————. *Joyce Carol Oates*. Boston: G.K. Hall, 1979.

Cunningham, Valentine. "Counting Up the Cost." *Times Literary Supplement*, March 20, 1981, 303.

Cushman, Keith. "A Reading of Joyce Carol Oates's 'Four Summers.' " *Studies in Short Fiction* 18 (Spring 1981): 137–46.

Dalton, Elizabeth. "Joyce Carol Oates: Violence in the Head." *Commentary* 49 (June 1970): 75.

Darrach, Brad. "Consumed by a Piranha Complex." *Life*, Dec. 11, 1970, 18.

Davenport, Guy. "C'est Magnifique, Mais Ce N'est Pas Daguerre." *Hudson Review* 23 (Spring 1970): 154.

Dean, S.L. "Faith and Art: Joyce Carol Oates's *Son of the Morning*." *Critique* 28 (Spring 1987): 135–47.

DeCurtis, Anthony. "The Process of Fictionalization in Joyce Carol Oates's *them*." *International Fiction Review* 6 (1979): 121–28.

DeFeo, R. "Only Prairie Dog Mounds." In *Critical Essays on Joyce Carol Oates*, edited by L.W. Wagner, 31. Boston: G.K. Hall, 1979.

DeMott, Benjamin. "The Necessity in Art of a Reflexive Intelligence." In *Critical Essays on Joyce Carol Oates*, edited by L.W. Wagner, 19–23. Boston: G.K. Hall, 1979.

Denne, Constance Ayers. "Joyce Carol Oates's Women." *Nation*, Dec. 7, 1974, 597–99.

Dickinson, Donald C. "Joyce Carol Oates: A Bibliographic Checklist." *American Book Collector* 2 (Nov.-Dec. 1981): 26–39; 3 (Jan.-Feb., 1982): 42–48.

Dike, Donald A. "The Aggressive Victim in the Fiction of Joyce Carol Oates." *Greyfriar* 15 (1974): 13–29.

Ditsky, John. "The Man on the Quaker Oates Box: Characteristics of Recent Experimental Fiction." *Georgia Review* 26 (Fall 1972): 297–313.

Duus, Louise. " 'The Population of Eden.' Joyce Carol Oates's *By the North Gate*." *Critique* 7 (Winter 1964): 176–77.

Edwards, Thomas R. "The House of Atreus Now" (review of *Angel of Light*). *New York Times Book Review*, Aug. 16, 1981, 1, 18.

Fossum, Robert H. "Only Control: The Novels of Joyce Carol Oates." *Studies in the Novel* 7 (Summer 1975): 285–97. Also in *Critical Essays on Joyce Carol Oates*, edited by L.W. Wagner, 49–60. Boston: G.K. Hall, 1979.

Fowler, Doreen A. "Oates's 'At the Seminary.' " *Explicator* 41 (Fall 1982): 62–64.

Franks, Lucinda. "The Emergence of Joyce Carol Oates." *New York Times Magazine*, June 27, 1980, 22 + .

Frenkiel, Nora. "Joyce Carol Oates." *New York Times Magazine*, June 27, 1980, 22 + .

Friedman, Ellen. "The Journey from the 'I' to the 'Eye': Joyce Carol Oates's *Wonderland*." *Studies in American Fiction* 8 (1980): 37–50. Also in *Critical Essays on Joyce Carol Oates*, edited by L.W. Wagner, 102–16. Boston: G.K. Hall, 1979.

————. *Joyce Carol Oates*. New York: Frederick Ungar, 1980.

Friedman, Lawrence S. "The Emotional Landscape of Joyce Carol Oates's 'By the River.' " *Cuyahoga Review* 1 (Fall 1982): 149–53.

Gardner, John. "The Strange Real World" (review of *Bellefluer*). *New York Times Book Review*, July 20, 1980: 1+.

Giles, James R. "The 'Marivaudian Being' Drowns His Children: Dehumanization in Donald Barthelme's 'Robert Kennedy Saved from Drowning' and Joyce Carol Oates's *Wonderland.*" *Southern Humanities Review* 9 (Winter 1975): 63–75.

———. " 'Suffering, Transcendence, and Artistic 'Form': Joyce Carol Oates's *them.*" *Arizona Quarterly* 32 (Autumn 1976): 213–26.

———. "From Jimmy Gatz to Jules Wendall: A Study of 'Nothing Substantial.' " *Dalhousie Review* 56 (Winter 1976–77): 718–24.

———. "Oates's 'The Poisoned Kiss.' " *Canadian Literature* 80 (1979): 138–47.

———. "Destructive and Redemptive Order: Joyce Carol Oates's *Marriages and Infidelities* and *The Goddess and Other Women.*" *Ball State University Forum* 22 (1981): 58–70.

Gillis, Christina Marsden. " 'Where Are You Going, Where Have You Been?': Seduction, Space, and a Fictional Mode." *Studies in Short Fiction* 18 (Winter 1981): 65–70.

Godwin, Gail. "An Oates Scrapbook." *North American Review* 256 (Winter 1971–72): 67–70.

Golightly, B. "Out of the Limelight." *Horizon* 27 (June 1984): 10.

Goodman, Charlotte. "Images of American Rural Women in the Novel." *Univ. of Michigan Papers in Women's Studies* 1 (June 1975): 57–70.

———. "Women and Madness in the Fiction of Joyce Carol Oates." *Women and Literature* 5 (1977): 17–28.

———. "The Lost Brother, the Twin: Women Novelists and the Male-Female Double Bildungsroman." *Novel: A Forum on Fiction* 17 (Fall 1983): 28–43.

Gordon, Jan B. "Gothic Fiction and the Losing Battle to Contain Oneself." *Commonweal* (Feb. 11, 1972): 449.

Grant, Mary Kathryn, R.S.M. *The Tragic Vision of Joyce Carol Oates.* Durham, N.C.: Duke Univ. Press, 1978.

———. "The Language of Tragedy and Violence." In *Critical Essays on Joyce Carol Oates*, edited by L.W. Wagner, 61–76. Boston: G.K. Hall, 1979.

Grant, Louis T. "A Child of Paradise." *Nation*, Nov. 1968, 475.

Gratz, David K. "Oates's 'Where Are You Going, Where Have You Been?' " *Explicator* 45 (Spring 1987): 55–56.

Hamilton, I. "Fatal Fascinations." In *Critical Essays on Joyce Carol Oates*, edited by L.W. Wagner, 5–6. Boston: G.K. Hall, 1979.

Harper, Howard M. "Trends in Recent American Fiction." *Contemporary Literature* 12 (Spring 1971): 204–29.

Harter, Carol. "America as 'Consumer Garden': The Nightmare Vision of Joyce Carol Oates." *Revue des Langues Vivantes*, Bicentennial Issue (1976): 171–87.

Harty, Kevin J. "Archetype and Popular Lyric in Joyce Carol Oates' 'Where Are You Going, Where Have You Been?' " *Pennsylvania English* 8 (1980–81): 26–28.

Healey, James. "Pop Music and Joyce Carol Oates' 'Where Are You Going, Where Have You Been?' " *Notes on Modern American Literature* 7 (Spring-Summer 1983): item 5.

Hicks, G. "What Is Reality?" In *Critical Essays on Joyce Carol Oates*, edited by L.W. Wagner, 13–15. Boston: G.K. Hall, 1979.

Higdon, David Leon. " 'Suitable Conclusion': The Two Endings of Oates's *Wonderland.*" *Studies in the Novel* 10 (1978): 447–53.

Hurley, C. Harold. "Cracking the Secret Code in Oates's 'Where Are You Going, Where Have You Been?' " *Studies in Short Fiction* 24 (Winter 1987): 62–66.

Janeway, Elizabeth. Review of *A Garden of Earthly Delights. New York Times Book Review*, Sept. 10, 1967, 5 +.

Jeannotte, M. Sharon. "The Horror Within: The Short Stories of Joyce Carol Oates." *Sphinx* 8 (1977): 25–36.

Johnson, Gregg. *Understanding Joyce Carol Oates.* Columbia, S.C.: Univ. of South Carolina Press, 1987.

Jong, Erica. Review of *Last Days. New York Times Book Review*, Aug. 5, 1984, 7.

"Joyce Carol Oates: Love and Violence." *Newsweek*, Dec. 11, 1972, 72 +.

Karl, Frederick P. *American Fictions, 1940–1980.* New York: Harper and Row, 1983, 420–22, 546–49.

Kazin, Alfred. "Oates." *Harper's* 243 (Aug. 1971): 78–82.

———. *Bright Book of Life: American Novelists and Storytellers from Hemingway to Mailer.* Boston: Little, Brown, 1974. Excerpt in *Critical Essays on Joyce Carol Oates*, edited by L.W. Wagner, 157–60. Boston: G.K. Hall, 1979.

Keller, Karl. "A Modern Version of Edward Taylor." *Early American Literature* 9 (Winter 1975): 321–24.

Kuehl, Linda. "An Interview with Joyce Carol Oates." *Commonweal* 91 (Dec. 5, 1969): 307–10.

Labrie, Ross. "Love and Survival in Joyce Carol Oates." *Greyfriar* 22 (1981): 17–26.

Leedom, Joann. "Out of the Riots—A Quest for Rebirth." *Christian Science Monitor*, Oct. 30, 1969, 12.

Leff, Leonard J. "The Center of Violence in Joyce Carol Oates' Fiction." *Notes on American Literature* 2 (1977).

Leonard, John. Review of *Bellefleur. New York Times Book Review*, July 20, 1980, 1.

Lercangee, Francine. *Joyce Carol Oates: An Annotated Bibliography.* New York: Garland, 1986.

L'Heureux, J. "Mirage-Seekers." In *Critical Essays on Joyce Carol Oates*, edited by L.W. Wagner, 16–18. Boston: G.K. Hall, 1979.

Lindemann, Bernhard. "Text as System and as Process: On Reading Joyce Carol Oates's 'Notes on Contributors.' " *Anglistik und Englischunterricht* 23 (1984): 95–109.

Liston, William T. "Her Brother's Keeper." *Southern Humanities Review* 11 (Spring 1977): 195–203.

Lundkist, Artur. *Fantasi med Realism.* Stockholm: Liber Förlag, 1979.

McConkey, James. "Joyce Carol Oates, *With Shuddering Fall." Epoch* 14 (Winter 1965): 185–88.

———. *"By the North Gate."* In *Critical Essays on Joyce Carol Oates,* edited by L.W. Wagner, 3–4. Boston: G.K. Hall, 1979.

McCormick, Lucienne P. "A Bibliography of Works by and about Joyce Carol Oates." *American Literature* 43 (March 1971): 124–32.

McGann, J. "Comment." *Poetry* 117 (Dec. 1970): 199–200.

Madden, David. "The Violent World of Joyce Carol Oates": In *The Poetic Image in Six Genres,* 26–46. Carbondale: Southern Illinois Univ. Press, 1969.

———. "Upon the Sweeping Flood." In *Critical Essays on Joyce Carol Oates,* edited by L.W. Wagner, 6–10. Boston: G.K. Hall, 1979.

Malin, Irving. "Possessive Material." In *Critical Essays on Joyce Carol Oates,* edited by L.W. Wagner, 39–41. Boston: G.K. Hall, 1979.

Markmann, C.L. "The Terror of Love." In *Critical Essays on Joyce Carol Oates,* edited by L.W. Wagner, 27–28. Boston: G.K. Hall, 1979.

Martin, Carol A. "Art and Myth in Joyce Carol Oates's *The Sacred Marriage." Midwest Quarterly* 28 (Summer 1987): 540–52.

Matsuyama, Nobunao. "What Manner of Women." In *American Literature: America Bungaku to New York* (report on Symposium of American Literature Society of Japan), 1982.

Mudrick, Marvin. "Fiction and Truth." *Hudson Review* 25 (Spring 1972): 142.

Norman, T. *Isolation and Contact: A Study of Character Relationships in Joyce Carol Oates's Short Stories.* Sweden: Acta I Universitat, 1984.

"*Ontological Proof of My Existence*" (review). *Newsweek,* Feb. 21, 1972, 99.

Parini, J. "A Taste of Oates." *Horizon* 26 (1983): 50–52.

Park, Sue S. "A Study in Counterpoint: Joyce Carol Oates's 'How I Contemplated the World from the Detroit House of Correction and Began My Life Over Again.' " *Modern Fiction Studies* 22 (Summer 1976): 213–24.

Petite, Joseph. " 'Out of the Machine': Joyce Carol Oates and the Liberation of Women." *Kansas Quarterly* 9 (Spring 1977): 75–79.

———. "The Marriage Cycle of Joyce Carol Oates." *Journal of Evolutionary Psychology* 5 (Aug. 1984): 223–36.

Phillips, Robert. "Joyce Carol Oates: The Art of Fiction LXXII." *Paris Review* 20 (Fall-Winter 1979): 199–226. Reprinted in *The Paris Review Interviews: Writers at Work,* 5th series, edited by George Plimpton, 359–84. New York: Penguin, 1981.

Phillips, R.S. *"Night-side."* In *Critical Essays on Joyce Carol Oates,* edited by L.W. Wagner, 42–43. Boston: G.K. Hall, 1979.

————. Review of *You Must Remember This. America* 157 (Nov. 14, 1987): 360.

Pickering, Samuel F., Jr. "The Short Stories of Joyce Carol Oates." *Georgia Review* 28 (Summer 1974): 218–26.

Pinsker, Sanford. "Isaac Bashevis Singer and Joyce Carol Oates: Some Versions of Gothic." *Southern Review* 9 (Autumn 1973): 895–908.

————. "Suburban Molesters: Joyce Carol Oates's *Expensive People.*" *Midwest Quarterly* 19 (Autumn 1977): 89–103. Also in *Critical Essays on Joyce Carol Oates*, edited by L.W. Wagner, 93–101. Boston: G.K. Hall, 1979.

————. "Joyce Carol Oates's *Wonderland*": A Hungering for Personality." *Critique* 20 (1978): 59–70.

————. "Joyce Carol Oates and the New Naturalism." *Southern Review* 15 (1979): 52–63.

————. "The Blue Collar Apocalypse or Detroit Bridge's Falling Down: Joyce Carol Oates's *them.*" *Descant* 23 (1979): 35–47.

————. "Speaking about Short Fiction: An Interview with Joyce Carol Oates." *Studies in Short Fiction* 18 (Summer 1981): 239–43.

————. "The Lamb of Abyssalia." *Studies in Short Fiction* 18 (Winter 1981): 111.

Pollock, John. "The Nouveau-Lipsian Style of Joyce Carol Oates." *San Jose Studies* 4 (1978): 32–40.

Prescott, Peter S. "Everyday Monsters." *Newsweek,* Oct. 11, 1971, 96. Also in *Critical Essays on Joyce Carol Oates*, edited by L.W. Wagner, 93–101. Boston: G.K. Hall, 1979.

Quirk, Tom. "A Source for 'Where Are You Going, Where Have You Been?' " *Studies in Short Fiction* 18 (Fall 1981): 413–19.

Reed, J.D. "Postfeminism: Playing for Keeps." *Time,* Jan. 10, 1983, 46–47.

Regan, Nancy. "A Home of One's Own: Women's Bodies in Recent Women's Fiction." *Journal of Popular Culture* 11 (1977–78): 772–88.

Ricks, Christopher. "The Unignorable Real." *New York Review of Books* 12 (Feb. 12 1970): 22–24.

Robeson, Mark B. "Oates's 'Where Are You Going, Where Have You Been?' " *Explicator* 40 (Summer 1982): 59–60.

————. "Joyce Carol Oates's 'Where Are You Going, Where Have you Been?' Arnold Friend as Devil, Dylan, and Levite." *Publications of the Mississippi Philological Association* (1985): 98–105.

Rubin, Larry. "Oates's 'Where Are You Going, Where Have You Been?' " *Explicator* 42 (Summer 1984): 57–60.

Sales, R.H. "Hawkes, Malamud, Richler, Oates." In *On Not Being Good Enough*, by R.H. Sak, 30–42. New York: Oxford, 1979.

Salholz, E. Review of *Mysteries of Winterthurn. Newsweek,* Feb. 6, 1984, 79.

Sanborn, Sara. "Two Major Novelists All by Herself." *Nation,* Jan. 1974: 20. Also in *Critical Essays on Joyce Carol Oates*, edited by L.W. Wagner, 32–35. Boston: G.K. Hall, 1979.

Schulz, Gretchen, and R.J.R. Rockwood. "In Fairyland, without a May: Connie's Exploration Inward in Joyce Carol Oates's 'Where Are You Going, Where Have You Been?' " *Literature and Psychology* 30 (1980): 155–67.

Showalter, Elaine. "My Friend Joyce Carol Oates: An Intimate Protrait." *Ms.*, March 1986, 44–46.

Siegal, R. "Comment." *Poetry* 130 (May 1977): 107–9.

Sjoberg, Leif. "An Interview with Joyce Carol Oates." *Contemporary Literature* 23 (Summer 1982): 267–84.

Spacks, Patricia Meyer. "A Chronicle of Women." *Hudson Review* 25 (Spring 1972): 168.

Stegner, Page. "Stone, Berry, Oates—and Other Grist from the Mill." *Southern Review* 5 (Jan. 1969): 273–301.

Sheppard, R.Z. "*You Must Remember This*" (review). *Time*, Aug. 31, 1982, 62.

Sterne, Richard Clarke. "Versions of Rural America." *Nation*, April 1, 1968, 450. Also in *Critical Essays on Joyce Carol Oates*, edited by L.W. Wagner, 11–12. Boston: G.K. Hall, 1979.

Sternhell, C. Review of *Last Days*. *Vogue*, Aug. 1984, 212.

Stevens, Peter. "The Poetry of Joyce Carol Oates." In *Critical Essays on Joyce Carol Oates*, edited by L.W. Wagner, 123–47. Boston: G.K. Hall, 1979.

Stout, Janis P. "Catatonia and Femininity in Oates's *Do with Me What You Will*." *International Journal of Women's Studies* 6 (May-June 1983): 208–15.

Sullivan, Walter. "Where Have All the Flowers Gone?: The Short Story in Search of Itself." *Sewanee Review* 78 (Summer 1970): 531–42.

———. "The Artificial Demon: Joyce Carol Oates and the Dimensions of the Real." *Hollins Critic* 9, no. 4 (Dec. 1972): 1–12. Also in *Critical Essays on Joyce Carol Oates*, edited by L.W. Wagner, 77–86. Boston: G.K. Hall, 1979.

———. "Old Age, Death, and Other Modern Landscapes: Good and Indifferent Fables for Our Times." *Sewanee Review* 82 (1974): 138–47.

———. "Gifts, Prophecies, and Prestidigitations: Fictional Frameworks, Fictional Modes." *Sewanee Review* 85 (Jan. 1977): 116–25.

"Sunday Dinner." *Nation* 211 (Nov. 16, 1970): 508.

Sweeney, Gail White. "*Do with Me What You Will*" (review). *Ms.*, Nov. 1973, 39–42.

Taylor, Gordon O. "Joyce Carol Oates: Artist in Wonderland." *Southern Review* 10 (1974): 490–503.

———. "Joyce 'after' Joyce: Oates's 'The Dead.' " *Southern Review* 19 (Summer 1983): 596–605.

Tierce, Mike, and John Michael Crafton. "Connie's Tambourine Man: A New Reading of Arnold Friend." *Studies in Short Fiction* 22 (1985): 219–24.

Tolomeo, Diane. "Joyce Carol Oates." In *American Writers:* Suppl. 2 pt. 2, edited by A. Walton Litz, 503–27. New York: Scribner's, 1981.

"Transformations of Self: An Interview with Joyce Carol Oates." *Ohio Review* 15 (Fall 1973): 50–61.

Updike, John. "What You Deserve Is What You Get." *New Yorker*, Dec. 1987, 119–23.

Uphaus, Suzanne Henning. "Boundaries: Both Physical and Metaphysical." *Canadian Review of American Studies* 8 (Fall 1977): 236–42.

Urbanski, Marie Mitchell Olesen. "Existential Allegory: Joyce Carol Oates's 'Where Are You Going, Where Have You Been?' " *Studies in Short Fiction* 15 (1978): 200–203.

Wagner, Linda W. "Oates: The Changing Shapes of Her Realities." *Great Lakes Review: A Journal of Midwest Culture* 5 (1979): 15–23.

———, ed. *Critical Essays on Joyce Carol Oates*. Boston: G.K. Hall, 1979.

———. *Joyce Carol Oates: The Critical Reception*. Boston: G.K. Hall, 1979.

———. "Oates's Cybele." *Notes on Contemporary Literature* 11 (Nov. 1981): 2–8.

Walker, Carolyn. "Fear, Love, and Art in Oates's 'Plot.' " *Critique: Studies in Modern Fiction* 15 (1973): 59–70.

Waller, G.F. "Joyce Carol Oates's *Wonderland*: An Introduction." *Dalhousie Review* 54 (Autumn 1974): 480–90.

———. *Dreaming America: Obsession and Transcendence in the Fiction of Joyce Carol Oates*. Baton Rouge: Louisiana State Univ. Press, 1979.

———. "Through Obsession to Transcendence: The Recent Work of Joyce Carol Oates." *World Literature Written in English* 17 (1978): 176–80.

———. "Through Obsession to Transcendence: The Lawrentian Mode of Oates's Recent Fiction." In *Critical Essays on Joyce Carol Oates*, edited by L.W. Wagner, 161–73. Boston: G.K. Hall, 1979.

Wegs, Joyce M. "Don't You Know Who I Am?: The Grotesque in Oates's 'Where Are You Going, Where Have You Been?' " *Journal of Narrative Technique* 5 (Jan. 1975): 64–72. Also in *Critical Essays on Joyce Carol Oates*, edited by L.W. Wagner, 87–92. Boston: G.K. Hall, 1979.

Westcott, Holly Mims. *Dictionary of Literary Biography Yearbook, 1981*, 119–25. Detroit: Gale Research Co., 1982.

White, William. "Place Names in *Childwold*." *Notes on Contemporary Literature* 15 (Jan. 1985): 2.

Wilson, Mary Ann. "From Thanatos to Eros: A Study of Erotic Love in Joyce Carol Oates's *Do with Me What You Will*." *Studies in the Humanities* 11 (Dec. 1984): 48–55.

Winslow, Joan D. "The Stranger Within: Two Stories by Oates and Hawthorne." *Studies in Short Fiction* 17 (1980): 263–68.

Wollcott, James. "Stop Me before I Write Again: Six Hundred More Pages by Joyce Carol Oates" (review of *A Bloodsmoor Romance*). *Harper's*, Sept. 1982, 67–69.

"Writing As a Natural Reaction." *Time*, Oct. 10, 1969, 108.

Zimmerman, Paul D. "Hunger for Dreams." *Newsweek*, March 23, 1970, 108, 110.

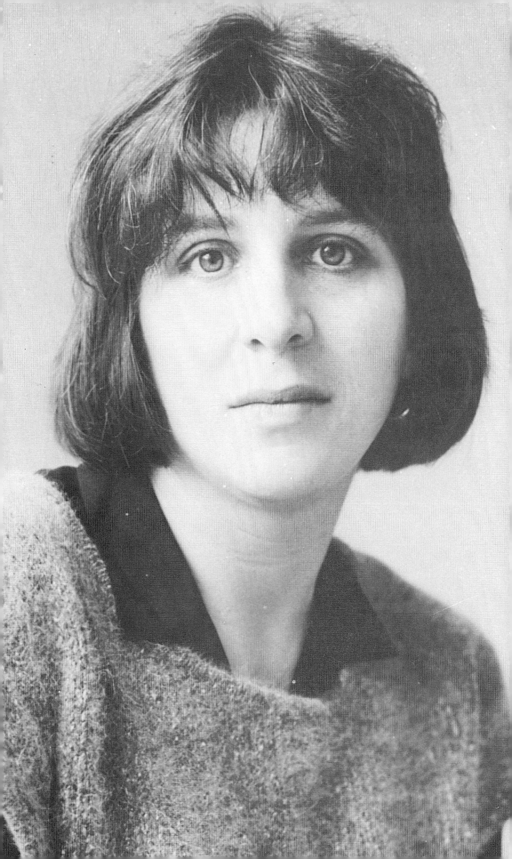

MARY GORDON

The Struggle with Love

John W. Mahon

Mary Gordon's third novel, *Men and Angels* (1985), introduces, for the first time in her fiction, a family in the ordinary sense of the word. Also for the first time, she eschews the Irish Catholic subculture that permeates her earlier novels, *Final Payments* (1978) and *The Company of Women* (1980). Despite this change in focus, Gordon seeks in all her work to explore how people love, or fail to love, each other in a world where belief in God is either a memory or an inconceivability. While the conventional family unit occupies the center of *Men and Angels,* Gordon's real concern extends beyond Anne and Michael Foster and their children to the wider human community outside their comfortable home.

In the first two novels, Gordon portrays communities where the traditional nuclear family plays little part. *Final Payments* opens on the day that Isabel's father is buried. Feeling responsible for her father's stroke eleven years before, she has devoted her life to nursing him. Ultimately, the novel is about coming to terms with death and accepting life with all its risks. It is only near the end that Isabel really mourns her father and begins to move beyond her guilt and self-hatred.

The narrative of *Final Payments* covers the several months following Joe Moore's death. Through flashback we learn that when Isabel is two her mother dies and her father hires the spinster Margaret Casey to keep house. Margaret, an odious, unlovable person, dislikes Isabel

Isabel and schemes to marry Joe, but Isabel uses her influence on her doting father to secure Margaret's dismissal. For the next seventeen years, until Joe's death, Isabel's family consists of her father, her school friends Eleanor and Liz, and Father Mulcahy. She finds a home with these three at various times after her father's death, until she gets involved with the "saintly" Hugh Slade. Chastened by the violent reaction of Hugh's wife to this latest adultery, Isabel relinquishes self-indulgence in favor of masochistic denial; she moves in with the hideous Margaret Casey, who, as ever, makes Isabel's life an ordeal. In the end, Isabel makes a "final payment" to Margaret by writing a check for all the money her father left behind. She then escapes Margaret in the company of her friends Eleanor and Liz, determined to try again for happiness with Hugh.

In *The Company of Women*, Felicitas, named for the virgin martyr mentioned in the Canon of the Mass, loses her father when she is six months old. She grows up surrounded by widows and spinsters, all under the domination of the dictatorial Father Cyprian. The importance of community here is implicit both in the title—the working title for this second novel had been *Fields of Force*[1]—and in the name of Felicitas, which appears in the Canon after these words: "We ask some share in the *fellowship* of your apostles and martyrs" (emphasis mine).

In Cyprian's look Felicitas reads the message: "You are the chosen one. Make straight the way of the Lord" (45);[2] like Isabel she is Mary, not Martha, destined for contemplation and study rather than concern about practical problems (Luke 10:40). Trained in the doctrines and ritual of the Church, Felicitas as an adult will provide her elders with vicarious satisfaction as she defeats the dragons of the secular culture. But the precocious Felicitas chooses to rebel, converts to the counterculture of the late sixties, sleeps with Robert Cavendish and another member of his "turned-on" community, and gets pregnant. Deciding literally at the last minute against an abortion, she returns to her mother, who takes charge and moves them both upstate to live permanently near Cyprian. Eight years after Linda is born, Felicitas elects to marry a local man who is simple but loving: "It is for shelter that we marry and make love" (243).

In these first two novels, Gordon writes virtual allegories of the search for community and love after the collapse of old certainties. The dilemma is exemplified in the life of Cyprian Leonard, one of Gordon's most important "minor" characters. His baptismal name was Philip, but he took the name of the early Christian martyr Cyprian, Bishop of Carthage, when he entered the Paraclete Order.

("Paraclete," a title applied to the Holy Spirit, means "advocate," "intercessor.") Like Felicitas, Cyprian is invoked in the Canon of the Mass. He reacts to change in the Church by growing more conservative, until he feels unwelcome among the Paracletists and begins a long exile, moving from one diocese to another before settling permanently in his hometown on his parents' property. Thus, Philip Leonard rejects his nuclear family to embrace the community of Paracletists: feeling betrayed by change, Cyprian Leonard rejects the community, returns home, and develops his own community, the "company of women" with Felicitas as the promise of a new generation. His reaction to upheaval is rejection; he thus anticipates the rebellion of his protégé, Felicitas, against him.

The experience of Isabel Moore and Felicitas Taylor also mirror those of the Catholic community from which they spring and against which they rebel. Both women spend years in a cloistered existence, and their break with the "cloister" mirrors the experience of Catholicism, especially American Catholicism, following the Second Vatican Council—long years of life in a carefully guarded fortress vanish before the onrush of the secular world and all its blandishments. Both Isabel and Felicitas function on one level as types, confronted with fundamental changes and loss of personal faith, forced to abandon familiar patterns and live outside the Catholic ghetto.

Both women break free of their cloistered environment through sex, an obvious route for repressed Catholic girls of their generation. The strictness of the cloister accounts in part for the extremity of their breaks. Isabel visits a gynecologist to get "some kind of birth control" (105) and chooses the IUD: "Never had I felt such pain, and there was an added sense of outrage in knowing that I had invited it" (108). Desperate to leave the doctor's office, she makes light of the pain: "I tried to make myself look Protestant" (109). After submitting in a moment of weakness to the odious John Ryan, husband of her friend Liz, she takes on the kindly Hugh Slade as a lover. Slade, every Catholic's idea of the solid WASP, talks of the "barbarous background" Isabel and her friends had (160); his unbelievably bland goodness is as grotesque as Ryan's chauvinism.

Felicitas rejects the control of the sternly conservative Cyprian only to fall into the lubricious arms of the odious Robert Cavendish, whose free-love harem is less attractive than the celibate community headed by Cyprian. Already under Cavendish's spell, Felicitas is unimpressed when her "aunt" Elizabeth tells her that Cyprian "loves you so much that he can hardly bear it." Felicitas responds that Cyprian "doesn't know anything about love." When Elizabeth observes that "None of us knows much," Felicitas thinks of Cavendish: "He knew about love" (106). In fact, love in any meaningful sense is a dirty word to Cavendish, and Felicitas learns to appreciate, if grudgingly, the love and shelter offered by her extended family, the company of women.

Shelter is an important word in Gordon's work, sought by all of her characters with more or less success. (It is no accident that the title for her collection of short stories [1987] is *Temporary Shelter*.) In the first two novels, love and shelter must be searched for outside the traditional family setting. Both Isabel and Felicitas find themselves members of a family in the extended sense. Struck by Eleanor's jealousy of her friendship with Liz, Isabel realizes, "We are connected. . . . I am not entirely alone" (121). Reflecting on the relationship among her friends, Felicitas's mother Charlotte realizes that "there was something between them, between all of them. They were connected to something, they stood for something. . . . When all of them came together, they were something" (18). It is this "something" that Felicitas rejects, to seek security in the Cavendish ménage, "more like a family, and Felicitas needed a lot of support" (156).

In *The Company of Women,* there is only one nuclear family, the one Cyprian leaves behind to enter the priesthood: "I would not be the son of my father, the brother of my brothers, bumbling and heavy and uncouth. I would be part of that glorious company, the line of the apostles. I would not be who I was" (278). The few families in *Final Payments* lack love. Liz and John Ryan find marriage more of a convenience for raising two children than a meaningful relationship. Liz finds fulfillment in a lesbian liaison, while John regularly commits adultery. Cynthia Slade has tricked Hugh into marriage and now taunts him with his infidelities.

The real love in the novel is between Isabel and her friends. Liz loves Isabel enough to confront her on occasion with difficult questions: Why fall for John Ryan? Do you realize the complications involved in loving Hugh? When Isabel retreats into her masochistic shell, it is Liz who tells her to get out of bed and confront life. It should be noted that Hugh, also, tries to jolt Isabel out of her self-hatred. How, after all, can you love others if you do not love yourself? Ultimately pushing Isabel to the decision to leave Margaret Casey, Father Mulcahy offers her money to improve her appearance, reminding her of the commandment against self-destruction.

Isabel's work for the county involves visiting families who are paid by the government to provide shelter for old people. Shelter can be provided, but love is not so easy to come by. Visiting one women,

Isabel wishes she could really help but thinks of St. Paul's statement in 1 Corinthians 13:4: "Charity suffereth long and is kind":

That was it, unless you were willing to suffer in your kindness, you were nothing. Barbarous, Hugh would have said. He would have said that most people feel nothing, that you can be kind in simpler ways. But with me I carried the baggage of the idea. Love and charity. One was that feeling below the breast, and the other was doing something, anything, to take people's pain away. I remembered the lettering on a bulletin board at Anastasia Hall: LOVE IS MEASURED BY SACRIFICE. And I remembered thinking how wrong that was, because the minute I gave up something for someone I liked them less.

"Ah," Sister Fidelis had said when I asked her, "you don't have to like someone to love them in God."

But who wants to be loved in God? I had thought then, and still thought. We want to be loved for our singularity, not for what we share with the rest of the human race. We would rather be loved for the color of our hair or the shape of our ankle than because God loves us. [168-69]

Isabel learns that some of the old people are happy while others are miserable. One old man gives her good advice about her relationship with Hugh and asks that, in return, she show him her breasts; she agrees. An old woman spends her days weeping and begs Isabel to recommend her transfer to a nursing home—there she can use the medication she has been saving to kill herself. She has, after all, nothing to live for, with both her son and husband dead: "What I want is to be with someone who wants me. Wants *me*. . . . Or else I want to die" (221). Isabel agrees to recommend her transfer: "That was charity, then. You let someone die if they wanted to. . . . If that was what you wanted—someone to love you for yourself more than anyone else (what I wanted from Hugh)—there was nothing worth living for once you lost it" (222).

In distinguishing between love and chaity, Isabel blurs the seamless nature of love in the Christian understanding, which is that God has a deeply personal love for each human being. Christians believe in the uniqueness of the individual and hold the cognate belief that Jesus died not for the race but for each person. The obligation of the Christian is to love others as God has loved each of us. By this definition the real lovers in Gordon's work are the mothers, who would die for their children "without a thought" (*Men and Angels*, 16); interestingly, Cyprian, not related to Felicitas by blood, feels the same way about her as Charlotte does and as Anne Foster feels about her children.

The "charity" that Isabel practices in exposing herself to the old man and helping the old woman commit suicide is a perversion of

Christian love. Through the love of her son and her husband, the old woman *has* experienced the kind of deeply personal love God has for each individual, but she has failed to find in human love the promise of God's love that would keep her from despair and suicide. Instead of helping the old woman to recognize the richness of the love in her life and to confront the pain of loss, Isabel helps her to opt out and fears the same end for herself if she risks loving Hugh.

Isabel has only a dim sense of what she knows her father would call the "error" (224) in this line of thought and action because, long before her father's death, she has lost her faith. Operating on the purely human level, she tries to give Hugh up and embrace life with Margaret: "If we can love the people we think are most unlovable, if we can get out of this ring of accident, of attraction, then it's a pure act, love; then we mean something, we stand for something" (243).

In fact, if she really loved Margaret, she would recognize her responsibility for Margaret's fate: Margaret reached out for human love with Isabel's father, but Isabel defeated the attempt. If she could love Margaret, Isabel would see her not as an ogre to be fobbed off with a check but as a person who has never been loved as Isabel herself feels people must be loved. If she really loved Margaret, who *has* hurt many people (including Father Mulcahy) and spread scandal, she would heed the advice of Jesus: "If thy brother shall trespass against thee, go and tell him his fault between thee and him alone: if he shall hear thee, thou hast gained thy brother" (Matt. 18:15). In short, if Isabel really loved Margaret, she would relate to her, and this she never does. Margaret Casey is an important "type" for Gordon, who will create a similar character in Laura Post in *Men and Angels*. Like Isabel, Anne Foster will encounter the unlovable; her actions will be somewhat different, but they too will be circumscribed by the limitations inherent in a response that cannot, or will not, transcend the human level.

Of course, Gordon's own experiences lie behind the struggle with love in all her work, behind the unconventional communities of the first two novels and behind the obsessive motherhood of the third. These experiences include her Catholic education in the fifties, when she would have learned by rote most of the Church's doctrines, as summarized in the Baltimore Catechism. My guess is that Mary Gordon, consciously or not, was profoundly influenced by the concept of the Mystical Body of Christ. In *The Company of Women*, Robert Cavendish praises Felicitas's abilities as a writer and declares: " 'I think the three women in this room could be at the vanguard of the new movement. Felicitas the head, Sally the hands and Iris the heart.' The mystical body of Christ, Felicitas thought, but said nothing" (144).

According to the Catechism, "the Catholic Church is called the Mystical Body of Christ because its members are united by supernatural bonds with óne another and with Christ, their Head, thus resembling the members and head of the living human body."[3] Since Catholics were also taught that every human being, either directly or by extension, belonged to the Church, the Mystical Body is, in fact, the human race with Christ as its head. The Church derives the notion of Mystical Body from Scripture: in John's gospel, Jesus says that "I am the vine, ye are the branches. He that abideth in me, and I in him, the same bringeth forth much fruit: for without me ye can do nothing" (15:5). Writing to the Ephesians, St. Paul says that the Father has made Jesus "head over all things to the church, which is his body" (1:22–3). In the chapter of 1 Corinthians that immediately precedes the famous disquisition on love that Gordon refers to in *Final Payments* and uses in the title *Men and Angels*, Paul writes most eloquently on this concept: "For as the body is one, and hath many members, and all the members of that one body being many, are one body: so also is Christ. For by one Spirit are we all baptized into one body. . . . And whether one member suffer, all the members suffer with it; or one member be honoured, all the members rejoice with it. Now ye are the body of Christ, and members in particular" (12:12–13; 26–27).

Every human being, then, is a member of the same family; blood ties matter far less than the unity all people share in Christ. The doctrine of the Mystical Body lies at the heart of Catholic belief; its concept of a community that makes no distinctions based on such human accidents as race or sex is an ideal the church has always sought to realize. Mary Gordon has said, "I guess what I see as valuable in the Church is a very high ethic of love which exists in the context of the whole of European civilization."[4]

Schooled in this approach to life, Gordon explores the boundaries of love, hopelessly limited on the merely human level but transformed when viewed in relationship to the transcendent. Very revealing are her selections for a 1985 symposium on "The Good Books: Writer's Choices":

Simone Weil, *Waiting for God*, George Herbert—a 17th-century poet—and the *Holy Sonnets* of John Donne. In Herbert, it is the perfection and the understatement of the language that allows for a simple encounter with the divine; the understatement allows for tremendous expansiveness. Simone Weil writes of a vision of God as love, and the relationship of the love of God to human life. It is rigorous, absolute, and passionate. In all three works, it is the link between spirituality and passion, as well as the absoluteness of vision. Much of my work deals with the limitation of human love; the vision of the absolute is the ideal that we as humans are striving against. If one talks about a spiritual quest, it is about this pursuit of absolute love.[5]

Gordon's choice of preposition in the penultimate sentence says a great deal. "We . . . humans strive *against* [emphasis mine]," not *toward*, the vision of the absolute, the ideal explored by Weil, Herbert and Donne. So far, her fiction has avoided the "spiritual quest," which would make "absolute love" its goal, and has focused instead on "the limitation of human love."

Therefore, her protagonists fail to acknowledge the divine dimension in human love; like the narrator in Francis Thompson's "The Hound of Heaven," they flee from the demands of absolute love, which is God, and try desperately to find substitutes for transcendence. In the first two novels, Isabel and Felicitas reject the Church at least partly because they do not really understand the substance of Christianity that lies beneath the accidents of discipline and ritual. Isabel seeks in vain for shelter in sex or in masochism. Felicitas seeks in vain for shelter in sex or in motherhood.

In her review of *Men and Angels*, Margaret Drabble notes that "this is a deliberately domestic, at times claustrophobic novel,"[6] one, indeed, in which very little happens on the surface. The Fosters plan to spend a year in France, where Michael will teach while a French colleague replaces him at Selby College in Massachusetts. But Anne decides to stay in Selby with the two children because an old friend, the art dealer Ben Hardy, offers her an opportunity to write the catalogue for an exhibition of paintings by Caroline Watson, an American artist who died in 1938. "Her misfortune was to be a merely first-rate painter in an age of geniuses" *Men and Angels* (22).

From the start, then, Gordon makes this "ordinary" family extraordinary by physically separating the parents; the Foster family is seriously weakened. Anne's decision to stay home precipitates the action, since she needs a live-in baby-sitter so that she can work. She reluctantly hires Laura Post, having conceived an instant dislike for this twenty-one-year-old who reads only the Bible. Laura is convinced that she is God's specially chosen creature (compare the status of Isabel and Felicitas!), destined to rescue Anne and her children from their pagan ways, their attachment to the flesh. Ultimately, she decides that she can rescue Anne only by taking her own life. Her suicide and its aftermath comprise the final movement of the novel.

In the earlier novels, the protagonist incorporates two extremes of behavior. Here, the extremes are split into two characters, who are meant to reflect one another; the masochist and the mother confront each other as distinct individuals. Early in the novel, Gordon goes to some trouble to suggest that Laura and Anne physically resemble each other. Thus, Anne has white skin and blue eyes, reddish hair, "a small bosom and no waist," and "comical size-eleven feet" (10). Laura has "the light blue watery eyes of many redheads, which her thick glasses clouded and enlarged. There was something opulent about her skin: it was white, translucent." If Anne has big feet, Laura has "large, protruding ears" (12). Later, Anne notes that Laura is wearing the same perfume and eye shadow Anne heself uses.

It would seem that no two people could be less alike than Laura and Anne, but this physical resemblance haunts the novel and forces the reader to consider that the all-too apparent obsessions of Laura are somehow related to the obsessive motherhood of Anne. Indeed, they share more than physical resemblance and makeup. With Michael they share the experience of mothers who failed them in one way or another. Lucy Foster, abandoned by her husband when Michael was four, could not handle domestic life: "Anne often wondered how Michael had physically survived his early childhood" (20). By the age of eight, he did all the shopping, cooking, and cleaning. But he never had cause to doubt his mother's love for him, despite her neglect of the house. Anne's mother not only disliked home life and failed during the simplest domestic crises; she never cared for Anne as Anne's father does; the mother has always feared that Anne's success would overshadow her sister, who even in adulthood resents Anne. Both Michael and Anne "had been, as children, mothers, both involved in the conspiracy at the center of the lives of children of deficient parents" (21).

Anne's only real failure in life occurs in 1974, when she loses her job at Boston's Gardner Museum: "She had felt shame then, as she had never in her life felt it before. . . . She knew, for the first time then, that failure made you feel like a criminal" (39). Unfortunately, Laura has never known success, and her lunacy derives directly from her brutal childhood. In *The Company of Women*, Felicitas recalls that, for some months, she was unable to treat Linda as her child: "I neglected Linda; I neglected her shamefully, but she is all right. I have read that a mother's rejection can cause autism and schizophrenia" (243).

A mother at seventeen, Mrs. Post rejects Laura because Laura's birth represents the end of her freedom. (Interestingly, Anne and Mrs.

Post are the same age: Anne could also have a twenty-one-year-old daughter; instead, her older child is only nine.) The damage is compounded by the passivity of Laura's father, who makes no effort to intervene when the mother mistreats Laura and favors their younger daughter. Mrs. Post withholds love from Laura and also destroys Laura's innocence, not only by tossing bloody menstrual napkins anywhere but by commiting adultery in the middle of the afternoon.

The Spirit first comes to Laura after a particualry vicious attack by Mrs. Post; her mother's rejection causes her to "find the Lord." From the start Laura's "Christianity" scorns and fears human love; so badly hurt by her mother, she avoids risking love and thus cripples her Christianity. Rejecting the possibility of human love, Laura leaves home and takes up with a sect of religious fanatics whose leader insists that the Lord desires the joining of his body and Laura's "flesh to flesh" (82). Later, she sleeps with Anne's philandering friend Adrian, whom earlier she had fantasized marrying, because she wants to keep him from Anne. "Laura did not understand marriage; the idea of it disgusted her: choosing a partner for the urges of the flesh, in filth creating children to be hurt and caused to suffer" (86).

Laura abhors sex and fears human attachments. When she fantasizes about marrying Adrian in Anne's house and living with him nearby, she catches herself: "They would love her but she would not love back as much. Because she still would have the Spirit. They would have to stay but she might leave at any time because she knew that attachments meant nothing. . . . She would have to be careful. Careful that she did not start to need, careful to remember that it was all nothing" (117-18). Ironically, Laura eventually dreams of a kind of celibate marriage with Anne; when Anne fires her for neglecting the children, she takes her life in order to win Anne's love, to win love that she has never known.

Presenting Laura with *Fear and Trembling* and *Waiting for God* as Christmas presents, Michael "tried to tell her about them. But she didn't care. Books would lead no one to the Spirit. In the Scripture she found all she needed" (147). Laura's tragedy is that she cannot find a human love to validate her love of God. She is completely isolated; she excommunicates herself from all human and religious community. Laura Post is the unloved child who never really understands the "whole point of the Gospels. She read them over and over, and she never got the point. . . . That she was greatly beloved." Unfortunately, "the love of God means nothing to a heart that is starved of human love" (231). The deranged Laura kills herself to save Anne Foster; ironically, her suicide does have a lasting effect; it destroys forever Anne's illusion that she can shelter her children from life and its dangers simply by the force of her motherly will.

Desiring to save her children from life, Anne exposes them to it sooner than she ever was exposed herself—indeed, she doesn't learn how awful it can be until confronted by Laura's suicide. Isabel in *Final Payments* decides that life is "monstrous: what you had you were always in danger of losing. The greatest love meant only the greatest danger. That was life; life was monstrous" (294). Anne recognizes this truth in the abstract, but it takes Laura to incarnate it for her, when she is thirty-eight years old. Gordon demonstrates Anne's obsessive love for her children in as much detail as she documents Laura's lunacy.

Anne's mother-love demonstrates the truth of a remark addressed to her at one point in the novel: "You're a great believer in the power of blood. A real primitive you are, aren't you?" (167). Early in the story, Gordon writes: "No one would ever know the passion she felt for her children. It was savage, lively, volatile. It would smash, in one minute, the image people had of her of someone who lived life serenely, steering always the same sure, slow course. As it was, they would never know, she was rocked back and forth, she was lifted up and down by waves of passion: of fear, of longing, of delight" (17).

At the crisis of the story, when Laura inadvertently allows the children to walk on an icy pond probably not firm enough to hold them, Anne brings the children to safety and then turns to Laura. "The desire to put her hands around Laura's throat, to take one of the large rocks on the shore and smash her skull, to break the ice and hold her head under the water till she felt her life give out was as strong as any passion Anne had ever known" (203). The gravity of the situation justifies Anne's anger. But it is also clear that Anne lives far from the extended families of the earlier novels and is unfamiliar with the concept of the Mystical Body, with its promise that blood is not all-important, that there are relationships that transcend the physical.

Long before this crisis, Gordon makes clear that religious belief is foreign to the Fosters; Anne's mother admits that her daughters "were both brought up quite irreligiously. I went to convent school for twelve years and had all I could take. Perhaps that was rash" (151). Consequently, "Anne had never understood the religious life. She could be moved by it when it led to some large public generosity. . . . But there was another side to it she couldn't comprehend. People led religious lives in the way that people wrote poetry, heard music" (41). As for the children, "Peter and Sarah hadn't been told anything about the devil" (14).

Yet someone Anne greatly respects and admires, Caroline Watson's daughter-in-law Jane, has a religious life and articulates some of the most important insights in the novel. It is Jane who realizes that Laura missed the "whole point of the Gospels" and who identifies Anne as "a great believer in the power of blood." Out of a sense of guilt over the death of her husband, Stephen, Caroline's illegitimate son, Jane "turned to faith because it showed the possibility of forgiveness for the unforgivable" (267).

Caroline's inability to love Stephen, her own flesh and blood, angers Anne, and Caroline's mistreatment of her son threatens Anne's ability to write about her objectively. "Whenever Anne thought of Caroline's treatment of Stephen she came upon a barrier between them that was as profound as one of language. . . . She couldn't imagine Peter or Sarah marrying anyone she would prefer to them, as Caroline had preferred Jane to Stephen" (68). Stephen's death at the age of twenty-eight was the result.

When Michael returns from France for Christmas, the Fosters visit Jane Watson. Michael notes that she has many of Simone Weil's books. Ben comments:

"Michael, be a dear boy and don't go on about Mademoiselle Weil. It's bound to make Jane and me come to blows. All that hatred of the flesh. . . ."

"It was Simone Weil who brought me to a religious life. Well, she and George Herbert."

"How so?" asked Michael.

Anne was embarrassed. She thought that religious people shouldn't talk about such things in public. . . . But Michael, she knew, had no such qualms. To him a religious disposition was only one more example of odd human traits quite randomly bestowed, like buckteeth or perfect pitch. Anne felt it was something powerful and incomprehensible. It made people behave extraordinarily; it made them monsters of persecution, angels of self-sacrifice. [161–62]

From her curious vantage point, Laura recognizes the emptiness of the lives around her. The reader is forced to wonder how long Anne and her family can survive in the culture of secular materialism that surrounds them. It is no accident, surely, that Laura's choice of suicide—slitting her wrists and bleeding to death in a bathtub that overflows down to the basement—destroys much of the fabric of the Foster home; possessions will not provide shelter, any more than mother-love can.

Laura's suicide is the desperate act of a deranged person. Yet it may force Anne to move beyond "blood" and mother-love to some concept of love that can embrace even the unlovable. Like Isabel with the old people in *Final Payments*, she practices "charity" on Laura, buying her beautiful clothing and fussing to celebrate her birthday. Unable to like Laura, Anne fails to love her, fails to provide her even a foster home. Loving Laura would mean taking some responsibility for her, providing her with real help, probably with psychiatric care.

Laura's death brings her the recognition she was denied in life: Anne could not love her, but she pledges to mourn for her. Weeping in Michael's arms, Anne reflects on the love that features so prominently in Gordon's work:

People were so weak, and life would raise its whip and bring it down again and again on the bare tender flesh of the most vulnerable. Love was what they needed, and most often it was not there. It was abundant, love, but it could not be called. It was won by chance; it was a monstrous game of luck. Fate was too honorable a name for it. . . . [Laura] was starved, and she had died of it. And Anne let her husband's love feed her. Let the shade of its wing shelter her, cover her over. But no wing had ever covered Laura. The harsh light had exhausted her until she could only go mad. And then the whip had fallen. And Anne knew that she had helped the whip to descend. [231–32]

In partially recognizing love's power, Anne may come to understand the love that transcends human love, that consoles even in cases like Laura's. At Laura's funeral service, for the first time in their lives, Peter and Sarah hear religious language as the priest recites several Psalms, including Psalm 121: "The Lord shall preserve thee from all evil: he shall preserve thy soul." The Fosters may come to recognize that familial love is not enough. But Gordon's focus, always, is on "the limitation of human love," and that limitation is nowhere more brilliantly presented than in *Men and Angels*.

Mary Gordon uses various strategies to explore how people live and relate to each other in the late twentieth century. In *Final Payments* and *The Company of Women*, she studies the Catholic subculture in disarray as certainties fade; shelter is offered by extended families, earthly echoes of the Mystical Body. But these families are flawed, even that of Father Cyprian, whose "company of women" is insular and isolated. There is no sense here of the universal community predicated by St. Paul or the Canon of the Mass. The third novel, *Men and Angels*, shifts the focus to an "average" American family. But the shelter offered here, in an a-religious environment, is so fragile that it cannot include the troubled Laura.

"Nobody wants to write about yuppies," Gordon herself has remarked. "It's much more interesting to write about a closed, slightly secret, marginal group."[7] This preference explains the first two novels, some of the short stories, and the work in progress, a treatment of the Irish immigrant experience. Yet *Men and Angels* is her "yuppy novel." As such it dramatizes forcefully the dilemma of our culture, which has left God and Church behind but not yet found a satisfactory substitute—the best it can offer is a Foster family.

NOTES

1. Mary Gordon, "Work in Progress," *New York Times Book Review,* July 15, 1979, 14.

2. In this essay page numbers from Mary Gordon's books are given in parentheses in the text.

3. John A. O'Brien, ed., *Understanding the Catholic Faith* (Notre Dame, Ind.: Ave Maria Press, 1955), 123.

4. Mary Gordon, "The Irish Catholic Church," in *Once a Catholic,* ed. Peter Occhiogrosso (Boston: Houghton-Mifflin, 1987), 77.

5. Karen Fitzgerald, ed., "The Good Books: Writer's Choices," *Ms.,* Dec. 1985, 30.

6. Margaret Drabble, "The Limits of Mother Love: *Men and Angels"* (review), *New York Times Book Review,* March 31, 1985, 30.

7. Joseph Berger, "Being Catholic in America," *New York Times Magazine,* Aug. 23, 1987, 65.

A Bibliography of Writings by MARY GORDON

John W. Mahon

BOOKS

Final Payments. New York: Random House, 1978.
The Company of Women. New York: Random House, 1980.
Men and Angels. New York: Random House, 1985.
Temporary Shelter (short stories). New York: Random House, 1987.

POEMS

"Poem for the End of the Year" *New York Review of Books* 28 (Dec. 17, 1981): 46.
"Wedding Photograph: June 1921." *Times Literary Supplement,* Dec. 25, 1981, 1501.
"Reading Auden while Nursing My Daughter." *New Statesman* 103 (June 18, 1982): 22.

ARTICLES, REVIEWS, STORIES

"Now I Am Married." *Virginia Quarterly Review* 51 (Summer 1975): 380–400. Reprinted in *Temporary Shelter.*

"The Other Woman." *Redbook,* Aug. 1976, 59–60. Reprinted in *Temporary Shelter.*

"The Thorn." *Ms,* Jan. 1977, 66–68. Reprinted in *Temporary Shelter.*

"Sisters." *Ladies Home Journal,* July 1977, 78–79.

"A Serious Person" (story). *Redbook,* Aug. 1977, 61–62.

"Kindness" (story). *Mademoiselle,* Oct. 1977, 224.

"The Writing Lesson." *Mademoiselle,* April 1978, 246. Reprinted in *Temporary Shelter.*

"Delia." *Atlantic,* June 1978, 42–45. Reprinted in *Temporary Shelter.*

"More Catholic Than the Pope: Archbishop Lefebvre and the Rome of the One True Church" *Harper's,* July 1978, 58 + .

"The Predicament" (review of *The Ambivalence of Abortion,* by Linda Bird Francke; *Abortion in America,* by James C. Mohr). *New York Review of Books* 25 (July 20, 1978): 37.

"The Magician's Wife." *Woman's Day,* Sept. 27, 1978, 52. Reprinted in *Temporary Shelter.*

"Swim or Sink" (review of *Other Shores,* by Diana Nyad). *New York Review of Books* 25 (Dec. 21, 1978): 52.

"Murder." *Antioch Review* 37 (Winter 1979): 106 + .

"The Habit of Genius: Flannery O'Connor, *The Habit of Being.*" *Saturday Review,* April 14, 1979, 42 + .

"Moving." *Southern Review* 15 (April 1979): 420 + .

"What Mary Ann Knew" (review of *Only Children,* by Alison Lurie). *New York Review of Books* 26 (June 14, 1979): 31.

"Women's Friendships." *Redbook,* July 1979, 31.

"Work in Progress." *New York Times Book Review,* July 15, 1979, 14.

"The Quest of Sister Mary Pelagia" (review of *The Glassy Sea,* by Marian Engel). *New York Times Book Review,* Sept. 9, 1979, 12.

Review of *Cannibals and Missionaries,* by Mary McCarthy. *New York Times Book Review,* Sept. 30, 1979, 1.

Review of *The Giant at the Ford,* by Ursula Synge. *New York Times Book Review,* April 27, 1980, 45 + .

Review of *China Men,* by Maxine Hong Kingston. *New York Times Book Review,* June 15, 1980, 1.

Review of *The Second Coming,* by Walker Percy. *New York,* July 28, 1980, 32.

"Company of Women" (Condensation of novel). *Redbook,* March 2, 1981, 145–67.

"On *A Room of One's Own:* The Fate of Women of Genius." *New York Times Book Review,* Sept. 13, 1981, 26, 28–29.

"A World of Baffled Love" (Review of *The Country,* by David Plante). *New York Times Book Review,* Oct. 4, 1981, 13.

"The Murderer Guest." *Redbook*, Nov. 1981, 29. Reprinted in *Temporary Shelter*.

"I Would Like to Have Written." *New York Times Book Review*, Dec. 6, 1981, 7.

"Coming to Terms with Mary: Meditations on Innocence, Grief, and Glory." *Commonweal* 109 (Jan. 15, 1982): 11 + .

Review of *Prince of Darkness and Other Stories* and of *Morte D'Urban*, by J.F. Powers. *New York Review of Books* 29 (May 27, 1982): 29.

"Safe." *Ms.*, June 1982, 50 + . Reprinted in *Temporary Shelter*.

"One Isolated World within Another" (review of *Felice*, by Angela Davis-Gardner). *New York Times Book Review*, June 6, 1982, 12.

"The Unexpected Things I Learned from the Women Who Talked Back to the Pope." *Ms.*, July/Aug. 1982, 65 + .

"The Only Son of the Doctor." *Redbook*, Aug. 1982, 45. Reprinted in *Prize Stories, 1983: The O. Henry Awards* and in *Temporary Shelter*.

"The Poor Man of Assisi" (review of *Francis*, by Tomie de Paola). *New York Times Book Review*, Aug. 22, 1982, 33.

"Books That Gave Me Pleasure." *New York Times Book Review*, Dec. 5, 1982, 9.

Review of *The Stories of William Trevor* and of *Fools of Fortune*, by William Trevor. *New York Review of Books* 30 (May 22, 1983): 53.

"The Hum inside the Skull (Authors Tell of Writers Who Most Influenced Them)." *New York Times Book Review*, May 13, 1984, 1.

Review of *Alfie Gives a Hand*, by Shirley Hughes. *New York Times Book Review*, June 24, 1984, 33.

"The Neighborhood." *Ms.*, July 1984, 70. Reprinted in *Temporary Shelter*.

"The Failure of True Love" (review of *A Fanatic Heart*, by Edna O'Brien). *New York Times Book Review*, Nov. 18, 1984, 1 + .

"The Imagination of Disaster." *Granta:Science* 16, (Winter 1985): 163–66.

"On Mothership and Authorhood." *New York Times Book Review*, Feb. 10, 1985, 1 + .

"Looking for Seymour Glass." In "How the City Shapes Its Writers." *World of New York* (Part 2 of *New York Times Magazine*), April 28, 1985, 32 + .

"I Married an Alien." *Vogue*, May 1985, 159 + .

"My Father's Daughter." *Mademoiselle*, May 1985, 184.

"Vanities of the Hunting Class" (review of *The Rising Tide* and *Devoted Ladies*, by M.J. Farrell). *New York Times Book Review* Sept. 29, 1985, 43.

"From the Council to the Synod." *Commonweal* 112 (Oct. 18, 1985): 569 + .

Review of *Occasional Prose*, by Mary McCarthy. *Esquire*, Nov. 1985, 249 + .

"Pig Tales" (review of *More Tales of Amanda Pig*, by Jean Van Leeuwen). *New York Times Book Review*, Nov. 10, 1985, 43.

"The Good Books: Writer's Choices." *Ms.*, Dec. 1985, 30.

"Let Us Now Praise Unsung Writers." *Mother Jones*, Jan. 1986, 27.

"The Life and Hard Times of Cinderella" (review of *Marya: A Life*, by Joyce Carol Oates). *New York Times Book Review*, March 2, 1986, 7.

"Why I Love to Read about Movie Stars" (reviews of books about Elvis Presley, Katharine Hepburn, Jane Russell, Ingrid Bergman). *Ms.*, May 1986, 22–23.

"Love in Heavy Armor" (review of *Half the Way Home: A Memoir of Father and Son*, by Adam Hochschild). *New York Times Book Review*, June 15, 1986, 7.

"The Dancing Party." *Ms.*, Aug., 1986, 64. Reprinted in *Temporary Shelter.*

"Sharon Gless and Tyne Daly." *Ms.*, Jan. 1987, 40+.

"What He Found, What He Lost" (review of *Faith, Sex, Mystery: A Memoir*, by Richard Gilman). *New York Times Book Review*, Jan. 18, 1987, 1.

"Violation." *Mademoiselle*, May 1987, 132. Reprinted in *Temporary Shelter.*

"Baby M: New Questions about Biology and Destiny." *Ms.*, June 1987, 25+.

"Chords of a Dissonant Choir: Leading American Catholics Critique John Paul." *Newsweek*, Sept. 21, 1987, 30.

"The Word for Children" (review of *The Book of Adam to Moses*, by Lore Segal, and *Adam and Eve*, the Bible story adapted and illustrated by Warwick Hutton). *New York Times Book Review*, Nov. 8, 1987, 29+.

"The Irish Catholic Church." In *Once a Catholic*, edited by Peter Occhiogrosso, 65–78. Boston: Houghton-Mifflin, 1987.

"Introduction to *Ethan Frome and Other Short Fiction*, by Edith Wharton. New York: Bantam Classics, 1987.

"Abasement Was Irresistible" (review of *Black Box*, by Amos Oz). *New York Times Book Review*, April 24, 1988, 7.

A Bibliography of Writings about MARY GORDON

John W. Mahon

Ableman, Paul. "Last Things: *Final Payments*" (review). *Spectator*, Jan. 13, 1979, 23–24.

Allen, Bruce. "*Final Payments*" (review). *Sewanee Review* 86 (Fall 1978): 616.

Armstrong, Marion. "*The Company of Women*" (review). *Christian Century* 98 (April 22, 1981): 454.

Auchard, John. "Mary Gordon." *Dictionary of Literary Biography* 6: 109–12. Detroit: Gale Research Co., 1980.

Bannon, Barbara. "PW Interviews Mary Gordon." *Publishers Weekly* 219 (Feb. 6, 1981): 274–75.

Becker, Alida. "*Men and Angels*" (review). *Book World—Washington Post*, March 31, 1985, 6.

Becker, Brenda L. "Virgin Martyrs: *The Company of Women*" (review). *American Spectator* 14, (Aug. 1981): 28–32.

Bell, P.K. *"Final Payments"* (review). *Commentary* 66 (Sept. 1978) 70.

Barret, Anthony J. "Religion and Comedy in Recent Fiction." *New Catholic World* 225 (1982): 254–56.

Billington, Rachel. "Women at Bay: *Temporary Shelter* (review). *New York Times Book Review,* April 19, 1987, 8.

Bras, Benvenuta. *"The Company of Women"* (review). *Critic* 39 (May 1981): 4.

Brown, Rosellen. *"Men and Angels"* (review). *New Republic,* April 29, 1985, 34.

Clark, Diana Cooper. "An Interview with Mary Gordon." *Commonweal* 107, May 9, 1980: 270–73.

Clemons, Walter. "Ah, They're on to Me," (interview). *Newsweek,* April 1, 1985, 75.

———. "Let Charity and Love Prevail: *Men and Angels"* (review). *Newsweek,* April 1, 1985, 75.

Cooper-Clark, Diana. "An Interview with Mary Gordon." *Commonweal* 107 (May 9, 1980): 270 +.

Costello, John. *"Men and Angels"* (review). *America* (July 13, 1985): 19.

Craig, Patricia. *"Men and Angels"* (review). *Times Literary Supplement,* Oct. 25, 1985, 1202.

De Mott, Benjamin. *"Final Payments"* (review). *Atlantic,* May 1978, 94.

———. *"The Company of Women"* (review). *Atlantic,* March 1981, 86.

Dillard, Annie. "Critics' Christmas Choices." *Commonweal* 106 (1979): 693–94.

Drabble, Margaret. "The Limits of Mother Love: *Men and Angels"* (review). *New York Times Book Review,* March 31, 1985, 1.

Dudar, Helen. "Portrait of the Artist as a Young Mom." *Wall Street Journal,* April 1, 1985, 20.

Duffy, Martha. *"Final Payments"* (review). *Time,* April 24, 1978, 92.

Eder, Richard. *"Men and Angels"* (review). *Los Angeles Times,* April 14, 1985, B3.

Feeney, Joseph J. "Imagining Religion in America: Three Contemporary Novelists." *Critic* 42 (Winter 1987): 58–74.

"Final Payments" (review). *Thought* 55 (Dec. 1980): 483.

Fitzgerald, Sally. *"The Company of Women"* (review). *Commonweal* 108 (June 19, 1981): 375.

Gilead, S. "Mary Gordon's *Final Payments* and the Nineteenth Century English Novel." *Critique* 27 (Summer 1986): 213–27.

Gray, Francine du Plessix. "A Religious Romance: *The Company of Women"* (review). *New York Times Book Review,* Feb. 15, 1981, 1 +.

Gray, Paul. *"Men and Angels"* (review). *Time,* April 1, 1985, 77.

Greenland, Colin. *"Men and Angels"* (review). *New Statesman* 110 (Nov. 1, 1985): 32.

Greenwell, Bill. "*The Company of Women*" (review). *New Statesman* 102 (July 7, 1981): 21.

Griffin, Emilie. "Man, Woman, Catholic III." *America,* July 11, 1981, 8–9.

Grumbach, Doris. "*Final Payments*" (review). *Saturday Review,* March 4, 1978, 32.

Harrison, B.G. "*The Company of Women*" (review). *Saturday Review,* Feb. 1981, 62.

Heller, Amanda. "*Final Payments*" (review). *Atlantic Monthly,* May 1978, 94.

Howard, Maureen. "Salvation in Queens: *Final Payments*" (review). *New York Times Book Review,* April 16, 1978, 1, 32.

Hulbert, Ann. "*The Company of Women*" (review). *New Republic,* Feb. 28, 1981, 33.

Hunt, George. "Man, Woman, Catholic II." *America,* July 11, 1981, 6–8.

Iannone, Carol. "The Secret of Mary Gordon's Success." *Commentary* 79 (June 1985): 62 + .

"Interview." *Vogue,* April 1985, 232 + .

Kakutani, Michiko. "Portrait of the Artist as a First Novelist." *New York Times Book Review,* June 8, 1980, 7.

———. "*Men and Angels*" (review). *New York Times,* March 20, 1985, C21.

Kolbenschlag, Madonna, G. Hunt, and E. Griffen. "Man, Woman, Catholic I." *America,* July 4–11, 1981, 4–9.

Lardner, Susan. "No Medium: *The Company of Women*" (review). *New Yorker,* April 6, 1981, 177–80.

Lee, Hermione. "The Perils of Safety: *Temporary Shelter*" (review). *Times Literary Supplement,* July 17, 1987, 765.

Lehmann-Haupt, Christopher. "*The Company of Women*" (review). *New York Times,* Feb. 13, 1981, C28.

———. "Effects a Writer Didn't Intend." *New York Times,* June 4, 1981, C17.

———. "*Temporary Shelter*" (review). *New York Times,* April 9, 1987, C25.

Levine, Paul. "Recent Women's Fiction and the Theme of Personality." In *The Origins and Originality of American Culture,* edited by Tibor Frank, 333–43. Budapest: Akademiai Kiado, 1984.

Lodge, David. "The Arms of the Church: *Final Payments*" (review). *Times Literary Supplement,* Sept. 1, 1978, 965.

"Mary Gordon." *Contemporary Authors* 102 (1981) 233 + .

"Mary Gordon." *Contemporary Literary Criticism* 13 (1980): 249 + .

———. *Contemporary Literary Criticism* 22 (1982): 184 + .

May, John R. "Mary Gordon." *Dictionary of Literary Biography Yearbook, 1981,* 81–85.

McKenzie, Madora. "*Final Payments*" (review). *Christian Science Monitor,* May 25, 1978, 23.

McNeil, Helen. "Miraculous Births: *The Company of Women*" (review). *Times Literary Supplement,* July 3, 1981, 747.

"*Men and Angels*" (review). *New Yorker,* April 29, 1985, 132.

"*Men and Angels*" (review). *Hudson Review* 38 (Autumn 1985): 771.

Mitgang, Herbert. "A Cabin of One's Own." *New York Times Book Review,* March 31, 1985, 30.

Morey, Ann-Janine. "Beyond Updike: Incarnated Love in the Novels of Mary Gordon." *Christian Century,* Nov. 20, 1985, 1059 + .

O'Rourke, William. "*The Company of Women*" (review). *Nation,* Feb. 28, 1981, 245.

Phillips, Robert. "*Men and Angels*" (review). *Commonweal* 112 (May 17, 1985): 308.

Pompea, N. "*Final Payments*" (review). *Choice* 15 (June 1978): 545.

———. "*Final Payments*" (review). *Best Sellers* 38 (Aug. 1978): 141.

Prescott, Peter S. "*Final Payments*" (review). *Newsweek,* April 10, 1978, 92.

———. "*The Company of Women*" (review). *Newsweek,* Feb. 16, 1981. 89.

Rawley, James M., and Robert F. Moss. "The Pulp of the Matter." *Commonweal* 105 (Oct. 27, 1978): 685–89.

Robertson, N. "Mary Gordon! Mary Gordon!" *Critic* 37 (Sept. 2, 1978): 4 + .

Sabolik, Mary. "*Final Payments*" (review). *America* June 17, 1978, 490.

Sandmaier, Marian. "*The Company of Women*" (review). *New Directions for Women* 10 (May-June 1981): 13.

Sanoff, A. P. "Growing up Catholic and Creative." *U.S. News and World Report,* Oct. 5, 1987, 74.

Schreiber, Le Anne. "A Talk with Mary Gordon." *New York Times Book Review,* Feb. 15, 1981, 26–28.

Sheed, Wilfrid. "The Defector's Secrets: *Final Payments*" (review). *New York Review of Books* 25 (June 1, 1978): 14–15.

———. "Mary Gordon: *Final Payments.*" In *The Good Word and Other Words,* edited by Wilfrid Sheed, 259–65. New York: Dutton, 1978.

Sheppard, R.Z. "*The Company of Women*" (review). *Time,* Feb. 16, 1981, 79.

Simon, Linda. "*Men and Angels*" (review). *Christian Science Monitor,* April 22, 1985, 21.

Slung, Michele. "*The Company of Women*" (review). *Ms.,* March 1981, 77.

Sorel, Nancy. "A New Look at 'Noble Suffering.' " *New York Times Book Review,* Jan. 26, 1986, 1 + .

Stetzmann, Rainulf A. "Verlassenheit, Gnade und Glück: Die Erstlingsromane Joseph Caldwells und Mary Gordons." *Stimmen der Zeit* 197 (1979): 65 + .

———. "Katholizismus und Frauenemanizipation: Die Romane Francine du Plessix Grays und Mary Gordons." *Stimmen der Zeit* 199 (1981): 641 + .

———. "Mit Menschen und mit Engelszungen: Gott und Welt in den Werken Christa Wolfs und Mary Gordons." *Stimmen der Zeit* 203 (1985): 693 + .

Sullivan, Walter. "Model Citizens and Marginal Cases: Heroes of the Day." *Sewanee Review* 87 (Spring 1979): 337–44.

Taliaferro, Frances. "*Final Payments*" (review). *Harper's,* April 1978: 84.

"*Temporary Shelter*" (review). *Time,* April 20, 1987, 74.

"*Temporary Shelter*" (review). *Book World* 17 (April 26, 1987): 8.

"*Temporary Shelter*" (review). *Village Voice,* May 19, 1987, 48.

"*Temporary Shelter*" (review). *Ms.,* June 15, 1987, 16.

"*Temporary Shelter*" (review). *Los Angeles Times Book Review,* July 12, 1987, 10.
"*Temporary Shelter*" (review). *London Review of Books,* July 23, 1987, 24.
Towers, Robert. "*The Company of Women*" (review). *New York Review of Books* 28 (March 19, 1981): 7.
Wiehe, Janet. "*Final Payments*" (review). *Library Journal* 103 (March 15, 1978): 683.
Wolcott, James. "More Catholic Than the Pope." *Esquire,* March 3, 1981, 21, 23.

JOAN DIDION

The Bond between Narrator and Heroine in *Democracy*

Katherine Usher Henderson

When Susan Stamberg told Joan Didion in a 1977 radio interview that she would never win the Nobel Prize for literature because her novels were too pessimistic, Didion readily agreed.

I think that's probably true. . . . One of the books that made the strongest impression on me when I was in college was *The Portrait of a Lady*. Henry James's heroine, Isabel Archer, was the prototypic romantic idealist. It trapped her, and she ended up a prisoner of her own ideal. I think a lot of us do. My adult life has been a succession of expectations, misperceptions. I dealt only with an idea I had of the world, not with the world as it was. The reality *does* intervene eventually. I think my *early* novels were ways of dealing with the revelation that experience is largely meaningless. [Emphasis mine.][1]

At the time of this interview, Didion had published three novels—*Run River* (1963), *Play It As It Lays* (1970), and *A Book of Common Prayer* (1977). To Stamberg's earlier challenge that she found *Play It As It Lays* and *Common Prayer* frightening, even distasteful, Didion had answered obliquely, "*A Book of Common Prayer* is . . . not a good deal more cheerful, but I think it's not as ugly."

By the end of *Common Prayer*, two of the four major characters are dead and a third, the narrator, is dying. Yet its atmosphere is not unreservedly ugly because it embodies a powerful existential moral:

Photo by Quintana Roo Dunne

In a world ruled by a capricious and elusive deity (or perhaps no deity at all), people must care for one another. Our conduct must evidence a "common prayer" of grace and love, for we are bound by common morality. Decent characters in the novel are defined by their attempts to care for those who are weak or endangered. Charlotte Douglas cares for her dying baby and for the children of Boca Grande. Leonard Douglas cares for Charlotte and even—an extraordinary act of generosity—for her dying first husband. Grace Strasser-Mendana tries desperately to save Charlotte's life. Despite the courage and concern of these characters, however, the novel affirms nothing beyond the existential fact of death as the measure of friendship and love.

In a perceptive essay on "The Didion Sensibility" written shortly before the publication of *Democracy*, Ellen G. Friedman stated that Didion "has no faith in the authority of individual choice and action. The individual in her view is not endowed with the power to recreate the world, imbue it with meaning, restore coherence and purpose."[2] As Friedman acknowledged, however, Didion's characters are often redeemed by an immense capacity for commitment and love, even when—as is usually the case—that commitment is doomed to fall far short of its purpose. In *Run River* Lily's commitment to Everett cannot save him from suicide; in *Play It As It Lays* Maria's commitment to her daughter cannot restore the child to health. While intense, the heroine's devotion is in both cases flawed; Lily contributes to Everett's destruction by her repeated infidelities, and Maria cannot accept the limitations of her daughter's illness. Although both women, like Charlotte and Grace in *Common Prayer*, are ennobled by love, the love is ultimately powerless to create coherence even within the family, far less within the community or the world.

At the end of her interview with Stamberg, Didion said, "My next novel is going to take place in Hawaii. I can't describe the picture, except that it is very pink and it smells like flowers, and I'm afraid to describe it out loud because if I describe it out loud I won't write it down."[3] For this novel, which she worked on over seven years, Didion created a new prototype of character and a new universe of personal relationships; for the first time in her fictional world, she created characters capable of successful loyalties and of purposeful lives. *Democracy* is not a fanciful novel—it includes a fair share of fools and villains—but it also portrays two strong and autonomous women whose lives mesh in a pattern of order and purpose. The novel is an uneasy affirmation of the possibility of personal meaning in a world where society and politics are defined by artifice and self-seeking.

The sensibility from which *Democracy* evolved was deeply affected by Didion's travels in Latin America and in Asia, where she stayed in both Jakarta and Kuala Lumpur. She has given us a full report of one of these visits, the trip to El Salvador that she took with her husband, the writer John Dunne, in June 1982. The long essay *Salvador* (1983) is an account of the events and impressions of their two-week stay. The techniques of *Salvador* are those that define her earlier journalism: a precise rendering of what she saw, heard, and felt, a complete absence of sentimentality, a bluntness of tone that serves to make the terror more palpable. In Salvador in the summer of 1982, no place and no one was safe; ordinary parking lots sported cars with bullet-shattered windshields and congealed blood on the upholstery; ordinary people disappeared to turn up (if ever) as viciously mutilated bodies.

Both in the book and in interviews about it, Didion stated that the trip was the most terrifying experience of her life. Reporter Leslie Garis asked them why they went.

> Dunne answers instantly, "Oh, we were desperate to go."
> "Desperate to go," Didion echoes. . . .
> "I was interested in what the United States was doing in El Salvador," she says.[4]

In her career as a reporter, Didion has always felt the pull of public and private catastrophes, often seeing them as emblems of our time. In the sixties she felt a personal need to witness the pain that seared the United States—the children on drugs in Haight-Ashbury, the Manson murder trial, the burial of young Americans killed in Vietnam. Since the late seventies, she has been drawn to the pain in *other* countries as well, especially those with which the United States has been involved.

Democracy reflects the inner changes in Didion that both led to and resulted from her trip to Salvador. It was no longer a novel set in Hawaii, but a novel spanning two continents, a novel in which personal and political lives are inextricably intertwined. The first Didion novel to contain portraits of fulfilling adult relationships, it is set—paradoxically—against a background of political violence and social chaos. From its opening sentence—"The light at dawn during those Pacific tests was something to see"—the novel projects a world contracted through technology into a single community existing under the threat of nuclear holocaust. Every major character is affected by the central political event of the novel, the fall of Saigon in the spring of 1975. Corruption and instability in government are mirrored throughout by disloyalty and disorder in the extended and nuclear family.

The very real chaos in the realms of politics and society today creates a challenge for the novelist, for the novel is that form of literature that traditionally defines the individual in relation to institutions such as family, community, and nation. When these relationships lose meaning, the characters must either be shown to find meaning from another source or life's insignificance will be tacitly affirmed. The voice and "self" of the narrator often assume a crucial importance in this question of the locus of life's larger meaning.

In Part I of *Democracy*, the narrative "self" that Didion projects is problematic. "I began thinking about Inez Victor and Jack Lovett at a point in my life when I lacked certainty, lacked even that minimum level of ego essential to the writing of novels, lacked conviction, lacked patience with the past and interest in memory; lacked faith even in my own technique" (17).[5] "Call me the author," she proclaims at the opening of chapter 2 but acknowledges that she has lost her author(ity) as novelist; she knows neither where nor how to begin. She lacks the easy confidence of the Victorian narrator (she mentions Trollope). She identifies with the "gold-feathered bird" in Wallace Stevens's poem "Of Mere Being," the bird who "sings in the palm, without human meaning, without human feeling, a foreign song" (16). She has no plot, only dreams, images, and fragments of poems. "I have those pink dawns of which Jack Lovett spoke. I have the dreams, recurrent, in which my whole field of vision fills with rainbow, in which I open a door into a growth of tropical green. . . . Consider any of these things long enough and you will see that they tend to deny the relevance not only of personality but of narrative, which makes them less than ideal images with which to begin a novel, but we go with what we have" (17).[6]

For the rest of this chapter and the first portion of the next, she tells us about the novel she is *not* writing, the historical novel of Hawaii that would trace the childhood and ancestry of Inez Christian, that was to have been written from Inez's point of view. *Democracy* is a later version of the novel originally entitled *Angel Visits*, begun shortly after the completion of *A Book of Common Prayer. Angel Visits* opened with Inez Victor's recollection of her mother; its first line was, "I have never seen Madame Bovary in the flesh but imagine my mother dancing."[7] In *Democracy, Angel Visits* has become "the shards of the novel I am no longer writing. . . . I lost patience with it. I lost nerve" (29–30).

The skeleton of a romantic novel is constructed and then deconstructed. The reader is mystified. The critics were, too, although some applauded and others panned. "What is Didion doing as character in her own novel?" was the question most insistently raised by reviewers.[8] If she is writing autobiography, is her story of Inez Christian and Jack Lovett and Harry Victor biography? (Mary McCarthy actually tried to find these people in *Who's Who*.) Didion employed unconventional narrative structures in earlier novels, but in none of them did she actually appear as a character.

The answer to the question raised by the reviews lies in Didion's self-definition as a writer. Writing is for her an act of self-discovery. "I write entirely to find out what I'm thinking, what I'm looking at, what I see and what it means. What I want and what I fear."[9] Relentlessly scrupulous in this pursuit, Didion abandons projects that do not lead to essential self-knowledge. Sometime before or after her trip to El Salvador in 1982, *Angel Visits*, narrated by Inez Victor, no longer felt right. It was too provincial, too limited in scope; it was not addressing Didion's private thoughts and fears. Her awareness of America's interventionist strategies in foreign countries intruded; the trips to Asia and El Salvador intensified her quest to understand herself as a North American and as a citizen of the larger world.

At the same time, her fictional characters Inez Victor and Jack Lovett had already seized her imagination, moved into her study. ("I think you identify with all your characters," she told Sara Davidson in an interview. "They become your family, closer to you than anyone you know. They kind of move into the house and take over the furniture."[10]) She had already developed a relationship with the characters and with certain images ("Those pink dawns of which Jack Lovett spoke") surrounding them. For all of these reasons, Didion entered a version of herself into her novel—not her private self, herself as mother/wife/friend—but herself as writer and reporter. In the final chapter of *Democracy*, she acknowledges, "It has not been the novel I set out to write, nor am I exactly the person who set out to write it" (220). A process of change is implicit in that of self-discovery.

Didion the narrator discovers herself most fully by entering the life of Inez Victor, her double, her alter ego. There are several kinds of twins in the novel: Jessie and Adlai, the twin children of Inez and Harry Victor; Harry Victor and Billy Dillon, the inseparable political team of candidate and manager; and most significant, Didion and Inez, two women born three weeks apart whose paths keep crossing, who share the perils of celebrity, who are both given to reticence and emotional control in their personal relationships.[11] The story of Inez led the narrator Didion to restored confidence and self-knowledge; in turn, Didion became Inez's closest friend and confidante. Neither character can be understood without appreciating the bond that subtly develops between them.

Democracy is a novel of correspondences: in addition to the correspondences between Inez and the narrator, there are numerous correspondences between the public and the private spheres, as well as a long series of literary correspondences (e.g., between Didion's Democracy and Henry Adams's Democracy; between the rhetoric assignment that Didion cites in chapter 2 of Part 1 and the structure of the novel itself). The most thematically central of these, however, is the parallel quest for life's meaning undertaken by Inez and the narrator, a quest pursued consciously and intellectually by the narrator and, until the end of the novel, fitfully and unconsciously by Inez. During the narrator's visit to Inez in Kuala Lumpur, Inez recurrently mentions coincidences of place that form a pattern in her relationship with Jack Lovett. "During the five days I spent in Kuala Lumpur Inez mentioned such 'correspondences,' her word, a number of times, as if they were messages intended specifically for her, evidence of a narrative she had not suspected" (230). Inez articulates the narrative primarily in terms of places and events; it is the narrator's rendering of the story, the novel itself, that will locate its real significance in the emotional and moral categories of love and loyalty.

For writer Didion the quest for meaning and the obsession with narrative are components of a single struggle. In the opening essay of The White Album, she wrote: "We tell ourselves stories in order to live. . . . We live entirely, especially if we are writers, by the imposition of a narrative line upon disparate images, by the 'ideas' with which we have learned to freeze the shifting phantasmagoria which is our actual experience" (11). Didion repeatedly describes herself as a writer who begins with a concrete image born of experience and then traces its path through her imagination. The narrator of Democracy can recover meaning and certainty only when she finds a form and structure in which to cast the disparate images of the gold-feathered bird, the pink dawns, and the tropical greens that dance through her imagination.

By following the images, painfully, faithfully, she ultimately succeeds in her appointed task. The images take on contexts, the contexts yield patterns, and the patterns yield meaning. One of the clearest patterns is of parallels and intersections between her life and that of Inez, together with a felt affinity between them. In 1960 she and Inez were both working for Vogue, and Didion first met Jack

Lovett when he dropped in to see her there. ("I had known Inez Victor for perhaps a year but I had never seen her smile that way" [33].) In 1972 Didion is present when a reporter from the Associated Press asks Inez what she regards as the greatest cost of public life. Her answer is "memory." When the reporter is puzzled, she elaborates, "You drop fuel. You jettison cargo. Eject the crew. You *lose track*" (52).

Three times in the course of the interview, Inez repeated the single word *memory* in answer to the reporter's question, but when the story appeared through the Associated Press wire, it read, "Inez Victor claims she is often misquoted" (53). Inez was trying to tell the reporter that her experience of life was jagged and discontinuous, that its pressures often led her to lose a former "self" as one might drop cargo from a plane. Clearly, this reporter did not understand. Didion did, however, and from this time she takes up the burden of Inez's story, piecing it together from various sources, trying to give it coherence. She needs to do this not primarily because Inez's memory is deficient—in fact, many of her memories are sharp and clear—but because they are scattered visual memories, usually dissociated from emotion. Didion also needs to do it to recover her sense of herself as a writer; if she can find the true narrative thread that defines Inez's experience, she can recover her own conviction of life's existential meaning.

Part 1 of *Democracy* might be called Didion's book; although we learn something of Jack's life and character and much of the history of Inez's marriage, Didion's presence dominates. The reader is drawn by her elegiac feelings of transience and dislocation, her sense of drowning in disconnected dreams, her need to show us the "shards of the novel" she is not writing. (That would have been an easy novel, a "provincial novel of manners.") As the book progresses, she gradually recovers a sense of purposeful writing—and the catalyst for recovery is her felt connection with Inez. A key moment in the forging of that connection is the interview in which Didion sits quietly in the background as Inez repeats the word *memory*. Didion had cited as one symptom of her malaise a lack of "patience with the past and interest in memory" (17). By the end of Part 1, her interest is mobilized, her mood raised, her narrative under way.

By the opening of Part 2 (Inez's book), she has charted a course (while still uncertain of precisely how to navigate it) that will traverse the love story of Inez and Jack from its inception through the crisis in Inez's family that brought it full circle. The markers in this course are events and feelings that she learned from observation, from Jack, whom she encountered from time to time in her travels, from Billy

Dillon and Harry Victor, and from Inez. The chief obstacles are enigmatic qualities within the lovers: "I have no memory of any one moment in which either Inez Victor or Jack Lovett seemed to spring out, defined. They were equally evanescent, in some way emotionally invisible; unattached, wary to the point of opacity, and finally elusive. They seemed not to belong anywhere at all except, oddly, together" (84).

By the sheer persistence of her quest, which gathers such momentum that it takes her finally to Kuala Lumpur, Didion penetrates most of the mystery of Inez Victor. The woman who emerges shares certain traits with earlier Didion heroines, although in fundamental ways she is radically different. Like both Lily Knight of *Run River* and Charlotte Douglas of *A Book of Common Prayer*, she is tough and outwardly composed under stress: she remains calm when her mother abandons her in Honolulu, when Janet lies dying in the hospital, when her daughter runs away to Saigon in the closing days of the war.

In other ways, however, she represents a fundamental departure from her predecessors. Unlike Maria Wyeth of *Play It As It Lays*, who imagines that she can one day live a normal life with her brain-damaged daughter, or Lily Knight, who believes that she can have serial affairs without damaging her marriage, or Charlotte Douglas, who lives in sentimental reveries of her "inseparable" relationship with her fugitive daughter, Inez nurtures no obsessive illusions about herself or other people. She recognizes the essential character of the separate members of her family; she has a realistic grasp of what is possible and what is not. Although she *believed* for many years that Harry would become president, the belief was in the realm of the possible, to be discarded the moment he lost the nomination. Her realism, together with the courage that sustains it, enables her to survive devastating losses and still reclaim and ultimately direct her life.

She also has firmer self-esteem than her counterparts in earlier Didion novels, all of whom look to men to validate their essential self-worth. Unlike Lily, Maria, or Charlotte, she does not fall into bed with any man who wants her, for her self-respect renders her incapable of casual affairs. Although her love for Jack is profoundly sexual, her sense of decorum prevents her from acting on these feelings while she is living with her husband.

"They did run into each other.
Here or there.
Often enough, during those twenty-some years during which Inez Victor and Jack

Lovett refrained from touching each other, refrained from exhibiting undue pleasure or untoward interest in each other's activities, refrained most specifically from even being alone together, to keep the idea of it quick" (92).

The affair between Inez and Jack is one of the most heroic and moving sexual and emotional relationships of contemporary American fiction. It is also quintessentially romantic, for it ultimately demands of Jack the risk of life itself and of Inez the courage to begin life over.

When Jack first meets Inez on her seventeenth birthday,. the image of her—in a white dress with a gardenia in her hair—becomes engraved in his imagination. Their affair begins a month later, when he rescues her from a drunken date, but they both know they cannot look forward to a conventional future together. When Jack predicts, "You'll go off to college and marry some squash player and forget we ever did any of it," Inez simply responds, "I suppose we'll run into each other. . . . Here or there" (89–90). Yet she forgets nothing that passed between them. When she marries Harry Victor in the spring of her sophomore year at Sarah Lawrence, two months pregnant with his child, she sends Jack an announcement with the words "Not a squash player" written across it.

From the moment of her marriage, her story becomes that of a woman defined by her role, the supporting role of wife to an ambitious public man. Plunged almost immediately into an active political life, she appears not to develop any core of identity, any private self. For the twenty years of her marriage to Harry, she had only two genuine interests—her twin children and a strong wish to work with refugees—a wish denied when Harry's political advisers decided that "refugees were an often controversial and therefore inappropriate special interest" (56).

For twenty years she played the role that Harry and Billy Dillon assigned to her. She was beside Harry as he rose on the tide of liberal politics—through his two years with the Justice Department, through the marches in Mississippi, through his three successful campaigns for Congress, through his brief period as senator and his failed bid for the 1972 presidential nomination. She did not protest volubly when Harry had affairs (" 'Inez, I'm asking you nice, behave, girls like that come with the life,' Billy Dillon said to Inez after Connie Willis and Frances Landau" [48]). She went on speaking tours and fact-finding missions and to fund-raisers. She behaved precisely as the wife of a politician should—in his interests.

Several critics suggested that the Inez-Harry relationship was modeled on that of either Jackie and Jack or Joan and Ted Kennedy. These suggestions may have elements of truth, but the portrait of Inez could represent equally the wife of *any* American politician aspiring to national prominence, women who sacrifice not merely their time and careers but their sense of continuity and even of identity. The sacrifice is enormous, not only because they must suppress cherished wishes (Inez's wish to help refugees), but because they must shape a self that is public property, that is constantly on display. The middle-class liberal constituency of Harry Victor felt that they knew Inez, when in fact they knew only media images: "These people had all seen Inez, via telephoto lens, drying Jessie's blond hair by the swimming pool at the house in Amagansett. These people had all seen Inez, in the *Daily News*, leaving Lenox Hill Hospital with Adlai on the occasion of his first automobile accident. These people had all seen photo after photo of the studied clutter in the library of the apartment on Central Park West. . . . These people had taken their toll" (49–50).

Although faithful at times, the media image is just as likely to be false. When CBS *Reports* did brief biographies of the candidates' wives during Harry's 1972 campaign, its representation of Inez as a woman with a "very special feeling for the arts" and a "very special interest in education" was largely a fictional construct. As part of the same program, her sister Janet in a live interview presented a certainly glamorized and probably incorrect version of incidents from their childhood. While watching the televised interview, Inez drew up a list of the names of the Star Ferry boats that crossed between Hong Kong and Kowloon. At the time, Didion says, she thought of this cool detachment as "the frivolous habit of an essentially idle mind"; she later recognized it as a protective mechanism "for living a life in which the major cost was memory" (70).

Yet to reconstruct an exhaustive list of the names of boats one has never taken requires the *capacity* of a retentive memory. Didion is using "memory" in a special sense that can be illuminated by a passage from her 1966 essay "On Keeping a Notebook," which appears in *Slouching toward Bethlehem.* "I think we are well advised to keep on nodding terms with the people we used to be, whether we find them attractive company or not. . . . We forget all too soon the things we thought we could never forget. We forget the loves and the betrayals alike, forget what we whispered and what we screamed, forget who we were" (143). Inez has unconsciously divided her life into discrete segments, and with each transition she tries to jettison painful experiences from memory. She can recall from an earlier period material that is not emotionally charged—such as the names of boats—but she refuses to remember painful events such as her abandonment by her mother. This defense saves the anguish of emotional work and may help her to survive and to function, but it at times gives a hard edge to her character, and it consistently disrupts the emotional continuity of her life. The only character in the novel who penetrates this defense is her tenacious friend Didion.

Inez does not often take her emotional pulse, nor does she often look at her past. On the few occasions when she does, there is a striking difference between the happy memories and the sad ones. The positive experiences are recalled with strong emotional overtones. "She recalled being extremely happy eating lunch by herself in a hotel room in Chicago, once when snow was drifting on the window ledges. There was a lunch in Paris that she remembereed in detail: a late lunch with Harry and the twins at Pre Catelan in the rain. . . . She remembered Jessie crowing with delight and pointing imperiously at a poodle seated on a gilt chair across the room. She remembered Harry unbuttoning Adlai's wet sweater, kissing Jessie's wet hair, pouring them each a half glass of white wine" (59).[12]

Her memories of tense, unhappy moments, on the other hand, are primarily visual, only faintly suggestive of emotion. After her discovery of Jessie's addiction to heroin, she and Harry run through three therapists before discovering the program in which Jessie is helped. "Inez remembered that the therapist was wearing a silver ankh. She remembered that she could see Jessie through a glass partition, chewing on a strand of her long blond hair, bent over the Minnesota Multiphasic Personality Inventory" (61).

It is Didion who portrays for us the losses and trials of Inez's life, sometimes telling us the source of her information, sometimes slipping into the role of omniscient narrator. When Inez finds Jessie on the floor of her bedroom begging to die, she remains calm and dry-eyed, despite the fact that Jessie is by this time (June 1973) the only member of her family to whom Inez feels bound. Harry has alienated her through infidelity and hypocrisy, and Adlai at seventeen is a crude carbon copy of his father, without feeling for the girl he almost killed through reckless driving, without feeling for his sister, whom he calls "the junkie." The bond between mother and daughter—in most Didion novels the strongest of emotional ties—is deftly implied in *Democracy* when Jessie calls Inez from the adolescent treatment facility in Seattle and reports that her job is "pretty cinchy"—"The bright effort in Jessie's voice had constricted Inez's throat" (64). As Inez's marriage moves slowly but steadily toward dissolution, she neither mourns nor rages; she simply prepares in the depths of her being to once again "jettison cargo" and "eject crew."

In March 1975, as the war in Vietnam is moving toward the fall of Saigon, Didion and Inez share a parallel experience of "homecoming," of returning after twenty years to the place each grew into adulthood. Didion is lecturing at Berkeley, feeling the personal nostalgia of teaching in the same rooms in which she had attended classes as an undergraduate and, with her preternatural response to public catastrophe, obsessively following the newspaper accounts of events in Southeast Asia. "In 1955 on this campus I had first noticed the quickening of time. In 1975 time was no longer just quickening but collapsing, falling in on itself, the way a disintegrating star contracts into a black hole" (72). Although she has asked her students to "consider the political implications of both the reliance on and the distrust of abstract words," their politics are radicalized, and they interpret the fall of Saigon not as disaster but as its liberation from imperialism. Thus, she is lonely, cut off from them, for her mind is focused on the specific, concrete events of the evacuation.

At the same time, Inez returns to personal catastrophe in Honolulu, for her father has been imprisoned for shooting her sister and the Nisei politician who was probably her lover, Wendell Omura. Omura is dead, and Janet lies dying in the hospital. Like Didion, Inez is surrounded by people who not only refuse to focus on the specific events of the tragedy but deny that a tragedy has taken place. Her uncle invites her to have a martini, and her aunt suggests that she and Billy tour the ranch. Dwight and Ruth Christian have no affective response at all, not wanting the surface of life ruffled. At one level they are satirical characters; when Inez insists on trying to learn how and why the tragedy occurred, her aunt challenges, "Why air family linen?" and her uncle agrees, "Why accentuate the goddamn negative?" (128).

More significantly, Inez's aunt and uncle are used by Didion to point to the absence of traditional Judeo-Christian values in the contemporary world. They are a family named "Christian" who display neither compassion, faith, nor charity. Janet's death, taking place the day before Good Friday, is in part a retelling of Christ's crucifixion. Although the insane Paul Christian casts himself as a martyr, it is Janet and Wendell Omura who are the Christ-figures. As Christ is abandoned by his apostles, so is Janet Christian abandoned by her family. During the twenty-four hours that pass before she is declared legally dead, only Inez cares enough to keep the vigil at the hospital. Her uncle plans a simple funeral ("the ashes to ashes business") from which the Twenty-third Psalm is to be specifically excluded. "Passive crap, the Lord is my shepherd. . . . No sheep in this family" (157).

Didion invokes the Christian myth to dramatize the spiritual impoverishment of Inez's family. Only she truly mourns; when choosing the dress for Janet's burial, she cries for the only time in the novel, sharing her grief not with her husband but with Jack Lovett. Her grief breaks through her usual suppression of memory; she remembers Janet's wedding and Janet's childhood identification with their absent mother. In the flood of genuine emotion caused by Janet's death—and by seeing Jack again—her feelings for Harry are like debris on the tide. When he criticizes her for going to the hospital with Jack while her sister was dying, she tells him that their marriage is over. In recounting the scene to Didion later, she admits to a failure of memory on one point. "She had either said 'Don't dramatize' to Harry that Saturday evening or she had said 'I love him' to Harry that Saturday evening. It seemed more likely that she had said 'Don't dramatize' but she had wanted to say 'I love him' and she did not remember which" (181).

Because Inez typically expresses her strongest emotions obliquely—not once in the novel does she tell Jack directly that she loves him—the reader can be confident that she said, "Don't dramatize." *Yet she told Didion what had been in her mind, what she felt at the core of her being.* This fact is a measure of the trust between the two women, of the powerful, mutually felt bond between them.

So strong is this bond that at times Didion's memory is indistinguishable from that of Inez, and the reader does not know how Didion "knows" the details of crucial scenes in Inez's story. One such scene takes place after Inez has said goodbye to Harry, when she goes with Jack to the bars where he hopes to learn of Jessie's whereabouts in Saigon.

Where Inez stood with her back against the jukebox and her arms around Jack Lovett. Where the Mamas and the Papas sang "Dream A Little Dream of Me." [187]

The novel keeps returning to a single line of dialogue from this scene, Jack's lament that Inez is married to a politician of national prominence, "Oh shit, Inez . . . Harry Victor's wife." Jack understands the likely personal consequences of his elopement with Inez. He knows that it will probably spell the end of his career as an undercover agent for the United States; he may also suspect that it will place his life in jeopardy. His willingness to suffer these consequences is the ultimate test and ultimate proof of love.

Of the cast of characters in *Democracy*, only Jack and Inez approach realization of the ideals their names suggest. Ruth Christian is perhaps the most ruthless character in the novel, concerned only with preserving appearances and avoiding all feeling and sentiment; Dwight Christian (unlike Dwight Eisenhower, who created unity among those around him) generates division by betraying Janet's husband in their business dealings. The bigoted and self-pitying Paul Christian is the opposite of the saint who welcomed all races into the Church. Harry Victor sustains only losses—the nomination, his wife, and almost his daughter. Only Inez embodies authentic Christian values, leaving her family on Easter night for a journey that will end with the sacrifice of comforts to a permanent, lonely commitment to serving the human community. Her description of her departure with Jack suggests resurrection and new life. "Inez said the 3:45 a.m. flight from Honolulu to Hong Kong was exactly the way she hoped dying would be. Dawn all the way."

Love for Jack is service and loyalty; he spends much of his life waiting for Inez, protecting her from rain and from danger, respecting her marriage until she herself denies it. It is her decision to flee the charade of "the correct thing" with which her aunt and uncle are obsessed, to acknowledge the hollowness of her marriage by resigning the role of supportive wife and public figure. The break is final and permanent; once again she has jettisoned cargo and ejected the crew of her past. This time, however, she will find her own place, be her own person. She is not an Isabel Archer, Didion's "prototypic romantic idealist," willing to remain imprisoned within a loveless marriage.

Part 3, covering the month of April 1975, is a transitional segment of the novel. Inez is in Hong Kong—for the most part alone, as Jack makes repeated trips to Saigon, both to gain strategic information and to find Jessie before the American evacuation is completed. The sexual component of their reunion is muted almost to complete silence, in keeping with the urgency of the occasion. Yet their relationship is tender and generous on both sides; for one entire night, Inez listens to Jack describe the madness that has taken over the leadership of the falling city, and when Inez expresses fears that Jessie may be lost, Jack promises to find her.

During the long days of solitude and waiting, Inez establishes a routine; she walks in the rain, reads American newspapers at the embassy, and spends much time watching Chinese children playing outside a nursery school. When Jessie's safety is assured, she realizes that her attitude and perspective toward herself and her family has radically changed. She feels separated from Harry and the children— and from her former "self"—by a vast emotional distance.

> It occurred to her that for almost the first time in twenty years she was not particularly interested in any of them.
> Responsible for them, yes, in a limited way, but not interested in them.
> They were definitely connected to her but she could no longer grasp her own or their uniqueness, her own or their difference, genius, special claim. . . . The world that night was full of people flying from place to place and fading in and out and there was no reason why she or Harry or Jessie or Adlai or for that matter Jack Lovett. . . should be exempted from the general movement. . . .
> Just because they were Americans. [207–8]

Like Didion, who anguished over events in Saigon, she now feels a member, not of a family or nation, but of the world community. Not fully understanding why, she is ready to forgo the privileged status of the American citizen. Since Inez is unable to define her own "uniqueness," Didion will attempt the definition by constructing the narrative of her life, probing its mystery.

In the summer of 1975, Didion travels thousands of miles to build her narrative—to learn events and their dates, to learn why Inez is in Kuala Lumpur and what happened to Jack. She travels to New York and to Martha's Vineyard to talk with Harry Victor and Billy Dillon and to Honolulu to speak with Dick Ziegler. She even talks briefly with Jessie and Adlai. But Inez remains inaccessible, politely but firmly rejecting Didion's repeated requests to see her—until the first week in December when she suddenly changes her mind and invites her to come to Kuala Lumpur.

Only to Didion does Inez communicate her memories of her sister and the details of Jack's death, as well as her view of their love affair. Didion is frustrated because Inez cannot remember those facts—places and dates—that are important to a reporter, but her memory is otherwise clear and full. For five days she recounts memories to Didion. She remembers her mother, slightly drunk, singing at her sister's wedding; she remembers that Janet as a child "had studied snapshots of Carol Christian and cut her hair the same way" (155). Her account of Jack's sudden death in Jakarta and her long trip with his body to Honolulu, where she negotiates an honorable burial space for him in the military cemetery at Schofield, is deeply moving, for this loss followed that of her sister by only four months. After burying

Jack under the jacaranda tree, Inez flies directly to Kuala Lumpur, without seeing or calling any member of her family.

Part 4 of the novel gives us a later perspective on the narrator's meeting with Inez in December 1975. (Since Adlai, who was eighteen in 1975, apparently has his law degree in the final chapter—he is clerking for a federal judge in San Francisco—the span of time since Didion's visit to Kuala Lumpur must be at least seven years.) Inez has seen neither Harry nor her children since the spring of 1975, although she writes to them—most often to Jessie. She also stays in touch with Didion and Billy Dillon, whom Didion occasionally meets for dinner. ("In some ways I have replaced Inez as the woman Billy Dillon imagines he wishes he had married" [233].) In a piece in the London *Guardian* about Southeast Asia's refugees, Inez is quoted as saying that "she would be in Kuala Lumpur until the last refugee was dispatched"—in other words, her lifetime.

The relationship between Didion and Inez might appear to be that of priest and confessor, or psychiatrist and patient, for the confidences flow only one way. However, Didion needs Inez as much as Inez needs Didion; through telling her story, Didion confirms her essential "self," the writer-reporter discovering meaning by understanding and ordering experience. The narrator senses rather than articulates the parallels of character and experience between herself and Inez. They are both realists with an irrepressible romantic streak. Inez has no illusions about Jack's marginally legal activities, yet her final vision of her relationship with him is a romantic affirmation. "We were together all our lives. If you count thinking about it." Didion is a ruthless seeker of truth, yet she is captive to romantic images of dancing—Inez leaning against the jukebox with Jack's arms around her, Inez dancing on the roof of the St. Regis. When she hears that Jessie is writing a novel, she fantasizes that it begins, "Imagine my mother dancing."

Inez is throughout the novel associated with images of height. At least five times Didion refers to the film clip of her dancing on the St. Regis roof, and Inez spends much of the novel on planes—during Harry's campaign, during the trip to Honolulu after her sister is shot, and, finally, her long flight in a small plane with Jack's body. These images enhance her heroic stature; by the novel's end, we can understand Jack's assessment of her as "'one of the most noble' women we had ever met" (40).

The narrator is *metaphorically* linked with images of height. She twice refers to herself as a tightrope walker.

Aerialists know that to look down is to fall.
Writers know it too.
Look down and that prolonged spell of suspended judgment in which a novel is written snaps, and recovery requires that we practice magic. We keep our attention fixed on the wire. [108]

In the book's final chapter, she explains her scattered narrative method (introducing crucial events early, providing their context later) as "the way I tried to stay on the wire in this novel of fitful glimpses" (232). Like a dancer, a tightrope walker must practice art; however, the aerialist traces a linear pattern—the narrative—while the dancer moves with less tension in graceful curves.

Another metaphor Didion invokes, a traditional image for a poet, is close to that of Inez flying about the world in planes. In the beginning of the novel, she was the bird in Wallace Stevens's poem who sang "without human meaning, without human feeling, a foreign song." But the story she has told—Jack's heroic love and Inez's discovery of her own place in the world—has affirmed the possibility of existential meaning in individual lives even amid the holocaust of contemporary madness and violence. For the character who is called Didion, the meaning of the story resided in her bonds with the woman who shared her capacity for solitude, her sensitivity to color and heat and moisture, and her stubborn resilience. In the novel's concluding sentence, the gold-feathered bird has recovered poignancy of feeling and memory. "I had a sudden sense of Inez and of the office in the camp and of how it feels to fly into that part of the world, of the dense greens and translucent blues and the shallows where islands once were, but so far I have not been back" (234).

NOTES

1. Susan Stamberg, "Cautionary Tales," interview with Joan Didion aired on April 4, 1977, on National Public Radio's "All Things Considered," published in *Joan Didion: Essays and Conversations*, ed. Ellen G. Friedman (Princeton: Ontario Review Press, 1984), 27.

2. "The Didion Sensibility: An Analysis," in *Joan Didion: Essays and Conversations*, 81.

3. Stamberg, "Cautionary Tales," 28. In 1977 this novel was tentatively entitled *Angel Visits* (an "angel" visit is one that is brief); by 1982 Didion was toying with the title *Pacific Distances*; when published in 1984, the novel was entitled *Democracy*.

4. "Didion and Dunne: The Rewards of a Literary Marriage," *New York Times Magazine*, Feb. 8, 1987, 18ff.

5. Page numbers from Joan Didion's *Democracy, The White Album*, and *Slouching towards Bethlehem* are given in parentheses in the text.

6. The crisis of confidence Didion describes echoes a similar period of her life (1966–1971) described in *The White Album*. "I was supposed to have a script, and had mislaid it. I was supposed to hear cues, and no longer did. I was meant to know the plot, but all I knew was what I saw: flash pictures in variable sequence, images with no 'meaning' beyond their temporary arrangement" (12–13).

7. The line and title are quoted in "A Visit with Joan Didion," a report of a 1977 interview conducted by Sara Davidson. *New York Times Book Review*, April 3, 1977, 1.

8. Joseph Epstein wrote, "Good as *Democracy* is, one cannot help feeling it would have been better if Miss Didion had left out the character called Joan Didion, the novelist" (*Commentary*, June 1984, 67). Mary McCarthy responded more dramatically. "Angels and ministers of grace defend us! What is a live fact—Joan Didion—doing in a work of fiction? She must be a decoy set there to lure us into believing that Inez Victor is real in some ghostly-goblin manner, as real anyway as the author herself is" (*New York Times Book Review*, April 22, 1984, 18).

9. Joan Didion, "Why I Write," *New York Times*, Dec. 5, 1976, 2.

10. "Visit with Joan Didion," 15.

11. Didion was born on Dec. 5, 1934; Inez Christian, on Jan. 1, 1935. It may also be significant that their first and last names (Joan/Inez and Didion/Victor) have the same number of letters.

12. Every Didion heroine has a similar memory of a particular moment when her family either seemed or was intact, inviolable, intimate. Maria Wyeth remembers "Kate's birthday, Kate laughing, Carter blowing out the candle." Charlotte remembers an Easter lunch at the Biltmore with her husband and daughter. Only Inez Victor and Lily Knight of *Run River*, however, realistically acknowledge that there is no turning back, no way of recovering these moments, except in memory.

A Bibliography of Writings by JOAN DIDION

Katherine Usher Henderson

BOOKS

Run River. New York: Obolensky, 1963; Penguin, 1963.
Slouching towards Bethlehem. New York: Farrar, Straus & Giroux, 1968.
Play It As It Lays. New York: Farrar, Straus & Giroux, 1970; Penguin 1970.

A Book of Common Prayer. New York: Simon & Schuster, 1977; Penguin 1977.
Telling Stories. Berkeley: Bancroft Library, 1978.
White Album. New York: Simon & Schuster, 1979.
Salvador. New York: Simon & Schuster, 1983.
Democracy: A Novel. New York: Simon & Schuster, 1984.
Miami. New York: Simon & Schuster, 1987.

ARTICLES, REVIEWS, STORIES

"Berkeley's Giant: The University of California." *Mademoiselle,* Jan. 1960, 88–91.
"San Francisco Job Hunt." *Mademoiselle,* Sept. 1960, 128–29.
"Self-Respect: Its Source, Its Power." *Vogue,* Aug. 1961, 62–63. Reprinted in *Slouching towards Bethlehem* as "On Self-Respect."
"Take No for an Answer." *Vogue,* Oct. 1, 1961, 132–33.
"When It Was Magic Time in Jersey." *Vogue,* Sept. 15, 1962, 33–35.
"Washington, D.C.: Anything Can Happen Here." *Mademoiselle,* Nov. 1962, 132–35.
"American Summer." *Vogue,* May 1963, 117.
"Passing Scene." *National Review* 15 (Sept. 24, 1963): 246+.
"I Can't Get That Monster out of My Mind." *American Scholar* 33 (Autumn 1964): 629–30f. Reprinted in *Slouching towards Bethlehem.*
"Silver to Have and to Hurl." *Vogue,* April 1, 1964, 60.
"Coming Home" (story). *Saturday Evening Post,* July 11, 1964, 50–52.
"World Was His Oyster" (review of *The Founding Father: The Story of Joseph P. Kennedy,* by Richard J. Whalen). *National Review* 16 (Dec. 1964): 1064–66.
"Bosses Make Lousy Lovers." *Saturday Evening Post,* Jan. 30, 1965, 34+.
"John Wayne: A Love Song." *Saturday Evening Post,* Aug. 14, 1965, 76–79. Reprinted in *Slouching towards Bethlehem.*
"The Insidious Ethic of Conscience." *American Scholar* 34 (Autumn 1965): 625–27. Reprinted in *Slouching towards Bethlehem* as "On Morality."
"Notes from a Native Daughter." *Holiday,* Oct. 1965, 76+. Reprinted in *Slouching towards Bethlehem.*
"Questions about the New Fiction." *National Review* 17 (Nov. 30, 1965) 1100–1102.
"Just Folks at a School for Non-Violence." *New York Times Magazine,* Feb. 27, 1966, 24+. Reprinted in *Slouching towards Bethlehem* as "Where the Kissing Never Stops."
"How Can I Tell Them There's Nothing Left?" *Saturday Evening Post,* May 7, 1966, 38–42. Reprinted in *Slouching towards Bethlehem* as "Some Dreamers of the Golden Dream."
"Hawaii: Taps at Pearl Harbor." *Saturday Evening Post,* Dec. 17, 1966, 22–29. Reprinted in *Slouching towards Bethlehem* as "Letter from Paradise."
"On Keeping a Notebook." *Holiday,* Dec. 1966, 10+. Reprinted in *Slouching towards Bethlehem.*

"Farewell to the Enchanted City." *Saturday Evening Post,* Jan. 14, 1967, 62–67. Reprinted in *Slouching towards Bethlehem* as "Goodbye to All That."

"Hippie Generation." *Saturday Evening Post,* Sept. 23, 1967, 25 + .

"Waiting for Morrison." In *The Age of Rock,* edited by J. Eisen, 385–88. New York: Random House, 1969.

"In Praise of Unhung Wreaths and Love." *Life,* Dec. 19, 1969, 2B.

"1950 Was More Than Twenty Years Ago." *Life,* Jan. 30, 1970, 20B.

"On the Last Frontier with VX and GB." *Life,* Feb. 20, 1970, 22.

"Piece of Work for Now and Doomsday." *Life,* March 13, 1970, 20.

"Ten Long Minutes in Punchbowl." *Life,* April 10, 1970, 26D.

"Scrapbook of a Pink Palace in the Sand." *Life,* April 24, 1970, 26B.

"Nine Bike Movies in Seven Vroom! Days." *Life,* May 8, 1970, 4.

"A Generation Not for Barricades." *Life,* June 5, 1970, 26.

"Best Selling Novelist Tells Why She Keeps a Notebook" (excerpt from *Slouching towards Bethlehem*). *Writer's Digest* 51 (Dec. 1971): 26–27.

[With John Gregory Dunne] "Panic in Needle Park." *Harper's Bazaar,* July 1971, 68.

"Shopping Center." *Esquire,* Dec. 1975, 98 + . Reprinted as "A Nation of Malls," *Esquire,* June 1983, 329–30.

"California Blue" (story). *Harper's,* Oct. 1976, 45–48.

"Why I Write." *New York Times Book Review,* Dec. 5, 1976, 1 + .

"A Book of Common Prayer" (excerpt). *Mademoiselle,* Feb. 1977, 148 + .

Review of *Falconer,* by John Cheever. *New York Times Book Review,* March 6, 1977. 1 + .

"Big Rock Candy Figgy Pudding Pitfall" (story). *Saturday Evening Post,* Dec. 1978, 38.

"Meditation on a Life" (review of *Sleepless Nights,* by Elizabeth Hardwick). *New York Times Book Review,* April 29, 1979: 1, 60.

"Letter from Manhattan" (review of *Manhattan, Interiors,* and *Annie Hall,* films directed by Woody Allen). *New York Review of Books,* Aug. 16, 1979, 18–19.

"I Want to Go Ahead and Do It" (review of *The Executioner's Song,* by Norman Mailer). *New York Times Book Review,* Oct. 7, 1979, 1 + .

"Nuclear Blue," *New West* 4 (Nov. 5, 1979).

"Mothers and Daughters." *New West* 4 (Dec. 12, 1979).

"Boat People." *New West* 5 (Feb. 25, 1980).

[With John Gregory Dunne] "The Need to Know." *New West* 5 (May 5, 1980).

"Without Regret or Hope" (review of *The Return of Eva Peron with the Killings in Trinidad,* by V.S. Naipaul). *New York Review of Books,* June 12, 1980, 20.

"Honolulu Days." *New West* 5 (July 14, 1980).

[With John Gregory Dunne] "True Confessions" (screen play). United Artists, 1981.

"Making Up Stories." In *The Writer's Craft,* edited by Robert A. Martin, 231–44. Ann Arbor: Univ. of Michigan Press, 1982.

Review of *Every Secret Thing,* by Patricia Hearst Shaw. *New York Review of Books,* March 18, 1982, 3 +.

"In El Salvador." *New York Review of Books,* Nov. 4, 1982, 9 +.

"In El Salvador: *Soluciones.*" *New York Review of Books,* Nov. 18, 1982, 31 +.

"El Salvador: Illusions." *New York Review of Books,* Dec. 2, 1982, 23–31.

Review of *Getting to Know the General: The Story of an Involvement,* by Graham Greene, and *Finding the Center: Two Narratives,* by V.S. Naipaul. *New York Review of Books* 31 (Oct. 11, 1984): 10.

"Miami." *New York Review of Books,* May 28, 1987, 43–48.

"La lucha." *New York Review of Books,* June 11, 1987, 15–18.

"Exiles." *New York Review of Books,* June 25, 1987, 5–9.

"Washington in Miami." *New York Review of Books,* July 16, 1987, 22 +.

"Kennedy, Reagan and After." *New York Times Book Review,* Oct. 25, 1987, 3.

A Bibliography of Writings about JOAN DIDION

Katherine Usher Henderson

Amis, M. "Joan Didion's Style." In *The Moronic Inferno and Other Visits,* 160–69. New York: Viking, 1987.

Anderson, Chris. "Joan Didion: The Cat in the Shimmer." In *Style As Argument,* edited by Chris Anderson, 133–74. Carbondale: Southern Illinois Univ. Press, 1987.

Brady, Jennifer. "Points West, Then and Now: The Fiction of Joan Didion." *Contemporary Literature,* 20, no. 4 (1979): 452–70. Reprinted in *Joan Didion: Essays and Conversations.*

Braudy, Susan. "A Day in the Life of Joan Didion." *Ms.,* Feb. 1977, 65–68, 108–9.

"California House of Joan Didion and John Gregory Dunne." *Vogue,* Oct. 1, 1972, 146–49.

Chabot, C. Barry. "Joan Didion's *Play It As It Lays* and the Vacuity of the 'Here and Now.' " *Critique: Studies in Modern Fiction* 21 (1980): 53–60.

Chace, James. "Betrayals and Obsessions" (review of *Miami*). *New York Times Book Review,* Oct. 25, 1987, 3.

Coale, Samuel. "Didion's Disorder: An American Romancer's Art." *Critique: Studies in Modern Fiction* 25, no. 3 (1984): 160–70.

———. "Joan Didion: Witnessing the Abyss." In *In Hawthorne's Shadow: American Romance from Melville to Mailer,*" 180–202. Lexington: Univ. Press of Kentucky, 1985.

Cohen, J.C. Review of *Miami. National Review* 39 (Nov. 20, 1987): 54 +.

Coradi, Juan E. "A Culture of Fear." *Dissent* 30 (Summer 1983): 387–89.

Crow, Charles L. "Home and Transcendence in Los Angeles Fiction." In *Los Angeles in Fiction: A Collection of Original Essays*, edited by David Fine, 189–205. Albuquerque: Univ. of New Mexico Press, 1984.

Daley, M. "PW Interviews." *Publishers Weekly* 202 (Oct. 9, 1972): 26–27.

Davidson, Sara. "A Visit with Joan Didion." *New York Times Book Review*, April 3, 1977, 1. Reprinted in *Joan Didion: Essays and Conversations*.

Diehl, Digby. "A Myth of Fragility Concealing a Tough Core." *Saturday Review*, March 5, 1977, 24.

Edwards, Thomas R. "An American Education." *New York Review of Books* 31, May 10, 1984, 23–24.

Epstein, Joseph. "The Sunshine Girls." *Commentary* 77 (June 1984): 62–67.

———. "The Sun-Girls: Renata Adler and Joan Didion." In Joseph Epstein, *Plausible Prejudices*, 238–53. New York: Norton, 1985.

Falcoff, Mark. "Two Weeks." *Commentary* 75 (May 1983): 66, 68–70.

Foust, Ronald. "Family Romance and the Image of Woman's Fate in *Play It As It Lays*." *Journal of Evolutionary Psychology*, March 5, 1984, 43–54.

Friedman, Ellen G. "The Didion Sensibility: An Analysis." Reprinted in *Joan Didion: Essays and Conversations*, 81–90.

———, ed. *Joan Didion: Essays and Conversations*. Princeton: Ontario Review Press, 1984.

Gardiner, Judith Kegan. "Evil, Apocalypse, and Feminist Fiction." *Frontiers* 7 (1983): 74–80.

Garis, Leslie. "Didion and Dunne: The Rewards of a Literary Marriage." *New York Times Magazine*, Feb. 8, 1987, 18 +.

Geherin, David J. "Nothingness and Beyond: Joan Didion's *Play It As It Lays*." *Critique: Studies in Modern Fiction*, 16 (1974): 64–78. Reprinted in *Joan Didion: Essays and Conversations*.

Gelfant, Blanche H. *Women Writing in America: Voices in Collage*, 41–42. Hanover, N.H.: Univ. Press of New England, 1984.

Goldman, M., and M.G. Goldman. "Click, Pop, Crack." *Working Woman* 9 (March 1984): 187 +.

Gregor, Charles, and Wm. Dorman. "The Children of James Agee." *Journal of Popular Culture* 9 (1976): 996–1002.

Hanley, Lynne T. "To El Salvador." *Massachusets Review* 24 (1983): 13–29.

Harrison, Barbara Grizzeti. "Joan Didion: The Courage of Her Afflictions." *Nation*, Sept. 29, 1979, 277–86.

Hart, James D. *The Concise Oxford Companion to American Literature*, 109. New York: Oxford Univ. Press, 1986.

Hearn, Pamela. "*Salvador*" (review). *Women's Studies International Forum* 7 (1984): 319.

Henderson, Katherine U. "Joan Didion." In *American Women Writers: A Critical Reference Guide from Colonial Times to the Present*, abridged ed., edited by Langdon Lynne Faust, 1: 166. New York: Frederick Ungar, 1979.

———. *Joan Didion*, New York: Frederick Ungar, 1981.

————. "*Run River*: Edenic Vision and Wasteland Nightmare." Reprinted in *Joan Didion: Essays and Conversations*, 91–104.

Hinchman, Sandra K. "Making Sense and Making Stories: Problems of Cognition and Narration in Joan Didion's *Play It As It Lays*." *Centennial Review* 29 (1985): 457–73.

Hollowell, John. "Against Interpretation: Narrative Strategy in *A Book of Common Prayer*." Reprinted in *Joan Didion: Essays and Conversations*, 164–76.

"Imagination of Disaster." *Time*, March 28, 1977, 87–88.

Jacobs, Fred Rue. *Joan Didion—A Bibliography*. Keene, Cal.: Loop Press, 1977.

"Joan Didion and Gregory Dunne." *Mademoiselle*, Nov. 1976, 162 + .

Johnson, Diane. "Should Novels Have a Message? Joan Didion, Bertha Harris, and Erica Jong." In *Terrorists and Novelists*, edited by Diane Johnson, 124–33. New York: Knopf, 1982.

Johnson, Nora. "Housewives and Prom Queens, 25 Years Later." *New York Times Book Review*, March 20, 1988, 1 + .

Kakutani, Michiko. "Joan Didion: Staking Out California." *New York Times Magazine*, June 10, 1979, 34–50. Reprinted in *Joan Didion: Essays and Conversations*.

Kapp, Isa. "Unearned Pessimism." *New Leader* 67 (May 14, 1984): 6–8.

Kasindorf, Martin. "New Directions for the First Family of Angst." *Saturday Review*, April 1982, 14.

Kaye, R. "1987: Miami's Year in the Literary Limelight." *Publishers Weekly* 232 (Nov. 13, 1987): 46–47.

Kazin, Alfred. "Joan Didion: Portrait of a Professional." *Harper's*, Dec. 1971, 112–22.

————. *Bright Book of Life: American Novelists and Storytellers from Hemingway to Mailer*. Boston: Little, Brown, 1973.

Kiley, Frederick. "Beyond Words: Narrative Art in Joan Didion's *Salvador*." Reprinted in *Joan Didion: Essays and Conversations*, 181–88.

Kuehl, Linda. "Joan Didion." In *Writers at Work: The Paris Review Interviews*," edited by George Plimpton 339–57. New York: Viking, 1981.

Lahr, John. "Entrepreneurs of Anxiety." *Horizon* 24 (Jan. 1981): 36–39.

————. "Joan Didion and John Gregory Dunne." In *Automatic Vaudeville*, 205–16. New York: Knopf, 1984.

Leppard, David. "Salvadorean Nights." *The Listener* 109 (April 28, 1983): 23–24.

McCarthy, Mary. "Love and Death in the Pacific" (review of *Democracy*). *New York Times Book Review*, April 22, 1984, 1.

McCreadie, Marsha. "The Culture Critics: Diana Trilling, Simone de Beauvoir, Joan Didion, and Nora Sayre." In *Women on Film: The Critical Eye*, 103–12. New York: Praeger, 1983.

Malin, Irving. "The Album of Anxiety." Reprinted in *Joan Didion: Essays and Conversations*, 177–80.

Mallon, Thomas. "The Limits of History in the Novels of Joan Didion." *Critique: Studies in Modern Fiction* 21, no. 3 (1980): 43–52. Reprinted in *Joan Didion: Essays and Conversations.*

Massing, Michael. "Snap Books: Big Writers and Little Countries." *New Republic,* May 4, 1987, 21+.

Merivale, Patricia. "Through Green-land in Drag: John Didion's *A Book of Common Prayer.*" *Pacific Coast Philology* 15 (1980): 45–52.

Merkin, Daphne. "Didion Looking Down." *New Leader* 62 (1979): 16–17.

Mickelson, Anne Z. "Joan Didion: The Hurting Woman." In *Reaching Out: Sensitivity and Order in Recent American Fiction by Women,* edited by A.Z. Mickelson, 87–111. Metuchen, N.J.: Scarecrow Press, 1979.

Morton, Brian J.W. "The Princess in the Consulate: Joan Didion's Fiction." *EDDA,* 1982, 73–87.

Natoli, J.P. "Phenomenological Perspectives on Literature: Freudian Dissidents and Non-Freudians." In *Psychological Perspectives on Literature: Freudian Dissidents and Non-Freudians,* by J.P. Natoli, 198–224. Hamden, Conn.: Archon Books, 1984.

Phillips, D.Z. "Mystery and Mediation: Reflections on Flannery O'Connor and Joan Didion." In *Images of Belief in Literature,* 24–41. New York: St. Martin's Press, 1984.

Pilger, John. "Having Fun with Fear." *New Statesman* 105 (May 6, 1983): 20–21.

Reed, J.C. "Postfeminism: Playing for Keeps." *Time,* Jan. 10, 1983, 46–47.

Romano, John. "Joan Didion and Her Characters." *Commentary* 64 (July 1977): 61–63. Reprinted in *Joan Didion: Essays and Conversations.*

Rothchild, J. "Revenge in a Hot Place" (review of *Miami*). *Washington Monthly* 19 (Dec. 1987): 45+.

Russell, G. "*Miami*" (review). *Commentary* 85 (Jan. 1988): 69–72.

Schow, H.W. "Out of Africa, The White Album, and the Possibility of Tragic Affirmation." *English Studies* 67 (Feb. 1986): 35–50.

Simard, R. "The Dissociation of Self in Joan Didion's *Play It As It Lays.*" In *Narcissism and the Text,* edited by L. Layton and B.A. Schapiro, 273–89. New York: New York University Press, 1986.

Stamberg, Susan. "Cautionary Tales." Interview aired on April 4, 1977, on National Public Radio's "All Things Considered." Reprinted in *Joan Didion: Essays and Conversations.*

Starr, N. *Miami* (review). *American Spectator* 21 (Feb. 1988): 37–39.

Stineback, David C. "On the Limits of Fiction." *Midwest Quarterly* 14 (1973): 339–48.

Strandberg, Victor. "Passion and Delusion in *A Book of Common Prayer.*" *Modern Fiction Studies* 27 (1981): 225–42. Reprinted in *Joan Didion: Essays and Conversations.*

Van Antwerp, Margaret A. "Joan Didion." In *Dictionary of Literary Biography Yearbook, 1981,* 56–61. Detroit: Gale Research Co., 1982.

Vincent, Sybil Korff. "In the Crucible: The Forging of an Identity as Demonstrated in Didion's *Play It As It Lays.*" *Perspectives on Contemporary Literature* 3 (1977): 58–64.

Westerbrook, C.L., Jr. "Coppola Now." *Commonweal* 106 (Sept. 28, 1979): 531–32.

Wilcox, Leonard. "Narrative Technique and the Theme of Historical Continuity in the Novels of Joan Didion." In *Joan Didion: Essays and Conversations,* edited by Ellen G. Friedman, 68–80. Princeton: Ontario Review Press, 1984.

Winchell, Mark Royden. *Joan Didion.* Boston: Twayne Publishers, 1980.

————. "Fantasy Seen: Hollywood Fiction since West." In *Los Angeles in Fiction: A Collection of Original Essays,* edited by David Fine, 147–68. Albuquerque: Univ. of New Mexico Press, 1984.

Wolff, Cynthia Griffin. "*Play It As It Lays*: Didion and the New American Heroine." *Contemporary Literature* 24 (Winter 1983): 480–95. Reprinted in *Joan Didion: Essays and Conversations.*

LOUISE ERDRICH

Of Cars, Time, and the River

Marvin Magalaner

*L*ove Medicine marks a new approach to the treatment of the American Indian in fiction. Louise Erdrich's Chippewa families on a twentieth-century reservation in the West bear no resemblance to the solemn "braves and squaws" of cowboy and Indian days. There's not a horse in the novel, not a peace pipe, and only a brief reference to nonfunctioning tribal gods. Where there is religion, it is Catholic; where there is hunting, it is by white police seeking Indian escapees from prison; where there is violence, it is from Indian family squabbles, husbands against battered wives, fathers caught in child abuse, and drunks in blind attacks against the animals they once venerated.

The noble savage becomes in this book, realistically enough, the ignoble citizen, reduced by externally imposed economic circumstances and the blandishments of media persuasion to a mean, degraded lowest common denominator of existence. Tonto no longer rides the plains beside the Lone Ranger's Silver. In an ironic shift, Albertine, the young student nurse in the novel (who ruminates that "Patient Abuse" can be interpreted two ways by Indians) drives back to the reservation in her "Mustang" car, soon to encounter her cousin, King, who arrives in his "Firebird."[1]

Yet Louise Erdrich in *Love Medicine* is attempting no historical panorama or sociological tract or study of ethnic relationships. The reader may legitimately infer the presence of these elements; the author's emphasis lies elsewhere. Her primary concern is to delineate the human condition as exemplified in two Chippewa families whose members' lives are recorded in fiction at critical moments, often in the words of narrators in the family, sometimes in the words of an unknown omniscient narrator. Erdrich stresses the interaction of family members as well as the relationship between two families, the Kashpaws and the Lamartines, but always to her the characters are more important than the trends or principles they may embody.

Her people are a strange and lively lot: the prostitute June, no longer young, who dies walking drunkenly through a snowstorm after a sexual encounter; Lipsha, her son, convinced that he has the "touch" necessary to dispense Love Medicine; Lulu, whose eight sons have eight different fathers; Sister Leopolda, who tries with boiling water and an iron hook to force the Devil out of young Marie Lazarre, later the Grandma Kashpaw of the novel; and many others equally vivid in their bizarre behavior.

Allowing characters of this ilk to act upon, and to interact with, one another should have produced a wild novel, replete with slapstick scenes, grotesque confrontations, weird, inexplicable visions, abnormal sexual interludes, and violent exchanges—and that is what indeed happens. June's husband, Gordie, drunkenly runs over a deer, which he then shoves into the rear seat of his car, only to become convinced that the animal is the wife he thinks he has murdered in his rage. June's son, King, also far-gone with drink, wildly attacks his own car in which his wife, Lynette, has locked herself to prevent being hurt by her husband. Senile Grandpa Kashpaw and promiscuous old Lulu Lamartine clumsily attempt a sexual liaison in the Senior Citizens Building's laundry room as young Lipsha watches. Or little Howard, King's son, enthusiastically betrays his father's presence to the police outside the apartment door by crying, "King's here."

Yet the effect of *Love Medicine* on the reader is anything but wild, outlandish, surrealistic. Quite the opposite, though the happenings may individually exhibit these qualities, the effect of the whole is cathartic; as a prose poem, it establishes an emotional equilibrium associated with writing of a high order.

The answer lies perhaps in Louise Erdrich's ability to place the petty, sensational lives of her characters in delicate balance with the enduring, changeless qualities of nature: air, sky, dust, water, snow, dandelions, darkness. This she accomplishes through her skillful employment of imagery and symbol. I should like here to examine at some length how she does this in a few illustrative instances.

In an interview published in *Belles Lettres*, Louise Erdrich confirms what any perceptive reader of *Love Medicine* does not take long to discover—that the controlling element of the novel is water,[2] as in her second novel, *The Beet Queen*, it happens to be air. Simply based on the frequency with which water is mentioned in the story, there is no doubt that the author has decided to concentrate on that element not merely in the development of plot but, beyond that consideration, in everything that has to do with the telling of the tale.

Though Erdrich's authorial control is unobtrusively apparent at every point, the events of the book seem to flow with the fluidity of a liquid. That the author decides to begin the action of the book with June's life and death in 1981, then take the story back to 1934 and return it in stages to periods of time after 1981, requiring a shimmery, ebb-and-flow movement temporally, may account in part for the choice of this element. It is no accident that the novel begins with Easter and June (the person and the month), before we are allowed to learn of June as a youngster and of the family events that occur after June's death.

In addition, Louise Erdrich's unusual decision to have successive chapters, and even sections of chapters, narrated by different characters lends to the novel a fluid mixture of voices, of speech patterns, of grammatical inflections, and of points of view quite unusual in fiction. Even Virginia Woolf, in *The Waves*, though she establishes set speeches by her six characters, has all of them speak in the sophisticated, literary voice of Virginia Woolf. In *Love Medicine*, on the contrary, we flow from the polished musings of Marie Kashpaw as she visits the dying Sister Leopolda to the jarring teen lingo of Lipsha Morrisey. In Marie's words: "I sat with her a long while, in silence. The earth was so mild and deep. By spring she would be placed there, alone, and there was no rescue. There was nothing I could do after hating her all these years" (122). And Lipsha's: "I never really done much with my life, I suppose. I never had a television" (189).

As has been said, the most pervasive image in *Love Medicine* is unquestionably water, in its numerous manifestations. Most obviously, the references are to bodies of water—rivers, lakes, brooks. But Louise Erdrich deals also in less cosmic terms with the image: the ability to shed tears or the curse of being unable to cry; the use of boiling water to exorcise the Devil from young Marie's body; the lack of rain, which leads to the pervading presence of dust as a realistic environmental factor and a rather obvious symbolic aura.

This paramount concern with water leads in turn to several associated though subsidiary motifs involving the relationships of her characters to water. The man ironically named King sees the body of water as engulfing him and associates himself with the smallest and most fragile of its denizens. " 'Minnows,' he said. 'It's like I'm always stuck with the goddamn minnows. Every time I work my way up—say I'm next in line for the promotion—they shaft me. . . . Stuck down at the bottom with the minnows.' " . . . " 'I'm gonna rise,' he said. " 'One day I'm gonna rise. They can't keep down the Indians. Right on brother, huh?' " (252)

The title of the first chapter, "The World's Greatest Fishermen," reveals the opposite facet of the motif, however ironically it may be interpreted. Traditionally, man has needed access to a river or ocean or stream to sustain life and to build a civilization. Only by making good use of nature's bounty (the water itself, the fish and other sea creatures for sustenance, the current for transporation, the tributaries for irrigation, and so on) has man been able to survive and to advance himself and his descendants. Especially in American historical lore has the availability of water, and its exploitation by indigenous Indian tribes, been central. The image of the Indian in a canoe holding aloft a fish just pulled from the waters below is almost a cliché of American art.

In Erdrich's novel, though King owns the hat identifying its owner as one of "The World's Greatest Fishermen," it is clear immediately that in King's physical and emotional state it is most unlikely that he could even hold a fishing pole, much less be successful in a battle with a fish at the end of his fishing line. Indeed, the bankruptcy of this contemporary Indian as fisherman (or breadwinner or head of household or transmitter of cultural arts and skills) is one of the incontrovertible points of the book. It is fitting, therefore, that he should abdicate his "King"-ship and, in a mock coronation scene, confer the crown on Eli, the only Indian in the family to follow the old ways, to live alone in his cottage in the woods, unsullied by an education in reservation schools (30).

Whatever else the river means in this context, it must be viewed as an element that no longer offers immediate sustenance to those who have lost the touch. As life-giving water brings death to Phlebas, the drowned Phoenician sailor in Eliot's "The Waste Land," so it swallows up Henry, the overwhelmed war veteran in *Love Medicine*. And Nector (Grandpa Kashpaw), a relic from an earlier generation, believes that he will survive the raging waters, as Ishmael and Ahab believe in *Moby-Dick*, but, senile and broken near the end, he appears buffeted by the forces of life he can no longer control.

In fact, the crucial moments in Nector's long life are narrated significantly through employment of the water metaphor. When his wife, Marie, describes a particularly meaningful sexual reconciliation with him in the early years of their marriage, Nector actually *becomes* a body of water. Marie thinks: "I went down beneath his hands and lay quiet. I rolled with his current like a stone in the lake. He fell on me like a wave. But like a wave he washed away, leaving no sign he'd been there" (72). Having compared herself to a stone in the lake, Marie expands the analogy on the next page. "I think of small stones. At the bottom of the lake, rolled aimless by the waves. . . . But I see no kindness in how the waves are grinding them smaller and smaller until they finally disappear" (73). Interestingly, in the course of another reconciliation between Marie and Nector, the husband returns drunk just after the wife has waxed the floor of their home, "which rolled and gleamed like a fine lake between us" (129). At a later point in the novel, Nector recalls his having posed in youth for a painting called *Plunge of the Brave*, in which he jumps off a cliff into a "rocky river." "I knew," he ruminates, "that Nector Kashpaw would fool the pitiful rich woman that painted him and survive the raging water." He will "let the current pull me toward the surface" and "get to shore" (91).

Nector's attempt to divide his time between two women, his wife Marie and his childhood sweetheart Lulu, is similarly described in aqueous terms. He is "swept" from one woman to another. "I only trusted that I would be tossed up on land when everyone who wanted something from Nector Kashpaw had wrung him dry" (102). The emotional conflict provoked by his having to choose between the two women is only resolved by a solitary late night drive to the lake and a swim. "I gave her [Lulu] up and dived down to the bottom of the lake where it was cold, dark, still, like the pit bottom of a grave. . . . Perhaps I should have stayed there. . . . But I didn't. The water bounced me up. I had to get back in the thick of my life" (103).

Finally, after Nector's (Grandpa Kashpaw's) funeral, Lipsha Morrisey's grief is couched in another metaphor of water. "As I lay there, falling asleep, I suddenly felt Grandpa's presence and the barrier between us like a swollen river" (213).

It should be manifest then that, whatever its merits, Louise Erdrich is exploiting the water theme for all it is worth. Space limitations preclude extensive treatment of the motif as applied to the other characters of the novel—to June, walking over the snow "like water" to her death; to King, trying to drown his wife by holding her head down in the kitchen sink; to Henry, deliberately drowning himself in the lake; to Lipsha, who doesn't want to be "like foam throwed off the waves of the lake, spin drift, all warped and cracked like junk and left to rot" (247).

The question still to be faced is why the author selected water in *Love Medicine* as the central metaphor. Even a casual reading of the history of the Ojibway (Chippewa) Indians impresses the reader with the pervasive presence and importance of water in their everyday lives and in the life after death prepared for them by the Great Spirit. Rivers, streams, lakes, oceans, ponds abound in the literature of the Ojibways as required for the existence of the nation; indeed, wars are fought over the possession of choice land with free access to water. When a group moves from one location to another, the availability of a body of water for transportation, for fishing, for drinking is paramount in the selection of a new site. Indian life, in the absence of a body of water, is thus unthinkable.

As George Copway reports, the goodness of the divine creator is evidenced in his concern to provide water for his people. "Benevolent Spirit . . . who made the earth. . . . His benevolence I saw in the running of the streams, for animals to quench their thirst and the fishes to live." In fact, material things are seen as ephemeral while Nature remains eternal. "Nature will be Nature still while palaces shall decay. . . . yes Niagra will be Niagra a thousand years hence! the rainbow . . . shall continue as long as the sun, and the flowing of the river. While the work of art, however impregnable, shall in atoms fall."[4] Further, in his history of the Ojibway Indians, William Warren tells how the soul departs the body at death and proceeds west until it reaches a "deep, rapid stream of water, under a bridge," in a land of spirits full of "clear lakes and streams."[5] Given such frequent reiteration of the religious and historical affinity of the Chippewa people with water, it is not surprising that Louise Erdrich chooses to build her novel around that element.

But life off and on the reservation for Erdrich's characters in the mid-twentieth century may no longer be energized by the blandishments of nature or the promise of the life beyond. The only instance in the book in which the author refers to Indian Gods is recited, tongue in cheek, by Lipsha.

Now there's your God in the Old Testament and there is Chippewa Gods as well. Indian Gods, good and bad, like tricky Nanabozho or the water monster, Missepeshu, who lives over in Lake Turcot. That water monster was the last God I ever heard to appear. It had a weakness for young girls and grabbed one of the Blues off her rowboat. She got to shore all

right, but only after this monster had its way with her. She's an old lady now. Old Lady Blue.
She still won't let her family fish that lake.
  Our Gods aren't perfect, is what I'm saying, but at least they come around. [194–95]

Deities, Christian or Indian, seem anachronistic in the century of
Vietnam and the Holocaust. Religious ecstasy has been replaced by
the worship of the beer can, which one of the characters crushes into
icon shape and sets up for adoration. Dust, rather than water, has
encroached upon the reservation in actuality and in symbolic import.
The myth of the Benevolent Spirit is losing ground to the myth of the
car, while true healing by the Gods is giving way to Lipsha's mumbo-
jumbo medicine.

Though the spiritual power of water is thus diminished in *Love
Medicine*, its power as a symbol and as a presence remains. The river,
for instance, endures as a direct link between the Indian past and the
less ennobling present. "I'd heard that this river was the last of an
ancient ocean, miles deep, that once had covered the Dakotas and
solved all our problems." Lipsha continues, "It was easy to still
imagine us beneath them vast unreasonable waves; but the truth is
we live on dry land" (272). The river also remains an awesome power
for life and death—a power even greater than that of the car in modern
existence. "Drowning," the reader is told in *Love Medicine*, "was the
worst death for a Chippewa to experience" (234). At the same time,
living without the proximity of water is a dreaded fate.

Finally, Louise Erdrich is aware of water as embodying time and
memory—elements that determine to a considerable extent the content and the shape of her novel: the multivoiced narration, the generational approach, the jumbled time sequence, the choice of motif and
metaphor, and the pattern of symbolic associations that makes the
book so rich.

If water is the all-pervasive symbolic link with the past, with
time past and to come, and with the natural environment, then the
unnatural present is epitomized by the automobile. Louise Erdrich
did not have to invent the symbol. More than half a century earlier,
Aldous Huxley had commented on a shift in deity from Our Lord who
art in Heaven to our Ford which art in Detroit. Evelyn Waugh had
followed with a scene in which racing cars careen wildly around a
circular track in an effort to return to the starting point first—a futile
exercise in getting nowhere fast. And Flannery O'Connor in her
stories often employs the image of the motorcar for whatever emotional mileage she can get out of it.

In *Love Medicine* the car is used by the author as a multipurpose tool to exhibit her Indian families adjusting (or failing to adjust) to their twentieth-century role. Required for life on and off the reservation, the car is at once as familiar as a hat or as a grocery bag, but, at the same time, invested with a mystique that engenders the awe and respect once reserved for venerated natural spirits. "It was as if the car was wired up to something. As if it might give off a shock when touched" (22). It is to the interior of this car that Lynette flees to take sanctuary from the threat of physical violence posed by King's drunken anger; and it is on this car that King takes frustrated revenge, seeking to get at his wife inside (32). The car, incidentally, is a Firebird, formerly an object of religious adoration by the Chippewa Indians.

From the beginning of the novel to the end, the car is there at moments of heightened intensity and dramatic climax—moments when life and death hang in the balance. In the first section of the opening chapter, the mud engineer's car is the scene of June's sexual encounter and the place where she becomes drunk enough to die in the snow shortly afterward. Indeed, though she seems unimpressed by the sexual prowess of her partner, it is the car itself that appears to acquire erotic characteristics. The heater's controls accidentally activated by the groping couple, "she felt it open at her shoulders like a pair of jaws, blasting heat, and had the momentary and voluptuous sensation that she was lying stretched out before a great wide mouth. The breath swept across her throat, tightening her nipples" (5). The car, personified, has its way with her (as the water monster had with the Blue maiden) as she lies ritually prone, "slipping along the smooth plastic seat" as on a sacrificial altar. And all this on the Easter weekend.

Fittingly, the final scene of the book, narrated by June's son, Lipsha, involves several of the same elements. Driving the car he has won from his brother, King, in a poker game (a car purchased with insurance money King received at his mother's death), Lipsha notices damage done to the car's exterior. "There was nicks and dents in the beautiful finished skin. I ran my hand up the racy invert line of the hood" (266). As his senses experience sensual enjoyment, his mind concentrates on the flight from the police of his father, Gerry Nanapush. "I knew my dad would get away. He could fly. He could strip and flee and change into shapes of swift release. Owls and bees, two-toned Ramblers, buzzards. . . . These forms was interchangeable with his" (266). Gerry, however, is *not* flying. He is at that moment hiding in the car trunk. "He was curled up tight as a baby in its mother's stomach, wedged so thoroughly it took a struggle to get him loose" (267). But if one's form is "interchangeable" with "two-toned Ramblers," it is no far stretch of the imagination to see his birth in the womblike depths of a Firebird car trunk. Gerry, constantly on the run from the police, is thus depicted as the offspring of a car; Lipsha's mother, June, as the sexual partner of one; and her legacy to their son, Lipsha, through King's bad luck at poker, the car bought with the insurance proceeds. It is highly significant that in this car the son, Lipsha, is atoned with the father at last, as it speeds toward the border and freedom.

It is perhaps unnecessary to multiply instances in the story in which the use of the car is central. When Lulu's husband, Henry, decides to take his life, he stops his car on the railroad tracks and waits for the death that swiftly claims him under the wheels of an even more imposing iron monster. When Lulu Lamartine determines that she will have Nector in middle age, as she has seduced him in youth, she invites him into her car for the attempt. Young Henry Lamartine calmly walks into the river to his death, overcome by his experience in the Vietnam War, at which point his brother, Lyman, drives their red convertible into the river, perhaps as tribute to the river god, perhaps as an offering to his drowned brother. For whatever motive, this swallowing up of the shiny, metallic new god by the hungry mouth of the old is an obvious but appropriate way for Erdrich to join the two.

The most dramatic and jarring employment of the car in the novel occurs in the "Crown of Thorns" chapter. Gordie, drunk, invokes the shade of his dead wife, June, by uttering her name. In horror he flees the apparition in his car, running down and injuring a deer on the highway. Having decided to drive off with the carcass of the animal, he discovers that he does not have the key to the locked car trunk, at which point he sees "clearly that the setup of life was rigged and he was trapped" (179). He is forced, therefore, to wedge the doe into the backseat. On the journey the deer revives and, through the rearview mirror, stares back at Gordie. "She saw into the troubled thrashing woods of him. . . . She saw how he'd woven his own crown of thorns" (180). Gordie kills her for good this time with repeated blows of a crowbar, but then, in a moment of dazed illumination believes that "he'd just killed June": "She was in the backseat, sprawled, her short skirt hiked up over her hips" (181). The enormity of his presumed act leads him to Sister Mary Martin for confession and then to flight from the authorities. "They heard him crying like a drowned person, howling in the open fields" (188). The animal has become a person, the person an animal.

The life in which Gordie and his contemporary fellows are trapped is represented as a car to whose locks the owner does not possess all the required keys—a hurtling, mechanical object driven drunkenly and unsteadily from point to point. It is not that the natural has been abandoned by the modern Indian; the natural has been perverted. To the actors nothing is what it seems to be. The "World's Greatest Fishermen," the mighty hunters, are reduced, as in Gordie's situation, to running over their prey and then bashing in the head with a tire iron. The hunted animal takes on human, noble qualities so lacking in the hunters. The deer's "look was black and endless and melting pure" (180). In the logical next step, to Gordie the animal is transformed into a human being, his dead wife, June, who had previously been described by the author as a "wild" thing. The vision of the deer-as-June that he experiences in the car, her clothing awry, sprawled on the vinyl seat, is very much a replay of the opening scene of the book in which June's animallike sexual encounter in the mud engineer's car is described. But even if the wife-June-prostitute echoes had not been introduced by Louise Erdrich, the incongruous and grotesque image of a deer perched upright like a human being in the backseat of a car—of the natural reduced to the unnatural, of the eternal placed in juxtaposition to the dated and the mechanically limited (was the car a used 1963 Buick?)—would have been more than enough to drive home the point. Maybe it is not even necessary for the author, in the final sentence of the episode, to depict Gordie as transposed into the hunted beast, "howling in the open fields."

It should be pointed out, incidentally, that Erdrich's fascination with the car as symbol extends to her second novel as well. In *The Beet Queen*, the most unusual section is the attempt of Dot's mother and Mary Adare to force Sita's body, stiff with rigor mortis, into their delivery truck and their subsequent ride in the parade of the Beet Queen, upright corpse and all, through the center of town. More than once, the interior of a car is described as a "cave," as a means of escape, of isolation, of enclosure, or of entrapment.

In *Love Medicine* imagery of enclosure abounds, partly, it seems clear, to highlight the dilemma of the Indian characters, savages now forced into tameness by material progress, by regimentation in the armed forces, by life on a reservation, by confinement in a prison, by employment in the tiny, stifling weighing hut, and even, as has been said here, by the necessity to adapt to the automobile. Only Eli, kept

out of school by his mother and sheltered from "civilizing" influences, retains a measure of openness to nature and his tradition. From
the very beginning of the book, the reader is confronted by this
unmistakable motif. Though June and her pickup are in a bar drinking "Angel Wings," she must stumble on all-too-human legs to a
bathroom stall and lock herself in. She even carries with her the
doorknob of her room as the only sure way to keep the door locked in
her absence. The second section begins with June "not only dead but
suddenly buried" in the last enclosed space of all. Further on in the
novel, describing Gerry and Dot's unborn child, Erdrich reinforces
the motif. "The child was as restless a prisoner as its father, and grew
more anxious and unruly as the time of release [from the womb]
neared. As a place to spend a nine-month sentence in, Dot wasn't
much. Her body was inhospitable. . . . The child was clearly ready for
a break and not interested in earning its parole" (163–64). Whether
the sense of enclosure is physical or emotional, it seems to be shared
by members of both the families in the book. Nector is trapped in his
mind. Lipsha is forced to witness Grandpa's sexual fumblings with
Lulu in the laundry room when he finds his tactful withdrawal cut
off. Lulu experiences entrapment in her burning house, while Gerry
temporarily entombs himself in the car trunk of King's automobile.
Finally, it is interesting to note that even June, liberated from her
boarding house room, freed from the toilet stall, released from the
mud engineer's car, a "free" spirit no longer confined to her skin and
bones, is yet compelled to appear to her husband at his call, presum-
ably from the grave, trapped as a wifely spirit for all time.

Reinforcing the theme of enclosure and entrapment as early as
the second paragraph of the novel and extending to the end is the
employment of the shell motif. That its first appearance should be in
connection with colored eggs on the counter of a sleazy bar during the
Easter weekend (on which the body of Christ was nailed to a cross but
on which He also attained the ultimate freedom through resurrection
into Heaven) must be noted. June's sex customer is first seen
"peeling" a blue egg—the "beacon" toward which June walks for the
last assignation of her life. The small talk between them is almost too
obviously pointed. He offers to peel a pink one for her because "it
matched her turtleneck." She corrects him, saying that her vest is
called a "shell." "He said he would peel that for her too." The sexual
innuendos serve to reveal June as egglike and fragile but enclosed in a
shell that permits her to ply her trade indifferently. When she locks
herself in the bathroom stall (a substitute for her shell), she recalls her
client's hand "thumbing back the transparent skin and crackling blue

peel." Sitting in the stall, "she seemed to drift out of her clothes and skin with no help from anyone," and she feels her body "pure and naked—only the skins were stiff and old." In the car, as the mud engineer removes June's slacks, Erdrich tells the reader that the fabric "crackled with electricity and shed blue sparks when he pushed them down," to balance perhaps with the description of the aftermath: after releasing the car door, June falls out "into the cold. It was a shock like being born. But somehow she landed with her pants halfway up." She adjusts her clothing and "pulled her shell down." At this point June plows through the drifts toward the reservation undaunted. "June walked over [the snow] like water and came home" (2–6).

The mixture of the vaguely religious and the specifically carnal in *Love Medicine*, focused on the peeling and unpeeling of Easter eggs, would not in itself sustain the motif for almost three hundred pages; Erdrich, however, supports the early allusions throughout the story. Her characters are almost all desirous of shedding their bodies to live as spirits. Marie has a vision of passing through walls. Nector leaves his body for a new one. Lulu, hemmed in by arms and legs, looks "forward to getting past them." Her hope is to "be out there as a piece of the endless body of the world feeling pleasures so much larger than skin and bones and blood" (226). Even Dot's baby longs to break out of the womb.

In her enthusiasm for the motif, Erdrich mentions shells as often as she can. The Easter eggs and June's sweater as shells have been mentioned. But the reader is also aware of Marie's toenails as "pink ocean shells" (40); Eli "had to save on my shells," (28) thinking how expensive ammunition was. And King, in his wild drunken rage, destroys the fruit pies so lovingly prepared by Zelda and Aurelia. "Bits of jagged shells were struck to the wall and some were turned completely upside down." Though Albertine tries to reconstruct the pies, she is unsuccessful, for "once they smash there is no way to put them right" (37–38).

In a novel of human relationships and the interactions between two families over a generation, the use of the egg and eggshell motif is very appropriate. Grandma Kashpaw is referred to as a hen or as a chicken on more than one occasion. The book is a chronicle of love and hate, of violence and sexual reconciliation, of attraction and repulsion, of attempts to connect and retreats to isolation. No wonder then that "peeling" and "shell" have such wide application throughout the story. Robert Frost's comments in "Mending Wall" on the dual use of a wall both to wall in and to wall out are particularly apposite here. Interesting too is the fact that among the Ojibway

Indians a giant shell, associated with the sun and with its setting and rising over water, is a major component of the religion—though its relevance in *Love Medicine* is tenuous.[6]

Louise Erdrich's novel is rich in much more than the vivid and poignant story she has to tell. Though on the surface it deals with simple people working out their daily lives in elemental flashes of love and hate and primitive violence, this is no Wild West adventure yarn. Rather, the narrative material is moulded with aesthetic precision, even when the narrator of the passage is untutored, ungrammatical, and illogical. The overriding aim appears to be the recreation of two families over a long period of time, for the basic unit of Chippewa life, as Erdrich sees it, is just that family structure. There may be constant strife among family members, there may be marked contrasts between the younger generation and the older, but the sense of belonging to the family is evident throughout, both in the memory of the family members and in their reactions to immediate familial crises.

Indeed, the images I have chosen to deal with here seem designed to advance the theme of family and to effectuate its presentation. The flowing of water has long been associated with the operation of memory. In *Love Medicine* the Chippewa family line, as well as the lines of the Kashpaws and the Lamartines, is filtered to the reader through the memory flow of family members: a quick-running stream of remembrance here, a slow and deliberately muddy flow of recollection there. Just as effectively, the movement of the young Chippewas from fishing and swimming to reckless driving in automobiles signals the encroachment of a mechanical and impersonal civilization upon the natural environment of the families. It is but a step from that conclusion to the author's pervasive interest in closed spaces (particularly, the interior of automobiles) as the logical and pernicious consequence of the families' retreat from nature. Louise Erdrich's employment of such imagery enormously enriches the novel in a work of artistic patterning at its best.

NOTES

1. In this essay page numbers from Louise Erdrich's *Love Medicine* are given in parentheses in the text.

2. Nan Nowik, "*Belles Lettres* Interview," *Belles Lettres* 2 (Nov.-Dec. 1986): 8–9.

3. George Copway, "The Life of Kah-ge-ga-gah-bowh," in *Touchwood: A Collection of Ojibway Prose*, ed. Gerald Vizenor, Many Minnesotas Project Number 3 (Minnesota: New Rivers Press, 1987), 47.

4. Ibid., 50.
5. William Warren, "History of the Ojibway Nation," in *Touchwood: A Collection of Ojibway Prose*, 20.
6. Ibid., 22–23.

A Bibliography of Writings by LOUISE ERDRICH

Mickey Pearlman

BOOKS

Imagination (textbooks). Westerville, Ohio: Charles Merrill Co., 1981.
Jacklight (poems). New York: Holt, Rinehart and Winston, 1984; 1986.
Love Medicine. New York: Holt, Rinehart and Winston, 1984; Bantam Windstone, 1985.
The Beet Queen. New York: Henry Holt and Co., 1986; Bantam, 1987.
Tracks. New York: Henry Holt and Co., 1988.

POEMS

"The Lesky Girls." *Carolina Quarterly*, Fall 1975.
"Tree Dweller"; "The Book of Water." *Decotah Arts Quarterly*, Summer 1977.
"All the Comforts of Home"; "His Deathmap"; "Certain Fields." *Decotah Territory*, Autumn 1977.
"The Rhubarb"; "Lise"; "From a Sentence in a Book of Italian Grammar"; "Tree Prayer." In *Tilt: An Anthology of New England Women's Writing*. Lebanon, N.H.: New Victoria Publishers, 1978.
"Maiden Sister"; "Insomniac's Journey." *Bloodroot*, Spring 1978.
"To Otto, in Forgetfulness"; "Here's a Good Word for Step-and-a-Half Waleski"; "My Name Repeated on the Lips of the Dead." *Louisville Review*, Fall 1978.
"The Red Sleep of Beasts." *Ellipsis*, Spring 1979.
"Turtle Mountain Reservation." *Shenandoah*, Spring 1979.
"Stripper." *Webster Review*, Summer 1979.
"In the Midlands." *Ms.*, Aug. 1979.
"Portrait of the Town Leonard"; "Leonard Commits Redeeming Adulteries with all the Women in Town." *Mss.*, Spring 1981.
"Jacklight"; "Indian Boarding School: The Runaways"; "Painting of a White Gate and Sky"; "The Strange People." *Frontiers*, Fall 1981.
"People." *Frontiers*, Fall 1982.

ARTICLES, REVIEWS, STORIES

[With Heidi Erdrich] "Listeners Unite." *Redbook*, March 1981.

"The Red Convertible." *Mississippi Valley Review,* Summer 1981.

"Scales." *North American Review* 267 (March 1982): 22–27.

"Nuclear Detergent." *New England Review*, Spring 1982.

[With Michael Dorris] "A Change of Light." *Redbook*, Oct. 1982.

"The World's Greatest Fisherman." *Chicago*, Oct. 1982.

[With Michael Dorris] "Alternate Life Styles"; "Music to His Ears." *Woman.* United Kingdom, 1983.

"Saint Marie." *Atlantic Monthly*, March 1984, 78–84.

"Lulu's Boys." *Kenyon Review* 6 (Summer 1984): 1–10.

"The Plunge of the Brave." *New England Review and Bread Loaf Quarterly,* Fall 1984.

"The Ballad of Moustache Maud." *Frontiers*, Sept. 1984.

"Crown of Thorns." *Chicago*, Sept. 1984, 206 +.

"Wild Geese." *Mother Jones*, Oct. 1984, 21 +.

"Flesh and Blood." *Ms.*, Oct. 1984.

"The Beads." *North Dakota Quarterly*, Fall/Winter 1984.

"American Horse." In *Earth Power Coming: An Anthology of Native American Fiction*, edited by Simon Ortiz. Tsaile, Ariz.: Navajo Community College Press, 1984.

"Excellence Has Always Made Me Fill with Fright When It Is Demanded by Other People, But Fills Me with Pleasure When I Am Left Alone." *Ms.*, Jan. 1985, 44 +.

"Destiny." *Atlantic Monthly*, Jan. 1985, 64–68.

"The Beet Queen." Paris Review 27 (Spring 1985): 10–26.

"Where I Ought to Be: A Writer's Sense of Place." *New York Times Book Review* July 28 1985, 1 +.

"The Little Book." *Formations*, Summer 1985.

"Mister Argus." *Georgia Review* 39 (Summer 1985): 10–26.

"The Air Seeder." *Anteus*, Fall 1985.

"Pounding the Dog." *Kenyon Review* 7 (Fall 1985): 18–28.

"Fleurs." *Esquire*, Aug. 1986, 52–55.

"Sita Kozka." *Ms.*, Aug. 15, 1986, 52 +.

"Scars." *Boston Globe Magazine*, Aug. 31, 1986.

[With Michael Dorris] "Cows, Colleges and Contentment." *New York Times*, Aug. 3, 1986.

"Knives." *Granta: More Dirt: The New American Fiction* 19 (Fall 1986) 135–149. *Chicago*, Aug. 1986, 108 +.

"Freight." *American Voice*, Summer 1986.

"Chez Sita." Minneapolis/Saint Paul, Magazine, Sept. 1986, 14.

"Mary Adare." *New England Review,* Fall 1986.

"My Urban Aunt." *New York Woman*, Nov. 1986.

[With Michael Dorris] "Sea to Sea on Route 2." *New York Times Magazine* (Sophisticated Traveler), March 15, 1987, 31–32, 43–48.

[With Michael Dorris] "On the Road with the Kids." *Boston Globe Travel Magazine*, March 1987.
"Snares." *Harpers*, May 1987, 60+.
Review of *Texasville*, by Larry McMurtry. *New York Times Book Review*, April 19, 1987, 1.
"Square Lake." *Working Woman*, Nov. 1987.
"Christmas Lights." *Seventeen*, Dec. 1987, 128.
[With Michael Dorris] "Bangs and Whimpers: Novelists at Armageddon." *New York Times Book Review*, March 13, 1988, 1+.
"Indian Boarding School: The Runaways" (poem). *New York Times Book Review*, June 19, 1988, 36.
"Matchimanito." *Atlantic Monthly*, 262, no. 1 (July 1988): 66-74.

A Bibliography of Writings about LOUISE ERDRICH

Mickey Pearlman

"American Indian Louise Erdrich Plumbs Her Heritage to Produce a Prize-winning First Novel." *People*, Feb. 18, 1985, 75.
A.S.A.I.L. Bibliography #9. *Studies in American Indian Literature: The Newsletter of the Association for the Study of American Indian Literature* Winter 1985, 37–41.
Banks, Russell. "*The Beet Queen*" (review). *Nation*, Nov. 1, 1986, 460–63.
Beddow, Reid. "*Medicine* Fiction Winner; First Novel Runaway Choice of Critics Circle." *Washington Post*, Jan. 15, 1985, C2.
"*The Beet Queen*" (review). *Library Journal* 112 (Jan. 1987): 55.
"*The Beet Queen*" (review). *New Yorker*, Jan. 12, 1987, 102.
Berkley, Miriam. "*Publishers Weekly* Interviews." *Publishers Weekly* 230 (Aug. 15, 1986): 58+.
Bly, Robert. "Another World Breaks Through." *New York Times Book Review*, Aug. 31, 1986, 2.
Bruckner, D.J.R. "*Love Medicine*" (review). *New York Times*, Dec. 20, 1984, C21.
Chase, Elise. "*The Beet Queen*" (review). *Library Journal* 111 (Aug. 1986): 168–70.
Contemporary Authors 114. Detroit: Gale Research Co., 1985.
Contemporary Literary Criticism Yearbook, 1985, 39:128–34. Detroit: Gale Research Co., 1986.

Cowin, Dana. "Speak Previews" (Some Excerpts from current books in progress culled from literary readings). *Vogue*, Feb. 1985, 236–37.

Cunningham, Valentine. "A Right Old Battle-Axe." *Observer*, Feb. 24, 1985, 27.

Dundar, Helen. "A Novel Partnership." *Wall Street Journal*, Oct. 24, 1984, 28–29.

Elle, Oct. 1986, 52.

Fraser, C. Gerald. "*Love Medicine*" (review). *New York Times Book Review* Dec. 15, 1985, 32.

Geeslin, Campbell. "*The Beet Queen*" (review). *People Weekly*, Sept. 29, 1986, 12–14.

Gilbert, Harriett. "Mixed Feelings: *Love Medicine*" (review). *New Statesman* 109 (Feb. 8, 1985): 31.

Gorra, M. "*The Beet Queen*" (review). *Hudson Review* 40 (Spring 1987): 136–48.

Harvey, Andrew. "The Voice of America: New Fiction from Our Most Talked-About Writers." *Vogue*, Sept. 1986, 410–12.

Howard, Jane. "Louise Erdrich: A Dartmouth Chippewa Writes a Great Native American Novel." *Life*, April 1985, 27 + .

Hunter, Carol. "*Love Medicine*" (review). *World Literature Today* 59 (Summer 1985:474.

Jahner, Elaine. "*Love Medicine*" (review). *Parabola* 10 (May 1985):96, 98, 100.

Kakutani, Michiko. "*The Beet Queen*" (review). *New York Times*, Aug. 20, 1986, 19, 21.

Kendall, Elaine. "*Love Medicine*" (review). *Los Angeles Times*, Dec. 20, 1984, 34.

Kessler, Jascha. "Louise Erdrich: *Love Medicine*." Radio broadcast on KUSC-FM, Los Angeles, Ca., Jan., 1985.

Kinney, Jeanne. "*Love Medicine*" (review) *Best Sellers* 44 (Dec., 1984): 324–25.

Kooi, Cynthia. "*Love Medicine*" (review). *Booklist* 81 (Sept. 1, 1984): 24.

Kroeber, Karl, ed. "Louise Erdrich: *Love Medicine*." Studies in American Indian Literature: The Newsletter of the Association for the Study of American Indian Literature 9 (Winter 1985): 1–29.

"Let Us Now Praise Unsung Writers." *Mother Jones*, Jan. 1986, 27.

Littlefield, D.F. "*Love Medicine*," (review). *American Indian Quarterly* 11 (Winter 1987): 71–73.

"*Love Medicine*" (review). *Kirkus Reviews* 52 (Aug. 15, 1984):765–66.

"*Love Medicine*" (review). *New York Times Book Review*, Dec. 8, 1985, 3.

Lovenheim, Barbara. "Hearing Echoes (Childhood Memories of Louise Erdrich)." *New York Times Book Review*, Aug. 31, 1986, 2.

Lyons, Gene. "In Indian Territory: *Love Medicine*" (review). *Newsweek*, Feb. 11, 1985.

MacDougall, Ruth Doan. "*Love Medicine*" (review). *Christian Science Monitor*, Nov. 27, 1984, 33.

Maynard, Joyce. "Reads for Ladies of Leisure (Authors' Summer Reading Recommendations)." *Mademoiselle*, July 1985, 158–60.

McDowell, Edwin. "National Book Critics Circle Picks Winners." *New York Times*, Jan. 15, 1985, 20.

McGrath, Anne. "National Book Critics Circle Awards" (column). *Wilson Library Bulletin* 59 (April 1985): 537.

Moyer, L.L. "*Love Medicine* and *The Beet Queen*" (reviews). *Christianity and Crisis* 47 (May 18, 1987): 198–99.

Nathan, P.S. "Offbeat Auction." *Publishers Weekly* 232 (Nov. 13, 1987): 40.

"NBCC Announces 1984 Award Winners." *Publishers Weekly* 227 (Jan. 25, 1985): 27.

"Novelist Who Found Her Native Voice." *New York Times Book Review,* Dec. 23, 1984, 6.

Nowik, Nan. "Interview with Louise Erdrich." *Belles Lettres,* Nov./Dec. 1986, 9.

O'Conner, Patricia T. "*Love Medicine*" (review). *New York Times Book Review,* Dec. 7, 1986, 84.

Parini, Jay. "*Love Medicine*" (review). *Saturday Review,* Nov./Dec. 1984, 83.

Peck, Claude. "Author Profile." *Minneapolis-St. Paul Magazine,* Sept. 1986, 84 + .

Portales, Marco. "People with Holes in Their Lives." *New York Times Book Review,* Dec. 23, 1984, 6.

Reuter, Madalynne. "NBCC Celebrates 10th Year in New, Scholarly Atmosphere." *Publishers Weekly* 227 (Feb. 15, 1985): 24.

Rothstein, Mervyn. "Louise Erdrich, Partner in a Conspiracy to Write; Michael Dorris Is Her Husband and Collaborator, Too." *New York Times,* Oct. 13, 1986, 17 + .

Rubins, Josh. "*The Beet Queen*" (review). *New York Review of Books* 33 (Jan. 15, 1987): 14–15.

Schreiber, Le Anne. "*Love Medicine*" (review) *Vogue,* March 1985, 330.

Shetley, Vernon. "*Jacklight*" (review). *Poetry* 146 (April 1985): 40–42.

Simon, Linda. "*The Beet Queen*" (review). *Commonweal* 113 (Oct. 24, 1986): 565 + .

Sokolov, Raymond. "*The Beet Queen*" (review). *Wall Street Journal,* Sept. 2, 1986, 24, 28.

Steinberg, Sybil. "*The Beet Queen*"(review). *Publishers Weekly* 230 (July 4, 1986): 60.

Stuewe, Paul. "*The Beet Queen*" (review). *Quill Quire* 52 (Oct. 1986): 49.

Towers, Robert. "Uprooted: *Love Medicine*" (review). *New York Review of Books* 32 (April 11, 1985): 36–37.

"What Next? Bestselling Authors Talk about Works in Progress." *Publishers Weekly,* Jan. 9, 1987, 62.

Wickenden, Dorothy. "The Beet Question: *The Beet Queen*" (review). *New Republic* 20 (Oct. 6, 1986) 46–49.

Yardley, Jonathan. "*Love Medicine*" (review). *Washington Post,* Nov. 14, 1984, D2.

ALISON LURIE

The Uses of Adultery

Katharine M. Rogers

By entitling her first novel *Love and Friendship*, Alison Lurie invited comparison with an author whom she resembles in her area of interest, in her disenchanted view of human nature, in her coolly ironic puncturing of pretension. Like Jane Austen, Lurie characteristically focuses on the development of a woman's identity, through increasing self-knowledge and decisionmaking, and portrays this through her character's relationships with men. But while Austen shows her heroines maturing as they move toward their proper choice in marriage, Lurie shows them maturing afterward, as they try other life choices, typically represented by an adulterous affair. Thus, she can deal with older women: while Austen's heroines, who must be marriageable in nineteenth-century terms, range from seventeen (Marianne Dashwood) to twenty-seven (Anne Elliot), Lurie's can range from twenty-seven (Emily Turner) to fifty-four (Vinnie Miner). Because adultery is no longer so heavily charged, morally and emotionally, as it was in the nineteenth century, Lurie is free to use it as a device for comic satire and intellectual exploration of character.[1]

When Frances Burney's Evelina writes to Mr. Villars on her marriage day, "All is over, . . . and the fate of your Evelina is decided!"[2] she is only making explicit an assumption traditional in fiction—one which to some extent reflected the actual situation in traditional society—that a woman's whole life was defined by her marriage. It followed that any developing she was going to do had to be accomplished before she chose her husband. Austen uses this crucial choice to reveal her heroine's basic character and force her to reject naive overconfidence and surmount immature limitations. As Elizabeth

Bennet learns to distrust her snap judgments and Emma Woodhouse to break through her complacent self-centeredness so as to know herself and other people, Anne Elliot learns to rely on her own judgment rather than deferring to older but not wiser authorities.

Lurie's heroines also assume that their marriages have determined the course of their lives. Coming of age in the fifties, they married right out of college and settled down to be wives to their husbands and mothers to their children. In middle age Erica Tate despondently thinks that she has already made her choices, taken the significant moral actions of her life long ago; now that she has more knowledge of herself and the world, she is "equipped to make choices, but there are none left to make" (*The War Between the Tates*, 58).[3] But in fact, unlike Austen's characters, Lurie's can change their partners and their life-styles. She presents them with choices that force them to examine their beliefs and values; whether they ultimately keep these or reject them, they have matured as human beings through having faced and made the decision. Typically, Lurie sets up the alternatives in the form of the heroine's husband and a lover. Such a choice is realistically momentous for these women, who are committed not only to firm and conventional moral principles but to a confident belief that they are happily married. But, at the same time, Lurie uses the lover symbolically to represent a radically different life-style and set of values.

When their stories begin, Lurie's heroines have reason to be pleased with themselves and their situation. Attractive and privileged, they are successfully married to successful men. They are intelligent, well-educated, and sophisticated; they have high moral standards and make a point of living up to them. Katherine Cattleman insists on inconveniencing herself to correct some typing errors, for she "did not like being in the wrong, and badly wanted to put" her obnoxious employer "back there where he belonged" (*The Nowhere City*, 159). Erica's "greatest ambition is to be right: seriously and permanently in the right. Until recently, that was where she usually felt she was" (WT, 25). They have no doubts about what is right or whether they can behave properly. Whether they are being the perfect wife and mother (Erica) or gracefully balancing the roles of creative writer and corporate wife (Janet Belle Smith of *Real People*), they enjoy "carefully constructed lives and self-images, glowing with conscious enlightenment."[4]

Their illusions are so plausible that at first they take in the reader as well as themselves. We do not realize that their apparent control of themselves and their lives is sustained by shutting out what they do not want to see. Nor do we notice that, although they are not totally conventional (Janet publishes stories, Emily Turner has married beneath her), none has seriously questioned the fundamental assumptions with which she has been brought up. Although theoretically they had many choices in life, they have acted as if they had none. Having accepted the feminine mystique of the fifties, they devote themselves wholly to their families and expect marriage and children to provide them with happiness and fulfillment. Erica can be cheered by a banal conversation that "reminds her that she is successfully married, whereas Helen is a widow, and her best friend Danielle Zimmern a divorcée; that Brian is an important professor who receives urgent business letters; and that he calls home every evening when he is out of town" (WT, 16).

Lurie proceeds to demolish her heroines' illusions of rectitude and well-being, usually by disrupting their marriages. The opening sentence of her first book announces, "The day on which Emily Stockwell Turner fell out of love with her husband began much like other days" (Love and Friendship 9). What jolts Emily into this realization is a conversation in which he refuses to talk to her about his work as a college English instructor. Having spent her day doing routine domestic tasks with no society but their four-year-old son and a garrulous cleaning woman, she feels a natural need for intellectual stimulation; but Holman would rather read his newspaper than exert himself in discussion, and then he can't imagine why she is offended. Is she perhaps having her period? So much for the theory that an intelligent woman can live through her husband's work.

Having aroused Emily's dissatisfaction with her superficially satisfactory marriage, Lurie presents her with an alternative in the form of a lover who is very different from Holman, so different that her relationship with him dislodges her preconceptions about herself and what she wants in a husband. The release of her previously constricted sexuality is less important than the opening of mental possibilities. Lurie's married heroines are trapped by their external situation—all but Janet are untrained for careers; their husbands oppose their working outside the home; they are tied down to households and children. But what she is more interested in is the internal factors that trap them: their need to be perfect wives and mothers, their fear of threats to their images of themselves and their situation.

Though the lovers are for the most part believable on the realistic level, they also symbolically represent what is missing in the heroine's marriage (or life situation, in Vinnie's case) and what is essential to eliciting the full range of her personality. Once she has done what had been unthinkable for her, she is ready to rethink her life in general, including the values she has been living by. Even if the woman chooses to remain in her original situation, as Emily does, this time she chooses it in an informed way.

Lurie's insight into the flaws of a seemingly ideal marriage, and into the complicity of even educated women in their own exploitation, is drawn from personal experience. (Her protagonists, from Mary Ann Hubbard in *Only Children* to Vinnie Miner in *Foreign Affairs*, are close to her own age at the time the story is set.) At Radcliffe Lurie and her fellow students sneered at the occasional woman who braved convention by attempting to get the professor's attention in a Harvard classroom.[5] In "No One Asked Me to Write a Novel," Lurie tells how family pressures, combined with rejection slips, persuaded her temporarily to give up writing and throw herself into a life like Erica's." "I organized family picnics and parties and trips; I baked animal cookies and tuna-fish casseroles. . . . I played monotonously simple board games. . . . I entertained my husband's superiors and flirted with his colleagues and gossiped with their wives. I told myself that my life was rich and full. Everybody else seemed to think so. Only I knew that, right at the center, it was false and empty. I wasn't what I was pretending to be. I didn't like staying home and taking care of little children; I was restless, impatient, ambitious."[6] Lurie's heroines (except for Janet) do not have a specific unused talent to pinpoint their dissatisfaction. Nevertheless, their lives do not fulfill their intellectual or emotional needs, although they have a strong stake in believing them "rich and full." Lacking a vocation, concerned only with the personal sphere, they are given the choice appropriate for them: between two men. By involving them in extramarital affairs, Lurie forces them to part with their cherished illusions and to see themselves more realistically.

Although Lurie uses this adultery plot in *Love and Friendship, The Nowhere City, Real People,* and *The War between the Tates,* it does not become boringly repetitious any more than Austen's marriage plot does.[7] Rather, the repetitive elements enable her to explore varied aspects of her themes of marital discontent and female consciousness-raising. In *The Nowhere City,* Lurie focuses on the negativism produced by acceptance of the feminine mystique, especially in a punctiliously righteous woman. Defining virtue as sacrificing her self-interest to her concept of ideal behavior, Katherine distrusts all enjoyment; imposing rigid controls on her desires, she fears anything that might unsettle the status quo. She wants men to be "reasonable, predictable, and considerate of her" (118); that is, they must not violate her expectations of proper behavior or challenge the adjustments that both protect and limit her. She is an intelligent and attractive woman, yet she has never been happy; in *The Nowhere City,* she suffers from a flagrantly unfaithful husband, an intrusive employer, an environment she hates, and sinus headaches. Not only is she convinced that these afflictions are irremediable, but she takes a certain self-righteous pleasure in them: the misbehavior of her husband and her employer highlight her own rectitude, as her loathing for Los Angeles proves her taste; through sinus headaches, which she cannot help, she can give vent to the pain and anger that she is too well conducted to express openly. Thus, her behavior patterns sustain her self-image even though they obstruct her happiness. She collaborates with her husband's inconsiderateness by masochistically expecting it. (In turn, his "impatient tolerance" of her limitations merely confirms her feeling that she cannot overcome them.)

Nevertheless, as the book progresses, she comes to realize how she contributes to her misery and that her protective shell is in fact a prison of inhibitions. It takes an aggressive lover, her exuberant employer, to break the shell. By openly expressing his feelings and sexuality, he forces her to recognize her own and to violate her limiting self-image as an irreproachable person. He makes her see that her concept of love is moralistic and self-destructive: "giving up everything for some other person in a very grudging, painful way" (240). This is not only unpleasant for her, but, since chronic self-sacrifice is no more natural for women than men, it leads to the sinus headaches which so annoy Paul. The result is that she critically examines the rigid standards which she had automatically accepted, opens her eyes to see if there are others which suit her better, and chooses a new life style.

The adjustment of Janet Belle Smith in *Real People* seems at first to be much more clear-sighted and constructive than Katherine's. Apparently she has achieved a happy balance between her roles as serious writer and wife; she even has a sympathetic male fellow-artist, a painter named Kenneth, with whom she can enjoy a platonic relationship without sullying her self-image. The only flaw she sees in her life is that her writing has become trivial and repetitious—something that will be corrected by a few weeks in Illyria, an idyllic artists' colony where she can become her "real self" (17). Or rather, *one* can become—Janet's preference for *one* over *I*, noted by Nick Donato, an outspoken fellow guest ("Janet has an imaginary friend named Wun. An Oriental," whom she makes responsible for her feelings [75]), suggests falsity in her ladylike self-image by giving away her need to disclaim emotion and egotism. At first we suppose, with Janet, that her sophisticated, impersonal style expresses her control over experience; gradually, we realize that it serves to insulate her from it. The first person point of view in *Real People* directly involves us in Janet's self-deception and the unpleasant self-recognition that follows.

Only a violently upsetting experience would be enough to shock Janet out of rationalizations that seem to serve her so well; and again, this comes in the form of a passionate affair with a man so unlikely that he upsets her deepest convictions about her own nature and possibilities. Unlike her husband and Kenneth, the vulgar pop artist Nick challenges her assumptions about what nice people do, whether she is a nice person, whether she ought to be. Janet enters Nick's studio as a slumming tourist gathering material for a witty anecdote.[8] She leaves after a passionate encounter that makes her recognize impulses in herself that do not at all fit her refined self-image: she not only has strong sexuality, but has responded to a man who violates all her standards of acceptable behavior. At the same time, Nick makes her see the truth about her genteel substitute for adultery and her compromise between niceness and artistic expression: Kenneth did not abstain from sexual overtures out of consideration and respect for her but because, as a homosexual, he was not interested; she cannot be a serious writer if she insists on censoring herself in order to maintain everyone's approval. Finally, Kenneth (embittered because her affair with Nick has shattered his illusions about her) forces her to see that the conformist pressure she has been blaming on an unsympathetic husband and stuffy friends is actually within herself: what she is really protecting is not her family, but "some idea of yourself that you're terribly fond of . . . the idea of this charming, intelligent, sensitive lady writer who lives in a nice house in the country with her nice family, and never makes any serious mistakes or has any real problems" (151–52).

Janet finally acknowledges that her "real self" includes ugly passions and that it is timidity that weakens her fiction and her life as well: between the external pressure to conform to a restrictive role and the internal pressure to behave properly in its terms, she had limited her options and blinded herself to anything that conflicted with her self-image. By the end of the novel, with a clearer picture of herself, she is free to consider alternative choices. Janet thought she would change simply by moving into Illyria, where she could pursue her work without interference and associate with sympathetic fellow-artists; but what she needs is something far more radical than new surroundings: she must be jolted out of her complacent certainties by perhaps the one event that could force her to change her view of herself.

In *The War between the Tates*, Lurie provides her most brilliant exposure of what her heroine once thought was a successful marriage. It is altogether a subtler work than *The Nowhere City:* Erica's masochistic self-righteousness is less obvious than Katherine's, Brian's selfishness more finely dissected than Paul's, the Tates' stresses not schematized by a move to another culture, and the ending ruthlessly realistic. Erica, once very satisfied with herself as the wife of a brilliant professional man and mother to two lovable children, now finds her children changed into brutish, ungrateful adolescents; her only consolation is "her friend and husband, Brian" (11). Then she discovers that he is having an affair with a mediocre young woman. This provokes her to reevaluate her "perfect" marriage, to see it for the unequal bargain it is. While Brian does interesting, prestigious work, she, with similar mental capacity and training, is expected to devote her days to the cheerful completion of routine tasks (vividly rendered in step-by-step descriptions and food imagery). If she does her work well, it is taken for granted; if anything goes wrong, she is blamed. She begins to question Brian's plausible doctrine of "separate spheres" in a marriage, whereby "if he lost his job (which had never been very likely and was now impossible, since he had tenure), it was his fault. If the children became uncontrollable, it was hers" (13).

Since her whole life was built around her family, Erica finds herself with nothing—no career, no satisfying social life, badly damaged self-esteem. She clings to behaving correctly herself but finds that this brings no rewards. The only alternative Lurie offers her is Sandy Finkelstein, the owner of an occult bookshop, who has worshiped her from afar since their graduate school days. He is a shabby dropout, a born loser of ridiculous appearance; but he is unselfish and loving, the only character in the book who is not involved in competition or "war." Erica turns to him in her misery, finds some consolation, and even, very briefly, thinks of going off with him. But though she can now value his freedom from convention and egotism and can recognize the wisdom of his saying that we must all some time adjust to being losers, she realizes that she needs the security and success that Brian offers.

So the Tates reunite, this time with more realistic expectations of life and each other. Erica is no longer trapped in her assumptions that she must listen to Brian because he is a just, objective moralist and must realize his and her own ideal of the perfect wife and mother of a perfect family. In an early scene, she had weakly let Brian talk her out of taking a part-time job by playing on her guilt, though even she recognized that his argument was shoddy (it might damage the children). Now she takes an interesting job and starts to let go of the children (which turns out to improve their behavior slightly). Having seen other possibilities, specifically life without Brian, she will be able to form independent views and defend them.

Sketched in *Love and Friendship*, developed in *The Nowhere City*, *Real People*, and *The War between the Tates*, Lurie's breaking marriage plot forces her heroine for the first time to examine the assumptions she has lived by. In terms of comic effect, we see the deflation of complacency, delightfully illuminating because the complacency is so high-level and sophisticated. In terms of character development, we see identity emerging as a result of breaking through constraints and facing truth.

Lurie uses surprising adulterous affairs not only to shock her protagonists out of their self-assurance but to explore the potentialities of her characters by mixing and matching them: Does prissy, repressed Katherine have it in her to accept Iz Einsam's open expression of feelings? Is snobbish, self-centered Vinnie Miner of *Foreign Affairs* capable of opening up to Chuck Mumpson's warmth? (Eighteenth-century women novelists did the same thing, less realistically, by supplying their heroines with five or six suitors.) Honey Hubbard in *Only Children* flirts with Dan Zimmern, who is more playful and sexually exciting than her stodgy workaholic husband; but in the end she prefers Bill's solid devotion to the casual exploitation that Dan would impose on any woman involved with him. Erica Tate is too conventional and success oriented to feel more than sympathy for Sandy, but her friend Danielle—less conventional and more angry at her sophisticated intellectual husband—can come to love the "pig pediatrician" Bernie Kotelchuk, though she takes care to settle the terms of their marriage beforehand to prevent misunderstandings produced by their different backgrounds. This process of considering possible men and settling for the one who is best for her indicates Lurie's realistically disenchanted view of marriage; she recognizes that every match is a compromise in which, at best, people find those who meet their most important needs.

She has a similarly disenchanted view of love, at least the romantic form; it is not an elevating or even an overwhelming passion in marriage or adultery. Lurie never loses sight of comic aspects, even in *Love and Friendship*, where she comes closest to presenting sexual passion as ecstasy. Early in their relationship, when Emily and Will are in a diner, Emily feels a marked pressure on her leg under the table; she feels flustered and guilty, knowing she should move her leg but somehow not doing so. How surprised she is when Will gets up and the pressure remains. Then she discovers a large crosspiece under the table.

In *Only Children* Lurie suggests that love may be both self-destructive and selfish; perhaps it is no more than urgent dependence, manifested as possessiveness by strong people like Bill, as propitiatory compliance by helpless ones like Dan's wife, Celia (252–53).[9] Anna, the wisest of the adults, is repelled by the idea of "complete merging of two souls": to know all another persons's thoughts and expect them to give themselves completely is enslavement. Celia, who thinks giving herself to "the right man" is beautiful, is pathetically exploited in her marriage (76).

On the other hand, in *Foreign Affairs* Lurie shows the unattractive consequences of not loving or being loved. Again, she uses an adulterous affair to open up possibilities to her heroine and make her question her values. The affair is literally adulterous only on Chuck's side, but considering the importance Vinnie attaches to culture, taste, and gentility, her relationship with Chuck, a crude, half-educated engineer, is as much a breach of cherished standards as were Katherine's and Janet's adulteries. Vinnie clings to her standards of elitism and self-control because they reassure her of superiority in a world that slights middle-aged single women. (At the same time that Lurie dissects Vinnie's single-minded pursuit of her own comfort and self-interest, she mocks the obtuseness of a world that expects "plain aging women" to be particularly self-effacing [4]). Vinnie has constructed a neat, superficially successful life for herself; but she is patronized by others, centered in herself, and dogged by self-pity, vividly personified as an imaginary dirty-white mongrel named Fido. Her first emotional response to Chuck is reluctantly to feel sorry for him, "perhaps even sorrier than she is for herself" (195); then she begins to appreciate his ingenuous friendliness and finally, as a result of their passionate affair, to recognize his worth.

Vinnie's first experience of mutual love frees her from her fear of emotional commitment and from the self-centeredness that cut her off from others and burdened her with Fido. Chuck's faith in her, produced simply by his ignorance of her social signals, forces her to try to live up to his image of her "as helpful and kindly" (240). At the beginning of the book, it appeared that Vinnie's life was as determined by her plainness as those of the other heroines were by their attractiveness; as they married without thought immediately after college and became dependent on their husbands, she developed a rigid and isolating self-sufficiency. As their identities are defined by their marriage, hers is by her career (10). (Plain men, less dependent on the approval of the opposite sex, are under less pressure than women like Vinnie to protect themselves by shrinking from emotional commitment.) Knowing Chuck makes Vinnie revise her standards and awakens her to her own capacities for joy and generous feeling. She resists the temptation to retaliate upon the daughter of a critic who has sneered at her; she puts herself to considerable inconvenience to help that daughter and her husband to reunite, even though these two young, beautiful, loved people might naturally evoke her envy. Her sophisticated friends would not have expected her to resist the temptation, but "Chuck Mumpson would take it for granted that she'd go" (373).

She is not, of course, totally transformed by her experience of love; when we last view her, she is accepting Fido as a permanent companion (but he is smaller than before). The same is true of Lurie's other protagonists, all of whom but Katherine return in the end to their husbands/life-styles. (We don't get enough detail on the new Katherine to know how radically she may have changed.) In every case, the lover's attractiveness to the heroine is outweighed by his deficiency in qualities essential to her. Lurie is too realistic not to recognize that, by and large, people's basic character and values are sufficiently formed by their late twenties to make total transformation impossible. But intelligent people can be brought to examine attitudes that they had unthinkingly developed and to recognize elements in themselves that they had repressed. Vinnie, Emily, Janet, Erica, and even Honey move toward examining their previously unexamined lives, a movement that is essential to their development as human beings even if not outwardly conspicuous.

Such an examination is particularly significant for women, because of the traditional pressure on them to accept rather than to question. A patriarchal society defines women's roles in terms of service to others and convinces them that not only their virtue but their fulfillment lies in putting other people's needs before their own, regardless of how those others behave. Thomas Gisborne, an eighteenth-century conduct-book writer, blandly asserted that women are naturally qualified by Providence to adapt happily to the wishes of those around them.[10] The feminine mystique that shaped the Lurie heroine's attitudes (and has not yet been dissipated by women's liberation) assumes that highly educated women can find fulfillment in caring for small children and promoting their husbands' careers and, moreover, that this job is so easy that it should be accomplished without strain. The less women examine these propositions, the more convenient for society. In the typical Lurie novel, a woman who has always prided herself on being reasonable and controlled suddenly finds herself overwhelmed by sexual passion. But her sexual awakening is less important than her realization that her ideals of rationality and self-control had been defined by patriarchal society and might be replaced by more genuine ones, based on experience and independent thought.

The pressure on women to conform to the status quo has tended to make them cautious and fearful of change. Erica's reaction is typical. "Whenever something sudden happens, her first impulse is to withdraw, consider the situation, regroup her forces" (335). Women are prone to accept their lives as set and may deny problems so as to avoid disbalancing a stable situation. This keeps them back, as has been pointed out by Donna Shalala, the former president of Hunter College. Going on to an even more prestigious position, she shocked her audience by remarking that women should always be prepared to move on. Most women, on the contrary, resist thinking about a major change unless prodded by some outside force such as Lurie provides for her characters. Her women are pushed into unfamiliar situations and end up enjoying them. In ironic contrast, her men, who seek change with virile adventurousness, are discomfited by it. Paul is as ridiculous in disreputable disguise at a beatnik coffeehouse as Brian is at the student pot-party to which Wendy drags him (NC, chap. 11; WT chap. 14). It is middle-aged Vinnie who grows and changes in *Foreign Affairs*, while young Fred comes out from his upsetting affair much as he went into it.

Women's traditional role in the family has sensitized them to other people's needs and led them to attach high importance to maintaining relationships.[11] This concern has strong positive effects (explored by Belenky, by Carol Gilligan in *In a Different Voice*, and others), but it can also impede women's development of individual selfhood, as it makes their concept of self-worth depend on the behavior of other people. Erica expresses this problem when she complains "that identity is at the mercy of circumstances, of other people's actions. Brian, by committing casual adultery, had turned Erica into the typical wife of a casually unfaithful husband: jealous and shrewish and unforgiving—and also, since she had been so easily deceived, dumb and insensitive. Her children, by becoming ill-mannered adolescents, had turned her into an incompetent and unsympathetic mother" (58).[12] Enmeshed in their family, women find it particularly difficult to define individual goals and to move resolutely toward them. By separating a woman from her accustomed context of family relationships, the adulterous affair gives her a chance to look at herself and her situation independently.

This concern with awakening her heroines to look critically at their lives is what makes Lurie a feminist author. It is true that doctrinaire feminists disapprove of her work[13] and that she subjects their slogans to the same witty deflation she applies to other forms of cant. Nevertheless, her encouragement of radical questioning, symbolized by the respectable wife's trying out of adultery, is liberating. So, in a lighter way, is her deadly accurate rendition of the irritations and frustrations usual in marriage—obtusely self-centered husbands, ungrateul children for whose deficiencies their mother is made to feel responsible, an endless round of routine tasks, none of which are appreciated. It is true that Lurie's husbands also have cause for dissatisfaction—Katherine's perpetual sinus headaches balance Paul's unthinking self-indulgence—but the focus is on men's routine exploitation of women in marriage. Lurie brilliantly exposes the obtuseness of otherwise intelligent, sophisticated men toward their wives. They cannot see that their marriage is an unequal bargain and that their wives have needs comparable to their own. Though Brian shows no interest in Erica's problems, he expects her to listen sympathetically to his. He is aggrieved by his children's misbehavior and doubly aggrieved because Erica is failing to handle them; he does not think of their effect on Erica, who has to see so much more of them. When Emily fails to keep house properly, Holman does not try to find out what is wrong with her but merely reflects, "Women went through these emotional periods, in his experience, and in his experience the best way to deal with them was to get out of their way" (*Love and Friendship* 222). Lurie's adultery plot not only punishes these husbands as they deserve but highlights the husband's obliviousnss to his wife's feelings and needs by contrasting it with the lover's attentiveness. The contrast is even sharper in the cases where the husband feels he is entitled to an extramarital affair because his wife is no longer giving him the devotion or excitement he considers his due.

Lurie has been criticized for exaggerating her characters and maintaining too great an emotional distance from them. Actually, these techniques are totally appropriate for an art that is comic as well as realistic, an art that (like Austen's) aims to deflate pretensions, expose rationalizations, and pinpoint incongruities. Moreover, Lurie is critical but not heartless. She makes us understand why her women are self-righteous and her men obtuse; we realize that these failings are society's fault as well as their own.

NOTES

1. This would, of course, be unthinkable in an Austen novel. The only adulterous wfe she includes, Maria Bertram Rushworth, is immediately banished from the world of *Mansfield Park*. Another adulteress, Colonel Brandon's dead sister-in-law, is only mentioned in retrospect in *Sense and Sensibility*. However, Austen evidently shared Lurie's doubts about marital bliss, since there are almost no examples of it within her novels, even though they culminate in happy marriages.

2. Frances Burney, *Evelina* (New York: W. W. Norton, 1965), 388.

3. In this essay Alison Lurie's novels will be identified in the following way, and page numbers are given in parentheses in the text. *Foreign Affairs* (FA); *Love and Friendship* (LF); *The Nowhere City* (NC); *Only Children* (OC); *Real People* (RP); *The War between the Tates* (WT).

4. Sara Sanborn, review of *The War between the Tates*, by Alison Lurie, *New York Times Book Review* (July 28, 1974): 1.

5. Lurie, "Their Harvard," quoted. *Something about the Author*, ed. Anne Commire (Detroit: Gale Research Co., 1987), 46:130.

6. Alison Lurie, "No One Asked Me to Write a Novel," *New York Times Book Review*, June 6, 1982, 47.

7. *Foreign Affairs* follows a similar pattern, as I shall argue below, even though Vinnie is unmarried. The exceptions are *Only Children*, which centers on the child Mary Ann, and *Imaginary Friends*, with a male protagonist. However, Mary Ann's mother, Honey, gets considerable attention; she flirts with adultery and does some examining of herself and her marriage. And even in *Imaginary Friends*, the protagonist is forced by his strong attraction to a person radically different from himself to question the assumptions he has complacently taken for granted.

8. H. Porter Abbott, *Diary Fiction: Writing as Action* (Ithaca: Cornell Univ. Press, 1984), 52.

9. Cf. Miranda Fenn's opinion: "The real life of romantic love, after its early flights, is nasty, brutish, and short. . . . Marriage is kinder, but it also lives on lies, little tame ones—one makes the best of the bargain" (LF, 212). Since Miranda has changed her name from Mary Ann, she may be the former Mary Ann Hubbard of *Only Children*.

10. Thomas Gisborne, *An Enquiry into the Duties of the Female Sex* (New York: Garland, 1974), 116.

11. Mary Field Belenky, et al., *Women's Ways of Knowing: The Development of Self, Voice, and Mind* (New York: Basic Books, 1986), 46–47.

12. It seems inconsistent that the same patriarchal tradition that holds wives and mothers responsible for everything that goes wrong in the household and pities the poor husbands and children driven to misbehavior also ridicules husbands for failing to keep their wives faithful and obedient. The

only constant is that women are blamed—whether for withholding goodness or for being so evil that they need to be controlled (and, simultaneously, so weak that a real man should be able to control them).

13. See, for example, Rachel Cowan's review "The Bore between the Tates," *Ms.*, Jan. 1975, 41–42.

A Bibliography of Writings by ALISON LURIE

Mickey Pearlman

NONFICTION

V.R. Lang: A Memoir. Privately printed, 1959.
V.R. Lang: Poems and Plays. New York: Random House, 1974.
[With Justin G. Schiller] *Classics of Children's Literature, 1631–1932 Series.* New York: Garland Publishing, 1977.
The Language of Clothes. New York: Random House, 1981.

FICTION

Love and Friendship. New York: Macmillan, 1962; Avon Books, 1962.
The Nowhere City. New York: Coward, 1965; Avon Books, 1965.
Imaginary Friends. New York: Coward, 1967; Avon Books, 1986.
Real People. New York: Random House, 1969; Avon Books, 1969.
The War between the Tates. New York: Random House, 1974; Avon Books, 1975.
Only Children. New York: Random House, 1979.
Clever Gretchen and Other Forgotten Folktales (juvenile). New York: Crowell, 1980.
The Heavenly Zoo (juvenile). New York: Farrar, Straus, 1980.
Fabulous Beasts (juvenile). New York: Farrar, Straus, 1981.
Foreign Affairs. New York: Random House, 1984; Avon Books, 1985.
The Truth About Lorin Jones. Forthcoming, 1988.
Manuscript Collection. Radcliffe College Library, Cambridge, Mass.

ARTICLES, POEMS, REVIEWS, STORIES

"Archer with His Arrow"; "In a Good Year"; "Trees, Being Neighbors" (poems). *Poetry* 70 (June 8, 1947): 126.
"The Boy Who Couldn't Grow Up." *New York Review of Books* 22 (Feb. 6, 1975): 11.
Review of *Shardik* by Richard Adams. *New York Review of Books* 22 (June 12, 1975): 34.

"A Tail of Terror," *New York Review of Books* 22 (Dec. 11, 1975): 26.

"Bunny Lang: Death among Friends" (except from *V. R. Lang, Poems and Plays* with a memoir by Alison Lurie). *Ms.* 4 (Dec. 1975): 118+.

Reviews of *On Human Finery,* by Quentin Bell; *Dress and Society, 1560–1970,* by G. Squire; *Hollywood Costume—Glamour! Glitter! Romance!* by D. McConathy. *New York Review of Books* 23 (Nov. 25, 1976): 17

"Fairy Tales for a Liberated Age." *Horizon* 19 (July 1977): 80–85.

"Beatrix Potter: More than Just Peter Rabbitt." *Ms.* 6 (Sept. 1977): 42–43.

Review of *The Book of Merlyn: The Unpublished Conclusion to "The Once and Future King,"* by T. H. White," *New York Review of Books* 24 (Nov. 24, 1977): 3.

Reviews of *Animals and Men: Their Relationship as Reflected in Western Art from Prehistory to the Present Day,* by K. Clark; *Freaks: Myths and Images of the Secret Self,* by Leslie Fiedler; and *A Fiedler Reader,* by Leslie Fiedler. *New York Review of Books* 25 (March 23, 1978):22.

Reviews of *The Woman's Dress for Success Book,* by J.T. Malloy; *Seeing Through Clothes,* by A. Hollander; *In Fashion: Dress in the Twentieth Century,* by P. Glynn; *Mirror, Mirror: A Social History of Fashion,* by M. and A. Batterberry; and *Avedon: Photographs, 1947–1977,* by R. Avedon with an essay by Harold Brodkey. *New York Review of Books* 25 (Dec. 7, 1978): 25.

Reviews of *The World Guide to Gnomes, Fairies, Elves and Other Little People,* by T. Keighttley; *A Field Guide to the Little People,* by N. Arrowsmith and G. Moore; *Gnomes,* by W. Huygen and R. Poortvliet; *Faeries,* by B. Froud and A. Lee, ed. by D. Larkin; *The Fairies in Tradition and Literature,* by K. Briggs; *The Vanishing People: Fairy Lore and Legends,* by K. Briggs; *An Encyclopedia of Fairies: Hobgoblins, Brownies, Bogies and Other Supernatural Creatures,* by K. Briggs; and *Fairy Tales and After: From Snow White to E.B. White,* by R. Sale. *New York Review of Books* 26 (March 8, 1979): 16; Lurie correction. *New York Review of Books* 26 (May 3, 1979): 46.

"Classics of Children's Literature." In *Children's Literature* 10, edited by A. Moss (Annual of the Modern Language Association Group on Children's Literature and the Children's Literature Association). New Haven: Yale Univ. Press, 1980–1984.

"Ford Madox Ford's Fairy Tales." In *Children's Literature* 8: 7–21 (Annual of the Modern Language Association Group on Children's Literature and the Children's Literature Association). New Haven: Yale Univ. Press, 1980–1984.

"Sex and Fashion" (excerpt from *The Language of Clothes*). *New York Review of Books* 28 (Oct. 22, 1981):38–46.

Review of *Kate Greenaway,* by R. Engen. *New York Review of Books* 29 (March 18, 1982): 15.

"No One Asked Me to Write a Novel: The Making of the Writer." *New York Times Book Review,* June 6, 1982, 46–48.

"The Steamy Side of Paradise." *House and Garden*, June 1983, 30 +.

Reviews of *American Beauty*, by L.W. Banner, and *Skin to Skin*, by P. Glynn. *New York Review of Books* 30 (June 2, 1983): 20.

"The Benevolent Tower." *House and Garden*, Sept. 1984, 174–75.

"E. Nesbit: Riding the Wave of the Future." *New York Review of Books* 31 (Oct. 25, 1984):19–22.

Review of *The Oxford Book of Children's Verse in America. New York Times Book Review*, May 5, 1985, 16.

"On the Road to Timbuktu: Exploring the Strange and Haunting Landscape of Mali." *House and Garden*, Sept. 1985, 46–50.

Review of *The Singing Game*, by Iona and Peter Opie, *New York Review of Books* 32 (Oct. 24, 1985): 35.

"Common Courtesy: In Which Miss Manners Solves the Problem That Baffled Mr. Jefferson." *New York Times Book Review*, Nov. 10, 1985, 13.

Reviews of *The Good Terrorist* and *The Diaries of Jane Somers: The Diary of a Good Neighbor* and *If the Old Could*, by Doris Lessing. *New York Review of Books*, 32 (Dec. 19, 1985): 8.

"Petals Personified" (review of J.J. Grandville's *The Court of Flora*). *Art and Antiques*, July 1986.

"To the Manner Born" (British fashion). *New York Times Magazine* Aug. 24, 1986; S150.

"Roly-poly Fun and Feasting" (review of *The Random House Book of Mother Goose*). *New York Times Book Review*, Nov. 9, 1986, 37.

Introduction to *Peter Pan*, by James Barrie. New York: Signet Classics, 1987.

"True Confessions" (review of *How I Grew*, by Mary McCarthy). *New York Review of Books* 34 (June 11, 1987): 19–21.

"Underground Artist: The Children's Books of William Mayne." New York Review of Books 35. (Feb. 18, 1988):11–13.

"*A Moody Retreat under Italy's Alps." New York Times*, April 3, 1988, XX13.

"E. Nesbit." In *Writers for Children*, ed. Jane M. Bingham, 423-30. New York: Scribner, 1988.

A Bibliography of Writings about ALISON LURIE

Mickey Pearlman

Abbott, H. Porter. *Diary Fiction: Writing as Action*, 40–53. Ithaca: Cornell Univ. Press, 1984.

Adams, Phoebe-Lou. "*The Language of Clothes*" (review). *Atlantic Monthly*, Dec. 1981, 92.

Adler, Constance. *Philadelphia Magazine*, July 1985, 89.

Aldridge, John W. "How Good Is Alison Lurie?" *Commentary* 59 (Jan. 1975): 79–81.

Alter, Ann Ilan. "*The Language of Clothes*" (review). *New Directions for Women* 11 (March-April 1982): 14.

Annan, Gabriele. "*Foreign Affairs*" (review). *New York Review of Books* 31 (Oct. 11, 1984): 37 + .

Bannon, Barbara A. "Publishers Weekly Interviews." *Publishers Weekly* 206 (Aug. 19, 1974): 6.

Bernays, Anne. "*Foreign Affairs*" (review). *New York Times*, Sept. 13, 1984, 23.

———. "What to Think about Chuck and Vinnie." *New York Times Book Review*, Sept. 16, 1984, 9.

Boston, Richard. "Minerva in London." *Punch*, Jan. 23, 1985, 52.

Bradbury, Malcolm. "The Paleface Professor." *Times* (London), Jan. 19, 1985, 6.

Bridges, Thomas. "*Only Children*" (review). *National Review* 31 (Dec. 7, 1979), 1576 + .

"Briefly Noted: *Only Children*." *New Yorker*, May 14, 1979, 174.

Burke, Jeffrey. "*Only Children*" (review). *Harper's*, July 1979, 78.

Butler, Marilyn. "Amor Vincit Vinnie" (review of *Foreign Affairs*). *London Review of Books*, Feb. 21, 1985, 5–6.

Chambers, Andrew. "In Winter, United States Writing Talent Pools on the Sensual, Timeless Port of Key West." *People Weekly*, Feb. 23, 1981, 24 + .

Champlin, Charles. "*Foreign Affairs*" (review). *Los Angeles Times Book Review* 103 (Oct. 21, 1984): 1.

"Child and Parents Reverse Roles." *Progressive* 43 (Sept. 1979): 60.

Clapperton, Jane. "*The Language of Clothes*" (review). *Cosmopolitan*, Dec. 1981, 22.

Clemons, Walter. "*Fabulous Beasts*" (review). *Newsweek*, Dec. 7, 1981, 101.

———. "*Foreign Affairs*" (review). *Newsweek*, Sept. 24, 1984, 80.

"Clever Gretchen" (review). *Publishers Weekly* 217 (Feb. 29, 1980): 13.

"*Clever Gretchen and Other Forgotten Folktales*" (review). *School Library Journal*, May 1980, 38.

Cloutier, Candace. *Contemporary Authors: New Revisions* 17:276–79. Detroit: Gale Research Co., 1980.

Commire, Anne, ed. *Something About the Author* 46:130. Detroit: Gale Research Co., 1987.

Conarroe, Joel. "Footnotes to Lovenotes." *Book World—Washington Post*, Sept. 30, 1984, 6.

Connaly, Bruce. Sound recording review. *Library Journal* 110 (Oct. 1, 1985): 89.

Contemporary Literary Criticism 4 (1975):305–7; 5 (1976):259–61; 18 (1980): 309–11; 39 (1986): 176–85. Detroit: Gale Research Co.

Corrigan, Maureen. "*Foreign Affairs*" (review). *Times Literary Supplement*, Oct. 1984, 5.

Cowen, Rachel B. "The Bore between the Tates." *Ms.*, Jan. 1975, 41–42.

Domowitz, Janet. "*Only Children*" (review). *Christian Science Monitor*, May 14, 1979, B4.

Dooley, Patricia. "*The Heavenly Zoo*" (review). *School Library Journal* 27 (Sept. 1980): 75.

Duffy, Martha. "It's That Old Short Story Again: Italian Designers Hope That Minis Will Bloom in the Spring." *Time*, Oct. 22, 1984, 108.

"Energy: Your Best Beauty Asset." *Glamour*, Feb. 1983, 210 + .

"*Foreign Affairs*" (review). *Books*, May 1984, 9.

"*Foreign Affairs*" (review). *Publishers Weekly* 226 (July 20, 1984): 71.

"*Foreign Affairs*" (review). *New York*, Sept. 24, 1984: 97.

"*Foreign Affairs*" (review). *New Yorker*, Nov. 5, 1984: 170.

Fox-Genovese, Elizabeth. "*The Language of Clothes*" (review). *Nation*, Nov. 21, 1981, 544 + .

Fraser, C. Gerald. "*Foreign Affairs*" (review). *New York Times Book Review*, Nov. 17, 1985, 50.

Glastonbury, Marion. "*The Language of Clothes*" (review). *New Statesman* 103 (May 7, 1982): 22 + .

Glendinning, Victoria. "Putting away Childish Things." *Book World—Washington Post*, April 29, 1979, M5.

Goodman, Walter. "*The Language of Clothes*" (review). *New York Times*, Jan. 17, 1982, 16.

Gordon, Mary. "*Only Children*" (review). *New York Review of Books* 26 (June 14, 1979: 31.

Greene, G. Letter to Alison Lurie. *New York Review of Books* 22 (Sept. 18, 1975): 60.

Hart, James D. *The Concise Oxford Companion to American Literature*, 238. New York: Oxford Univ. Press, 1986.

"*The Heavenly Zoo*" (review). *Publishers Weekly* 217 (June 6, 1980): 82.

Heins, Ethel L. "*Clever Gretchen and Other Forgotten Folktales*" (review). *Horn Book* 56 (April 1980): 180 + .

Helfand, Michael S. "The Dialectic of Self and Community in Alison Lurie's *The War between the Tates*." *Perspectives on Contemporary Literature* 3 (1977): 65–70.

Heron, Liz. "*Foreign Affairs*" (review). *New Statesman* 109 (Jan. 25, 1985): 31.

Hite, Molly. "Interview with Alison Lurie." *Belles Lettres* 2 (July/Aug. 1987): 9.

Hollander, Anne. "*The Language of Clothes*" (review). *New York Review of Books* 29 (April 15, 1982): 38 + .

Howard, Jane. "*The Language of Clothes*" (review). *Mademoiselle*, Feb. 1982, 46 + .

"*Imaginary Friends*" (review). *New York Times Book Review*, July 6, 1986, 24.

"Interview with Alison Lurie." *Weight Watchers*, May 1982, 12.

Jackson, David. "An Interview with Alison Lurie." *Shenandoah* 31 (1980): 15–27.

Jebb, Julian. "Ordinary Life." *London Magazine,* Dec. 1974/Jan. 1975: 125–28.

Johnson, Margot. *"Clever Gretchen and Other Forgotten Folktales"* (review). *Christian Science Monitor,* May 12, 1980, B8.

Kaufmann, James. *"Foreign Affairs"* (review). *Christian Science Monitor,* Oct. 19, 1984, 24.

Koenig, Rhoda. *"The Language of Clothes"* (review). *New York,* Dec. 14, 1981, 100+.

Kroll, Jack. "Only Children" (review). *Newsweek,* April 23, 1979, 98.

Lanes, Selma G. *"Clever Gretchen"* (review). *New York Times,* April 27, 1980, 62.

"The Language of Clothes" (review). *Books,* May 1987, 9.

"The Language of Clothes" (review). *Weight Watchers,* May 1982, 12.

Lasdun, James. "The Great or the Good." *Encounter* 65 (July-Aug. 1985): 47–51.

Lehman, David. "A Kind of Witchery" (interview). *Newsweek,* Sept. 24, 1984, 80.

Lehmann-Haupt, Christopher. *"The Language of Clothes"* (review). *New York Times,* Nov. 18, 1981, 25, 32.

———. *"Foreign Affairs"* (review). *New York Times,* Sept. 13, 1984, C21, 23.

Milton, Edith. "Looking Backward: *Only Children.*" *Yale Review* 69 (Oct. 1979): 96–97.

Mitgang, Herbert. "Out of War, into Love." *New York Times,* May 20, 1979, 63.

Morris, James McGrath. "Pulitzer Winner Alison Lurie: Still 'Driven to Writing.' " *Washington Post,* April 25, 1985, B12.

Oates, Joyce Carol. "Honey and Bill and Dan and Celia: *Only Children*" (review). *New York Times Book Review,* April 22, 1979, 7, 27.

O'Brien, Darcy. *"Only Children"* (review). *New York,* April 30, 1979, 106.

O'Connor, Patricia T. *"The War between the Tates"* (review). *New York Times Book Review,* March 30, 1986, 28.

"Only Children" (review). *New York Times,* May 11, 1980, 47.

Parini, Jay. "The Novelist at Sixty (Alison Lurie)." *Horizon* 29 (March 1986): 21+.

Pechter, Kerry. "Silent Signals: What You're Really Saying (Successful Interaction often Nonverbal)." *Prevention,* Aug. 1982, 58+.

Peters, Margaret. *"Foreign Affairs"* (review). *Wall Street Journal,* Oct. 10, 1984, 30.

"Prince Myshkin, Gigi, and Dr. Johnson: Prominent People Choose Favorite Book Characters." *New York Times,* Dec. 2, 1984, 42+.

Reed, J.D. *"The Language of Clothes"* (review). *Time,* Nov. 30, 1981, 95+.

Rinzler, Carol E. *"Foreign Affairs"* (review). *Cosmopolitan,* Oct. 1984, 42.

Sage, Lorna. "Adventures in the Old World." *Times Literary Supplement,* Feb. 1, 1985, 109.

Sanborn, Sara. *New York Times Book Review,* July 28, 1974, 1–2.

Satz, M. "A Kind of Detachment: An Interview with Alison Lurie." *Southwest Review* 71 (Spring 1986): 194–202.

Schoen, Elin. "*Foreign Affairs*" (review). *Mademoiselle*, Nov. 1984, 86.

Shapiro, Anna. "*The Language of Clothes*" (review). *Saturday Review*, Nov. 1981, 80+.

Shapiro, Harriet. "*Foreign Affairs* Earns Novelist Alison Lurie Domestic Acclaim and a Place beside Henry James." *People Weekly*, Dec. 3, 1984, 73+.

Shappard, R.Z. "*Foreign Affairs*" (review). *Time*, Oct. 15, 1984, 104.

Stickney, J. "A Novelist Studies Fashion and Finds Tongue-in-chic Proof That You Are What You Wear." *People Weekly*, Nov. 30, 1981, 95+.

Stokes, Geoffrey. "*Foreign Affairs*" (review). *Vogue*, Sept. 1984, 570.

Stones, Rosemary. "*Clever Gretchen and Other Forgotten Folktales*" (review). *New Statesman* 100 (Nov. 14, 1980): 20.

Stuttaford, Genevieve. "*The Language of Clothes*" (review). *Publishers Weekly* 220 (Oct. 9, 1981): 58.

Talmey, Allene. "*Only Children*" (review). *Vogue*, April 1979, 41.

Thompson, Andrea. "*Fabulous Beasts*" (review). *McCall's*, Nov. 1981, V-18.

Tindall, Gillian. "Alison Lurie," *Contemporary Novelists*, 4th ed.

Tyler, Anne. "The Glass of Fashion." *New Republic*, Dec. 23, 1981, 32+.

"Uncivil War" (review of *The War between the Tates*). *Newsweek* 84 (August 5, 1974): 64+.

Wendling, R. *America*, May 4, 1985, 379.

Wickenden, Dorothy. "Love in London" (review of *Foreign Affairs*). *New Republic*, Oct. 8, 1984, 34–36.

Wilkie, Everett, & Josephine Helterman. *Dictionary of Literary Biography II: American Novelists since World War II*. Detroit: Gale Research Co., 1987.

Williamson, Barbara Fisher. "*Foreign Affairs*" (review). *Ms.*, Oct. 1984, 142.

"Winners of Pulitzer Prize in Journalism, Letters and the Arts." *New York Times*, April 25, 1985, 17, B10.

SUSAN FROMBERG SCHAEFFER

The Power of Memory, Family, and Space

Mickey Pearlman

Susan Fromberg Schaeffer is known for a certain kind of long, elaborate, complicated novel—what used to be called a saga—where reading "is rather like falling into a time warp . . . experiencing events through total immersion in the mind of the protagonist."[1] She writes of gentile families in nineteenth-century New England in *Time in Its Flight*, where "she livens [things] up with epidemics, marriages, a suicide by hanging, insanity, a murder trial, philosophy via daguerreotypes, reports of the American Civil War and twenty or thirty deaths."[2] She writes of Jewish families in Brooklyn in *Love*, her fourth novel, where she "takes us trudging through Russian snows, dancing through Jewish weddings, noshing in Brooklyn kitchens. She gives us childbirth, divorce and nightmares that come true . . . murder, pogroms and talking dogs."[3] And she has contributed successfully to the Jewish American genre with *Anya*, a book not "about suffering, nor about the horrors of the holocaust [but a] fictionalized memory which seeks to dwell on human goodness more than depravity and evil."[4] Schaeffer returned to turn-of-the-century New England with *The Madness of a Seduced Woman*, a gothic tale of romance, passion, and murder. This novel is based on newspaper clippings of an actual event, which Schaeffer disovered during the research for *Time in Its Flight*, a novel about "family history versus personal freedom."[5]

All of these novels, while variously praised for their imagery, use of informative details, and "photographic genius,"[6] have at the same time been criticized for overabundance, careless editing, and confusion. There is, said Cynthia MacDonald of *Time in Its Flight*, "too much. More shaping, more order, more discarding were needed."[7]

But something new happens in Schaeffer's most recent fiction—*Mainland* (1985), the story of Eleanor, a college professor in Brooklyn, and *The Injured Party* (1986), a story set again in the home of a Brooklyn author, in this case Iris Otway. And in spite of criticism that *The Injured Party* is largely a retelling of the details in *Falling* (1973), Schaeffer's first and extraordinary novel, and that the housekeeper Emmeline of *Mainland* reappears as Etheline, and so on, these two novels say something valuable and provocative about the concept of enclosed space, as women experience it, about the often negative power of memory, and about what Sheila Ballantyne calls "the unspoken tension that exists between Family and Outsider."[8]

Schaeffer's vision of the past in *The Injured Party* is unexpectedly, and somewhat ironically, Faulknerian for a northern, urban writer so far from the gothic world of light and evil; she repeatedly makes the point that the past flows irrevocably and irretrievably into the present or, as Faulkner would have it, "there is no was." Schaeffer's protagonist, Iris Otway, has returned to her doll and memento-laden Brooklyn house after a six-week hospital stay for a mysterious and poorly treated fever, ostensibly the result of her undilutable anger over the bad review of her last novel. She realizes, for instance, during the repeated taking of her personal history by practicing interns, that "she was merely suffering from rage. Her fever rose to 104 at eleven in the morning and stayed there until three in the afternoon, when it fell to normal and did not rise again until midnight, and by two A.M. it was gone. She had an explanation for this: the fever rose during the hours she would normally be writing" (111).[9] Frustration produces anxiety; anxiety promotes illness.

After experiencing the disappearance of various terminally ill roommates in the "dead" of night (the nurses report, on questioning by Otway as to their whereabouts, that they have "gone home"), she finally leaves the enclosed and suffocating space of the hospital, probably sicker than when she arrived. It is only later that her former lover explains "that [she] got too close. . . ." "You started to cross over" (90). " 'I tried to raise the dead,' said Iris" (90).

She had, in fact, provided in her own psyche a final resting place for the unresolved pain of her former fellow patients, an emotional space already overburdened with her own frustration and a plethora of unresolved conflicts. What Schaeffer is addressing here is more than the obvious debilitating effects of illness and the sense of dependency experienced by all patients. She is writing about memory, about the interlocking structure of emotional and physical space and the comfort and discomfort associated with the past as it manifests itself in the present. Iris Otway goes from her hospital bed in the Bronx to her bed at home in Brooklyn with "the carved wooden sun [on] the headboard. "Someone," she says, "had believed enough in the sun to carve it at the head of that bed . . . because he was afraid that one day the sun would not return" (11). There she spends interminable hours looking out the window at a bleak winter landscape, where the tree "branches were no longer branches but massed black crosses, swaying desperately in the wind as if to keep evil spirits back. Thick branches were crossed by thin bony ones, at right angles, at oblique angles, a mob of crazily drawn crosses, sketched hastily, as if there were only seconds in which to draw, to fill the window" (4). These are images that sustain the idea of limited space as negative and tomblike, as opposed to positive and restorative. Iris is emotionally locked in, entombed, with "swaying" crosses marking an uneasy resting place.

Here Iris Otway proceeds to vegetate. (Her husband stood "in the doorway to their bedroom, looked at his wife and thought, I am married to a stone, a drift of snow"[3]). She becomes a bedridden, almost lifeless form encased in woolen socks provided by the housekeeper, who washes her hair once a week to prevent the onset of lice. This image, of a corpse invaded by insects, underscores the connection of enclosure, enervation, and death. Otway's husband, children, and housekeeper seem powerless to reverse this almost comatose state until the arrival of Otway's former lover of twenty-six years ago, he of the symbolic name John Stone, and himself dying of amyotrophic lateral sclerosis with possible complications of multiple sclerosis. The winter motif of death and nonviability is combined now with gravelike rooms, silence, lethargy, and stones, all interwoven to stress the power of memory and the past, here unresolved, and its power for women in Schaeffer's vision in these novels, which is to cause paralysis. Enclosed spaces, in this case the rooms and apartments and laboratories of the University of Chicago shared by Stone and Otway, cause paralysis when the people are unable to get beyond the negative power of memory and into the future. As Schaeffer says in her novel *Anya*, "Memory is a form of reality after all" (9). So we are not only locked into the events of the past, she suggests, but into our perceptions of that past. What we choose to remember from the past becomes part of the reality of the present. How we choose to incorporate those memories into the present determines our perception of emotional and actual space.

This motif is further underscored by the three-part division of the book. Part One is called "The Room"; Part Two is "The House"; and the final section, where Otway goes to Cornwall, England, to scatter the ashes of the now-dead Stone on the reefs, surrounded by the open spaces of the English countryside, is called "Outside." It is only in such open spaces and in the unfurnished rooms of her borrowed cottage that Otway is able to reconcile both the death of Stone and the emotional termination of a relationship that ended, in actuality, long before her marriage to her husband, Mike.

Otway is a collector, and much is made in the novel of her dollhouses, gimcracks, the secondhand furniture retained from her student apartments with John, a "forest of cut-glass perfume bottles, jewelry boxes made of pink marble, of Chinese cloisonné, three necklace strands, acrylic stems surmounted by antique doll heads . . . a gingerbread clock, . . . angels, little pillows covered with string lace" (67), the "small mosaic pieces that made up her soul" (69). The memorabilia are visible symbols of the past, bringing it in a tangible way into the present. All of it is a kind of material clutter that provides Iris with a fantasy world of protection and succor, a kind of "doll's house," complete with heavy velvet drapes that block the outside in her Victorian dining room, closed off during the winter to preserve the heat. And none of it works because Iris Otway lives also with her emotional clutter. Otway's only moments of peace and lucidity are related to the window and later to the countryside, to the emotional voyage out. When Otway finally chooses to leave the house for an excursion with John Stone, they go to her favorite neighborhood cemetery (to which she has a key), surrounded again by death and rococo angels. Like her house it is a closed space disguised by the decorative. (Because of Stone's stubbornness, they find themselves in a closed car, in a locked cemetery, which is patrolled by vicious guard dogs.) Schaeffer does not explain why a previously healthy woman would have wanted a key to that cemetery. It is not, after all, the only grassy spot in Brooklyn. But it *is* a repository of memory, of the past, and it is both protected (guarded, in fact), an enclosed space, safe, and a place where there are no demands.

The flyleaf of *The Injured Party* refers to it as "a passionate and utterly absorbing portrait of a woman at that dangerous point of life," an allusion to the supposed identity dilemmas of fortyish women entering middle age. But Sheila Ballantyne's review in *The New York Times* alluded to those identity dilemmas from a different angle of vision. She says that "in both novels a heroine brings into her family a man with whom she is connected outside of it, with the expressed intention that he become a 'member.' The attempt to integrate old lives into the fabric of that exclusive knot raises an interesting possibility: that by definition the family is an impenetrable unit, permitting no real interaction of its members' past attachments into its inner circle."[10] But Ballantyne's erroneous assessment is the antithesis of what actually happens in *Mainland* and *The Injured Party.* In both novels the outsider *is* integrated into the "inner circle"; John Stone is there before he actually appears, in the form of memory, and in *Mainland* the outsider becomes, so to speak, one of the children. In fact, the impetus for growth, for rapprochement with an unresolved past, is resolved *through* the introduction of an outsider, and in this novel and in *Mainland*, the outsider is a man.

Eleanor, a Brooklyn College professor who has a husband, Tom, but no last name, is suffering from premature cataracts caused largely by the inept treatment of the neighborhood "eye doctor" ("dubbed The Maniac" [58]) whose incompetence and shaky professionalism would be apparent to any Ph.D. in the "real" world. But for Eleanor the clubby waiting room, with its neurotic nurse, Challah (a Yiddish term for a twisted bread), and assorted picturesque patients, becomes another space that she enters eagerly for one year until it becomes apparent, even to the shortsighted Eleanor, that she is going blind. Blindness, it should be noted, is another kind of space, which blocks off the intrusion of seeable reality, and, beyond its value as a traditional metaphor for the unknown and the unknowing, ideas that permeate both novels, it is an especially apt physical affliction for Schaeffer's kind of heroine. And it is worth noting that "Eleanor" is a name related to "Helen," which means "light."

Eleanor likes silence, privacy, and enclosure. She, too, has a house filled with toys, "a gingerbread clock hung with necklaces . . . stuffed pillows impaled with rhinestone pins . . . urns draped with hair ribbons" (264), but she is particularly addicted to her solitary drives on the East River Drive into Manhattan for business lunches with agents, publicists, and editors, trips that must now be shared with a Chinese student—with the symbolic name Toh (pronounced "tow"), who is hired to drive her back and forth over the Brooklyn Bridge, "beautiful, encrusted as it is with memories" (66). The car quickly becomes their space; they become lovers, albeit with little ostensible passion (". . . not an affair, really . . . a state of mind" [218]), and the romance moves to "a one-room apartment in Chinatown he has borrowed from a friend. She recognizes it as one recognizes something seen in a dream many times before. It is not a room but a world, a mainland cut off from all other land not by water but by a zone of time. The room floats, bobs gently, like a boat on water. As she walks into the center of the room, the rest of the world ceases to exist" (115). The room is the idyllic safe space. There, Eleanor says to herself, "How long can [I] stand at the window, looking out?" (26). Toh becomes part of her family; her children appropriate him, even fall in love with him as Iris Otway's children appropriate and fall in love with John Stone in *The Injured Party.*

The interesting component of this assimilation of the male "stranger" in Schaeffer's recent fiction is that it essentially desexualizes the male. By making him part of the family, it neutralizes the sexual tension between female protagonist and intriguing male visitor. He becomes, in both cases, a vehicle for the female's enlightenment, gains a surrogate family, and allows the woman to remain secure in the circle of her original family. (John Stone even leaves his estate to Otway's children.) And if the husbands in *The Injured Party* and *Mainland* are indicative of male consciousness in the eighties, the intruders are no threat to them either. Mike, Iris's husband, is jealous. Certainly, he misses the physical and sexual contact with his emotionally absent wife, but there is little sense of the outrage or anger one would expect. He is, apparently, so desperate for Iris's recovery, dependent as it is on John Stone, that he can control his emotions when John, Iris, and his children go off to Vermont for the weekend. He is similarly understanding when Iris and John spend long hours alone together in the house. Schaeffer's vision of educated, middle-aged women, at least in these novels, is of childish females, out of control and with limited emotional resources, who are physically sick or "injured" and depressed, repressed, and often obsessed. But the men are stoical, with ultratight upper lips, limitless patience, and a marked practical and analytical approach to life that is in noticeable contrast to the women. Tom, Eleanor's husband (in *Mainland*), is a distant figure who makes "important" decisions about who can borrow the car and how to find a driver for Eleanor but seems oblivious to his wife's growing involvement with a young Chinese student. He seems almost organically connected to his computers, not so much uncaring but unconscious, a kind of responsible but absent father figure for Eleanor, Toh, and his two children.

The question in Schaeffer's recent fiction is why female epiphany has to be a product of male intervention, if unexpected, and why it comes from such strange sources: a dying man and a barely verbal foreigner? One suggestion is that both of these men, for different reasons, are not threatening, which makes sense given the childlike nature of the women. Toh is not only Chinese, a student, and a virgin, but at twenty-seven, he is significantly younger, both in age and in mileage, than Eleanor, who is forty-one. Eleanor reacts to his threats that he will return to China with crying fits and pouting, reemphasizing Schaeffer's vision of woman as crybaby; her greatest fear is that he will no longer be a part of her family's future. The novel ends with the introduction of Mai, the Chinese student whom he will marry. "He is, thinks Eleanor, the illuminated letters of the text of my life. The text will change if only because he keeps changing it, but the illuminations will remain. . . . Soon they will be having children and the children will be running about this porch and they will call her Grandmother. It is time . . . to prepare for a small horde of plump Chinese children, every one of whom she will wish she had borne, to prepare for years of envying the girl, in whose place she would like to be" (285). In this way Toh becomes the vehicle for new memories, and his continued presence becomes the reverberating echo of the past, which Eleanor attempts both to retain and to relinquish. "His children will polish the magic false words *we live forever* from her windows until they are clear and she can see the bony, hard landscape beneath the greenery. They will polish the indisputable facts of this life until they shine white and glorious like the bleached bones struck by sun on sand. So there was a price to pay after all. In this way, Toh will be her particular punishment and her joy" (285).

This idea of braided, complicated images of insight/sight and memory/actuality pervades both novels. Toh's youth, sensitivity, and ability to "see" become the impetus for Eleanor to get beyond her metaphorical blindness. And he is perceptive as well about their relationship. He understands the temporary nature of their affair; he says, "If our lives tangle too much, they choke each other" (243). Toh, too, is a caring but somewhat aloof and analytical male to whom Schaeffer's women seem inordinately attracted. The women become imprisoned in their unresolved emotions and memories; the men, unencumbered by symbolic or real injuries, are unemotional but free. This is true even of John Stone, who faces his terminal illness with more equanimity than believability.

In *The Injured Party*, Iris Otway also has problems with her eyes; she has "floaters," explains John, and a symbolic name (Iris), and she has problems, as she tells her husband, Mike, understanding "what happened." "So many things," she thinks, "have nothing to do with one another. But how do you know which things do and which things don't? How do you know when to drop a line that will twist and strangle you if you hold onto it?" (18), voicing once again the ideas that we are all entangled in memories, that much of life makes no sense, and that existential disorder is the common denominator of experience. But here the imagery of eyes and the idea of space are combined with a discussion of dreams, since dreams are an excursion into buried memory, intangible artifacts of the struggle for identity and the submerged anger of daily existence. John Stone and Iris Otway exchange dreams, as they exchange notebooks filled with memories, the suggestion being that their lives are so inextricably linked that they share a communal subconscious. One day Iris rests on the "fainting" couch and John on the chair; the next day they exchange places. The dreams are fraught with negative visions of space—dead family members beckon from various mausoleums.

"How do you know I had your dream?" [Iris] asked suddenly. "Describe it to me."
"It starts out with a fog or a black slab, and sooner or later I go down into a mausoleum and my family's eating there, and they keep asking me to come and eat with them. They don't actually speak but I know what they're saying, and I float back and forth and wake up frightened. I hate that dream."
It was [says Iris] the same dream. [78]

Again, Schaeffer links family to enclosed space and enclosed space to the power of memory.

A similar idea permeates *Mainland*. Here the dreams take the form of daydreams, or of uninvited visits from Eleanor's maternal relatives who underscore again the premonitions of disaster, the idea that whatever can go wrong will, and that an emotional winter, a vision of spiny crosses and brittle branches, is barricading every window. Eleanor may have blurred vision, but the hovering crones who star in her daydreams, her long dead mother and grandmother, have no such problem, and what they see are accumulated missteps and miscalculations. " 'Look how old you can get and still have no brains,' says her grandmother" (21). " 'Those whom the gods would betray, they first make stupid, ' . . . walking out of the mirror, holding a pencil wth an eraser top now worn down to the gold metal band" (21). And the sine qua non of all parents: " 'How could you do this to me?' asks her mother, bursting into tears. She has turned toward her daughter, the iron still hot on the white shirt sleeve, not replaced on its safe metal triangle: this must be important . . . her mother was about to cremate an article of clothing, purchased, as she has so often told her, with her father's blood" (22). " 'Stop drifting,' says her grandmother. 'What are you? A rowboat?' " (35). " 'See?' says her grandmother, 'I may not see what you do, but God does. You see? You skinned that knee because you didn't do your homework' " (60).

This kind of black-cloud syndrome is associated in *Mainland* and *The Injured Party* with family, particularly with the parents of Iris Otway, Eleanor, Mike, and John Stone. In *Mainland* Eleanor's maternal relatives are an updated version of a borscht belt comedian's routine on the Jewish family, kvetching their way through eternity. But there is a bitter coating here: no chicken soup, no emotional or actual swaddling; just vinegar, Brooklyn-style nihilism, and diatribes.

"That's right, Eleanor," says her mother, "always expect the worst."
"If she expects the worse, she'll never be disappointed," says her grandmother.
"Expect the best, live through the rest," says her mother from the cloud she and her grandmother are now scouring. (11)

The grandfather who takes her for drives in a stretch limousine and pampers her "wails . . . tearing his hair, 'Women! Women!' (Is the entire family up there on that cloud? Is heaven full of front porches?)" (129). "And Iris's father, rail[ing] about her paternal grandmother, says . . . 'For a smart woman . . . she can be a brainless cantaloupe' " (237).

The point here is that the images of maternal and paternal relatives in these novels by Schaeffer are negative and verging on the cruel, although they are a somewhat less grotesque, updated version of the collection of child beaters and abusers who populate the pages of *Falling*, her first novel. What parents and grandparents have in common in *Falling*, *The Injured Party*, and *Mainland* is that they devastate egos, reprimand, punish, and degrade and by doing so, ensure that female children will grow older, but not up.

Iris Otway's husband, Mike, is afflicted by family, too, but their sins spring more from omission than commission, and he, consequently, is a person who believes that "recovery was not in the natural order of things. It was something marvelous" (19). Like Iris's grandmother he "expects the worst," but for different reasons. Schaeffer makes the point that families damage as much by distance as by the suffocation associated with familial closeness. "[Mike] could [still] hear his father's voice on the answering machine: 'Mike, your mother's in the hospital. Call this number.' 'Mike, your mother's very sick. Call this number.' 'Your mother's dying. Call this number.' 'Your mother just died. Call me at your aunt's house' " (19). This scene would be hilarious if it were not so numbing. But it, and others like it, reflect an idea in *Mainland* about "another one of my theories. No one gets over anything. You find some way to move the pieces around, that's all" (164). And this idea may be the most profound in either of the novels, products of the late eighties, a decade marked by self-help books, articles, and videos on how-to-fix-it, forget-it, rearrange-it, and change-it "it" being life, memories, identity, and the past. And Schaeffer's answer here is that you can't: fix, forget, rearrange, or change it.

John Stone's family, described by Schaeffer as the so-called perfect Protestants, Baptists from Nebraska, are not spared either. Iris reminds John of the daily migraines he suffered during the summer visits to "that house of horrors, his childhood" (166), with his mother, "who proceeded to clean the house in a kind of religious fury, saying, as she dusted, that only a fire could get the house really clean" (72), and his father, "a man happy to be in the world but not at ease in it" (142). When Iris visited, she hid in the linen closet with a book and Moonshine, the "fierce" family cat. This scene is reminiscent of a pivotal section in Sue Miller's *The Good Mother*, where the adult Anna Dunlop reinterprets the memories of her own summers at her grandfather's house in the woods of New England and the stultifying effects those summers had on her emergence into adulthood. Iris Otway thinks about "the terrible silences in her house when she was a child, of which she understood nothing" (94). Silence and its enervating effect is a preoccupation in many novels by women. It functions as an emotional space that separates people, blocks the interweaving of husband and wife, and intensifies the often childlike atmosphere surrounding the lives of women. It is a weapon and a defense mechanism.

John Stone is not only a victim of an angry mother and a distant father; his second wife and his daughter both die, and his sister is in a mental institution. All of this agony is related to an essay on "What I know about Life" that Eleanor (in *Mainland*) writes in grade school. "Eleanor's entire composition consisted of one sentence. 'Nothing remains the same' " (80), "the first truth Eleanor came upon on her own" (80) and one she has continued to trust. This concept, that no person, situation, or emotion is secure or dependable, is the philosophical underpinning of both novels and certainly of *Falling*. And in a world perceived by Schaeffer as precarious and untrustable, it is not surprising that her novels are peopled by female characters who are temporarily disabled physically and permanently disabled emotionally in spite of their Ph.D.'s and published books or that the males are either the vicious, domineering, often sadistic fathers of *Falling* or the more shadowy figures discussed here.

Both of these dark comedies emerge as intelligent, incisive statements about the power of memory, particularly when it is intertwined with unresolved issues about family and identity and the ways in which women, particularly, often emerge as the injured parties. And Susan Fromberg Schaeffer, the author, is an undervalued interpreter of the spatial relationships, familial disenchantments, and identity crises that, to some extent, are part of every contemporary reader's experience.

NOTES

1. Sybil S. Steinberg, review of *Madness of a Seduced Woman*, *Publishers Weekly* 223 (April 8, 1983): 60.

2. Webster Schott, "Happy Family," *New York Times Book Review,* Aug. 13, 1978, 34.

3. Susanne Freeman, *Washington Post*, Jan. 26, 1981.

4. William Novack, *New York Times Book Review,* Oct. 20, 1974.

5. Rosellen Brown, *New York Times Book Review,* May 22, 1983, 144.

6. Clifton Fadiman, *Book-of-the-Month Club News*, July 1978.

7. Cynthia McDonald, *Book World—Washington Post*, Nov. 17, 1974.

8. Sheila Ballantyne, "Dinner in the Crypt," *New York Times Book Review*, Nov. 16, 1986, 15.

9. In this essay page numbers from Susan Fromberg Schaeffer's *The Injured Party* and *Mainland* are given in parentheses in the text.

10. Ballantyne, "Dinner in the Crypt," 16.

A Bibliography of Writings by SUSAN FROMBERG SCHAEFFER

Mickey Pearlman

BOOKS

The Witch and the Weather Report (poetry). New York: Seven Woods Press, 1972.

Falling. New York: Macmillan, 1973; New American Library, 1974.

Granite Lady (poetry). New York: Macmillan, 1974.

Anya. New York: Macmillan, 1974: Avon Books, 1986.

Rhymes and Runes of the Toad (poetry). New York: Macmillan, 1975.

Alphabet for the Lost Years. San Francisco: Gallimaufry, 1977.

The Red, White, and Blue Poem. St. Paul, Minn.: Ally Press, 1977.

Time in Its Flight. Garden City, N.Y.: Doubleday, 1978; Pocket Books, 1979.

The Bible of the Beasts of the Little Field. New York: Dutton, 1980.

The Queen of Egypt and Other Stories. New York: Dutton, 1980. (Contains "The Exact Nature of Plot," an O. Henry Award winner, and "Why the Castle?" a Best American Short Stories nominee.)

Love. New York: Dutton, 1981; Pocket Books, 1982.

The Madness of a Seduced Woman. New York: Dutton, 1983; Bantam Books, 1984.

Mainland. New York: Linden Press/Simon and Schuster, 1985; Bantam Books, 1986.

The Dragons of North Chittendon (young adult novel). New York: Simon and Schuster, 1986.

The Injured Party. New York: St. Martin's Press, 1986.

The Four Hoods and Great Dog (young adult novel). New York: St. Martin's Press, 1988.

Buffalo Afternoon. New York: Alfred A. Knopf, forthcoming.

SELECTED POEMS

"Proverbs"; "A Suicide." *Poetry* 120 (April 1972): 6–17.

"Winter Wood." *Mademoiselle,* Dec. 1972, 104.

"Widow" (limited to 100 copies, Numbers 1 to 30 signed by the poet). Rushden, Northamptonshire, England: Sceptre Press, 1973.

"Lightning Storm." *American Scholar* 42 (Spring 1973): 281–82.

"Age." *Esquire* 79 (June 1973): 197.

"May Day: Two Views." *Commonweal* 99 (Oct. 5, 1973): 13.

"Picture Frame." *Chicago Review* 26 (1974): 89.

"End." *Prairie Schooner* 48 (Spring 1974): 76.

"Weather lately"; "Room"; "Tree"; "Sabbatical." *Texas Quarterly* 17 (Autumn 1974): 82.

"Next." *Encounter* 43 (Oct. 1974): 38.

"Poor." *Prairie Schooner* 48 (Fall 1974). Also in *Encounter* 43 (Dec. 1974): 259–60.

"Rest"; "Picture: In the Park"; "Nymph." *Chicago Review* 27 (Winter 1975): 128–31.

"Backyard." *Poetry* 125 (Feb. 1975): 256.

"Dry River." *Prairie Schooner* 49 (Fall 1975): 252–53.

"Jubilate Agno: Thomas Car." *Ms.* 4 (July 1975): 62–63.

"Climbing the Mountain." *American Scholar* 44 (Summer 1976): 457–61.

"Tulips Again." *Mademoiselle,* 82, Nov. 1976, 90.

"Confession in April." *Ms.* 5 (April 1977): 84.

"Angel"; "King's Destinies"; "King's Melancholy"; "Exit"; "Away." *Midwest Quarterly* 20 (Summer 1979): 368–76.

"Leavetaking." *Southern Review* 16 (Winter 1980): 139–46.

"Mercury"; "Cobalt"; "Uranium." *Prairie Schooner* 55 (Spring/Summer 1981): 297–302.

"Season"; "In the Time." *Southern Review* 18 (July 1982): 538–39.

"Damp;" "Visitors." *Literary Review* 29 (Fall 1985): 28–29.

"In Dreams." *Literary Review* 30 (Summer 1987): 532–36.

ARTICLES, REVIEWS, STORIES

"The Editing Blinks of Vladimir Nabokov's *The Eye.*" *University of Windsor Review* (1972).

"*Bend Sinister* and the Novelist as Anthropomorphic Deity." *Centennial Review* (1973).

" 'It is Time That Separates Us': Form and Theme in Margaret Atwood's *Surfacing.*" *Centennial Review* 18 (1974): 319–37.

"Taxi." *Triquarterly* 1 (Winter 1976): 55–57.

"The Unwritten Chapters in *The Real Life of Sebastian Knight.*" *Modern Fiction Studies* (1977).

"The Exact Nature of Plot." In *Prize Stories of 1978: The O. Henry Awards.* edited by William Abrahams, New York: Doubleday, 1978.

"Under the Chronoscope: A Study of Peter Redgrove's *Weddings at Nether Powers.*" *Poetry Review* (England), Redgrove Special Issue (1981).

"In the Hospital and Elsewhere." *Prairie Schooner* 55 (Winter 1981/1982): 42–63.

"The Unreality of Realism" (in "Artists on Art"). *Critical Inquiry* 6 (1982): 727–37.

"Virginia: Or, A Single Girl." *Prairie Schooner* 57 (Fall 1983): 3–40.

"Making New or Making Known: The State of Fiction Today." In *Great Ideas Today,* annual publication of *Encyclopedia Britannica,* 1984.

"Stanley and the Women." *New York Times Book Review,* Sept. 22, 1985, 9 + .

Review of *Things Invisible to See,* by Nancy Willard. *New York Times Book Review,* Feb. 3, 1985, 12 + .

"Charlotte Brontë's *Villette.*" Introduction to Bantam Books classic edition. New York: Bantam, 1986.

"The Object of My Affection." *New York Times Book Review,* March 22, 1987, 7.

"The Lover Had a Brother" (review of *Lives of the Twins,* by Rosamund Smith [pseud. for Joyce Carol Oates]). *New York Times Book Review,* Jan. 3, 1988, 5.

A Bibliography of Writings about
SUSAN FROMBERG SCHAEFFER

Mickey Pearlman

Allen, Carol J. "*Alphabet for the Lost Years*" (review). *Prairie Schooner*, Fall 1977.

"A Reindeer Fawn Goes to College." *New York Times*, Nov. 29, 1981, 36, 74.

Avery, Evelyn Gross. "Tradition and Independence in Jewish Feminist Novels." *MELUS* 7 (1980): 49–55.

Ballantyne, Sheila. "*The Injured Party*" (review). *New York Times Book Review*, Nov. 16, 1986, 15.

Bannon, Barbara A. "*Love*" (review). *Publishers Weekly* 218 (Nov. 28, 1980): 45.

Bell, Pearl K. "From Brooklyn and the Bronx." *New Leader* 61 (Aug. 6, 1973): 15–16.

Bilik, Dorothy S. "Schaeffer's Romantic Survivor." In D.S. Bilik, *Immigrant Survivors: Post-Holocaust Consciousness in Recent Jewish-American Literature*, 101–11. Middletown, Conn.: Wesleyan Univ. Press, 1981.

Booth, Wayne C. "Elizabeth's Fight for a Life of Her Own" (review of *Falling*). *New York Times Book Review*, May 20, 1973, 56–57.

Brandmark, Wendy. "*The Injured Party*" (review). *New Statesman* 112 (Dec. 5, 1986): 29.

Brown, Rosellen. "*The Madness of a Seduced Woman*" (review). *New York Times Book Review*, May 22, 1983, 14+.

Camper, Cathryn A. "*The Dragons of North Chittendon*" (review). *School Library Journal* 33 (Sept. 1986): 139.

Contemporary Literary Criticism. 6 (1976), 11 (1979), 22 (1982). Detroit: Gale Research Co.

Dickstein, Lore. "Trouble, Trouble" (review of *Love.*) *New York Times Book Review*, Jan. 11, 1981, 10, 30.

Dillingham, Thomas. Review of *Granite Lady*. *Open Places* 20 (Fall/Winter 1975/1976): 63.

Epps, Garrett. "The Writer in Her Own Backyard." *Book World—Washington Post*, Feb. 3, 1980, 12.

Fisher, Ann H. "*The Injured Party*" (review). *Library Journal* 111 (Sept. 15, 1986): 101.

Geeslin, Campbell. "*Mainland*" (review). *People Weekly*, Aug. 19, 1985, 13–15.

Gies, Judith. "Books in Short: *The Queen of Egypt*." *Ms.*, Feb. 1980, 39–40.

Gold, Ivan. "Short Fictions: *The Queen of Egypt*." *New York Times Book Review*, Feb. 24, 1980, 15.

Greenstein, Julie. "*The Madness of a Seduced Woman*" (review). *Ms.*, July 1983, 22.

Havercamp, L. "*Granite Lady*" (review). *Chicago Review* 29 (Summer 1975): 192–96.

Johnson, G. "*The Madness of a Seduced Woman*" (review). *Southwest Review* 69 (Winter 1984): 93–96.

Karp, Lila. *Ms.*, Aug. 1973, 34.

Kavounas, Alice. *Times Literary Supplement*, Dec. 3, 1971.

Korelitz, Jean Hanff. "*The Injured Party*" (review). *Times Literary Supplement*, Dec. 12, 1986, 1409.

Kress, Susan. "Susan Fromberg Schaeffer." In *Dictionary of Literary Biography* 28: *Twentieth Century American-Jewish Fiction Writers*, 276–80. Detroit: Gale Research Co. 1984.

McPherson, Judith. "*The Bible of the Beasts of the Little Field*" (review). *Library Journal* 104 (Dec. 1, 1979): 2575.

———. "*The Queen of Egypt*" (review). *Library Journal* 105 (Jan. 1, 1980): 121.

Mintz, A. "*Anya*" (review). *Commentary* 59 (March 197): 88–90.

Mintz, Jacqueline A. "The Myth of the Jewish Mother in Three Jewish, American, Female Writers." *Centennial Review* 22 (1978): 346–55.

Muske, Carol. "*The Madness of a Seduced Woman*" (review). *Los Angeles Times*, July 24, 1983, 6.

Nichols, K. L. "*Queen of Egypt*" (review). *Midwest Quarterly* 23 (Summer 1982): 450–52.

Novack, William. *New York Times Book Review*, Oct. 20, 1974.

Nowik, Nan. "*The Injured Party*" (review). *Belles Lettres* 2 (March/April 1987): 8.

O'Conner, Patricia T. "Surveying the Inner Landscape" (review of *Mainland*). *New York Times Book Review*, July 7, 1985, 6.

———. "*Mainland*" (review). *New York Times Book Review*, Aug. 10, 1986, 28.

Parisi, Joseph. "Comment" (review of *Granite Lady*). *Poetry*, July 1975, 239–41.

Pearlman, Mickey. "An Interview with Susan Fromberg Schaeffer." *Belles Lettres* 3 (May-June 1988): 9.

Piercy, Marge. "*The Queen of Egypt* and *The Bible of the Beasts of the Little Field*" (review). *Chicago Tribune Book World*, May 11, 1980, 1.

Pritchard, William H. *New York Times Book Review*, May 18, 1975.

"Publishers Weekly Interviews." *Publishers Weekly* 223 (April 8, 1983): 60–61.

Ratner, Rochelle. "*The Bible of the Beasts of the Little Field* and *The Queen of Egypt*." *American Book Review* 3 (Jan.-Feb. 1981): 10–11.

Ribalow, Harold U., ed. "A Conversation with Susan Fromberg Schaeffer." In *The Tie That Binds: Conversations with Jewish Writers*, 77–92. San Diego and New York: A.S. Barnes, 1980.

Rinzler, Carol E. "*Mainland*" (review). *Cosmopolitan*, Aug. 1985, 32.

Roback, Diane. "*The Dragons of North Chittendon*" (review). *Publishers Weekly* 229 (June 27, 1986): 91.

Schott, Webster. "Happy Family: *Time in Its Flight*" (review). *New York Times Book Review*, Aug. 13, 1978, 34.

Schwartz, Lynn Sharon. "*Time in Its Flight*" (review). *Saturday Review*, June 24, 1978, 35.

See, Carolyn. "*Mainland*" (review). *Los Angeles Times*, Aug. 20, 1985, 8.

Silbert, Layle. "Writers and Poets." *Present Tense* 6 (Summer 1976): 36–40.

Skow, John. "So Well Remembered." *Time*, Oct. 14, 1974, 88, 90.

Spacks, P.M. "*Time in Its Flight*" (review). *Hudson Review* 31 (Winter 1978–79): 663–76.

Steinberg, Sybil S. "*Madness of a Seduced Woman*" (review). *Publishers Weekly* 223 (April 8, 1983): 60+.

———. "*Mainland*" (review). *Publishers Weekly* 227 (May 10, 1985): 223.

———. "*The Injured Party*" (review). *Publishers Weekly* 230 (Aug. 1, 1986): 70.

"Susan Fromberg Schaeffer Writes First Children's Book." *Publishers Weekly* 229 (April 25, 1986): 36.

"The Four Hoods and the Great Dog." *Publishers Weekly* 233 (April 8, 1988): 95.

"*The Madness of a Seduced Woman*" (review). *Publishers Weekly* 223 (Feb. 25, 1983): 80.

"*The Madness of a Seduced Woman*" (review). *New York Times*, June 12, 1983, 35.

Thurman, Judith. "Unchanged by Suffering?" *Ms.*, March 1975, 46–47.

"*Time in Its Flight*" (review). *Publishers Weekly*, April 17, 1978, 63.

"*Time in Its Flight*" (review). *Saturday Review*, June 24, 1978, 35.

"*Time in Its Flight*" (review). *New Yorker* 54 (July 31, 1978): 78–80.

Toth, Susan Allen. "*Mainland*" (review). *New York Times*, July 7, 1985, 6.

White, Edmund. "*The Madness of a Seduced Woman*" (review). *Nation*, July 9–16, 1983, 57–58.

Wickenden, Dorothy. "Book Briefs: *Love*." *Saturday Review*, Jan. 1981, 70, 72.

Wiegner, Kathleen. *American Poetry Review*, Jan.-Feb. 1976, 41–43.

TONI CADE BAMBARA

The Dance of Character and Community

Martha M. Vertreace

T he question of identity—of personal definition within the context of community—emerges as a central motif for Toni Cade Bambara's writing. Her female characters become as strong as they do, not because of some inherent "eternal feminine" quality granted at conception, but rather because of the lessons women learn from communal interaction. Identity is achieved, not bestowed. Bambara's short stories focus on such learning. Very careful to present situations in a highly orchestrated manner, Bambara describes the difficulties that her characters must overcome.

Contemporary literature teems with male characters in coming-of-age stories or even female characters coming of age on male typewriters. Additional stories, sometimes written by black authors, indeed portray such concerns but narrowly defined within crushing contexts of city ghettos or rural poverty. Bambara's writing breaks such molds as she branches out, delineating various settings, various economic levels, various characters—both male and female.

Bambara's stories present a decided emphasis on the centrality of community. Many writers concentrate so specifically on character development or plot line that community seems merely a foil against which the characters react. For Bambara the community becomes

Photo by Sandra L. Swans

essential as a locus for growth, not simply as a source of narrative tension. Thus, her characters and community do a circle dance around and within each other as learning and growth occur.

Bambara's women learn how to handle themselves within the divergent, often conflicting, strata that compose their communities. Such learning does not come easily; hard lessons result from hard knocks. Nevertheless, the women do not merely endure; they prevail, emerging from these situations more aware of their personal identities and of their potential for further self-actualization. More important, they guide others to achieve such awareness.

Bambara posits learning as purposeful, geared toward personal and societal change. Consequently, the identities into which her characters grow envision change as both necessary and possible, understanding that they themselves play a major part in bringing about that change. This idea approximates the nature of learning described in Paulo Freire's *Pedagogy of the Oppressed*, in which he decries the "banking concept," wherein education becomes "an act of depositing, in which the students are the depositories and the teacher is the depositor."[1] Oppressive situations define the learner as profoundly ignorant, not possessing valuable insights for communal sharing.

Although many of Bambara's stories converge on the school setting as the place of learning in formal patterns, she liberates such settings to admit and encourage community involvement and ownership. Learning then influences societal liberation and self-determination. These stories describe learning as the process of problem solving, which induces a deepening sense of self, Freire's "intentionality."[2]

For Bambara the community benefits as both "teacher" and "student" confront the same problem—that of survival and prospering in hostile settings, without guaranteed outcomes. The commonality of problems, then, encourages a mutual sharing of wisdom and respect for individual difference that transcends age, all too uncommon in a more traditional education context. Bambara's characters encounter learning within situations similar to the older, tribal milieus. The stages of identity formation, vis-à-vis the knowledge base to be mastered, have five segments: (1) beginner, (2) apprentice, (3) journeyman, (4) artisan, and (5) expert.

Traditional societies employed these stages to pass on to their youth that information necessary to ensure the survival of the tribe, such as farming techniques, and that information needed to inculcate tribal mores, such as songs and stories. Because of Bambara's interest in cultural transmission of values, her characters experience these stages in their maturational quest. In her stories these levels do not correlate with age but rather connote degrees of experience in community.

The beginner deeply experiences, for the first time, the kind of world into which she is born, with its possibilities of joys and sorrows. In "Sweet Town" fifteen-year-old Kit apprehends the "sweet and drugged madness" (122)[3] of her youth. Teetering on the edge of young adulthood, she writes fun notes to her mother. "Please forgive my absence and my decay and overlook the freckled dignity and pockmarked integrity plaguing me this season" (121).

Falling in love with the handsome but irresponsible B.J., Kit experiences his loss as a typical teenager might, vowing to search for him from town to town. Bambara is too skilled a storyteller to ascribe to her characters an unexplained superhuman source of wisdom that transcends their natural maturational state. Rather, she portrays the community as interceding on Kit's behalf, providing her with a sense of rootedness that protects her from emotional injury by putting the entire experience in proper perspective. Kit comes to realize that "days other than the here and now . . . will be dry and sane and sticky with the rotten apricots oozing slowly in the sweet time of my betrayed youth" (125). Kit weathers this experience, learning that the community becomes the source of wisdom lacking in the beginner.

Ollie, in "Happy Birthday," does not experience such communal affirmation and support. That no one remembered her birthday becomes symptomatic of the community's withdrawal from her, its failure to provide her with a nurturing environment, its indifference to strengthening communal ties. Bambara catalogs the friends and family members who have forgotten, suggesting that this is the most recent of a succession of omissions. When one woman, Miss Hazel, suggests that Ollie will be happy to forget birthdays when she grows old, Ollie dissolves in tears. Most societies mark birthdays with cultic response. Children learn to ritualize birthdays as a way of reestablishing communal links. Forgetting is inconceivable, tantamount to willfully breaking or, worse, ignoring such bonds.

The community provides a structure of rules for the beginner that governs the interpretation of human experience. Within such rules the beginner can explore life without risking either self-destruction or alienation from the community. If the rules themselves fall into question, however, the beginner questions the trustworthiness of the community that generated them. Hazel experiences adults, in "Gorilla, My Love," as contradictory and therefore problematic. At a showing of "Kings of Kings," Hazel wonders at a God who would passively allow his son to die when no one in her family would do that. Yet these same adults "figure they can treat you just anyhow. Which burns me up" (15). I get so tired of grownups messin over kids just cause they little and can't take em to court" (16).

The familial setting encourages Hazel's independence and strength of character. Granddaddy Vale, for example, trusts her to sit in the "navigator seat" (13) of the car and read the map as he drives, calling her "Scout" (13). But at school her teachers dislike her "cause I won't sing them Southern songs or back off when they tell me my questions are out of order" (17). A spunky little girl, Hazel has already begun to understand the societal forces that impinge on her world.

In spite of the fact that "my word is my bond" (18), Hazel learns that adults define "word" and "bond" differently when addressed to children. When her favorite uncle, "Hunca Bubba," becomes Jefferson Winston Vale" as he prepares for marriage, Hazel feels betrayed. Once when babysitting her, Hunca Bubba had playfully promised to marry her when she grew up. Hazel had taken him seriously, had taken his word as his bond. Losing her faith in the only community she trusts, her family, Hazel realizes that "I'm losing my bearings and don't even know where to look on the map cause I can't see for cryin" (20). Adults seem to slide between two different definitions for "word" and "bond"—one for themselves and one for children. Because children never know which definition is being used, the supportive ground of community can never be fully trusted. Children, as Hazel says, "must stick together or be forever lost, what with grownups playing change-up and turning you round every which way so bad. And don't even say they sorry" (20).

Beginners become very self-conscious, as rules provide the structure and stability they require. Rules confirm expectations. Beginners struggle with limited vision, however, as the total context of an experience lies outside their purview. These stories show young girls as beginners, at pivotal points in their understanding of themselves within the framework of community. Kit emerges whole, without the bitterness that both Ollie and Hazel develop. The difference was the role of the community, supportive of Kit while hostile to Ollie and fickle to Hazel.

Hazel's misinterpretation stemmed from her lack of experience with adults she can trust. Because a beginner can have many painful experiences, she needs a teacher from whom she can learn, who provides a supportive environment, who acts as a guide. At the level of apprentice, the second step, the learner moves from dependence on concrete situations to an ability to generalize to the hypothetical. At this point the learner relates consciously to the experience of a teacher, someone who can show her the ropes, help her see beyond shortsighted rules.

The movement from beginner to apprentice occurs when the beginner confronts a situation not explained by known rules. Someone steps in who breaks open the situation so that learning can occur. For Sylvia, in "The Lesson," Miss Moore was that person. Sylvia was an unwilling apprentice, resenting Miss Moore's teaching.

Miss Moore wants to radicalize the young, explaining the nature of poverty by taking her charges from their slums to visit Fifth Avenue stores, providing cutting-edge experiences for the children, making them question their acceptance of their lot. When asked what they learned, various ideas surfaced. "I don't think all of us here put together eat in a year what that sailboat costs"; (95) "I think that this is not much of a democracy if you ask me. Equal chance to pursue happiness means an equal crack at the dough, don't it?" (95).

The children, encouraged by Miss Moore, coalesce into a community of support that encourages such questions. For these children these questions represent rules that no longer work, assumptions that are no longer valid. The adult Miss Moore has stepped out of the adult world to act as guide to the children. Sylvia, for her part, profoundly affected by the day, concludes, "She can run if she want to and even run faster. But ain't nobody gonna beat me at nuthin" (96).

Sylvia's determination to defeat her poverty represents movement to the next level, that of journeyman. No longer hampered by a strict adherence to established rules, the journeyman feels confident enough to trust instinct. Risk becomes possible as the journeyman extrapolates from numerous past experiences to stand alone, even if shakily. At this point the community must provide support without heavy-handed restraint or control as the journeyman ventures forth.

The generation gap gives Miss Hazel a chance to step out on her own, in "My Man Bovanne." At a benefit for a political candidate, Miss Hazel dances with Bovanne, a blind man whom the kids like, "or used to fore Black Power got hold their minds and mess em around till they can't be civil to ole folks" (3). Her children cast aspersions on her " 'apolitical self" (5), but she perceives that, notwithstanding their concern for the movement, they "don't even stop a minute to get the man a drink or one of them cute sandwiches or tell him what's goin on" (4).

Hazel knows that power concerns roots, not surface features such as hairstyles or handshakes. Hazel's children want her to form the

Council of Elders, encouraging them to become politically active. Hazel, however, keeps company with Bovanne, "cause he blind and old and don't nobody there need him since they grown up and don't need they skates fixed no more" (9). She knows the importance of historical continuity that the Elders represent and how unimportant, but politically seductive, passing fads are to youth.

Hazel's experience gives her the perspective she needs to reflect on her present, a possibility denied her children who seem ignorant of their history. Consequently, Hazel retreats from the currently popular expectations, fully confident in her risk taking because she knows that the youth must learn wisdom from the old if the community is to survive and prosper. Bambara shows that Hazel's awareness of the needs of the total community empowers her to remember the source of her strength. Her children, still beginners lacking visionary perspective, cannot recognize these needs concretized in the person of Bovanne, preferring instead to engage in an abstract level of political discourse. They cannot see the ultimate irony in soliciting the political support of the elders, yet failing to provide for their care.

Having experienced the encouragement that the community offers, the journeyman progresses to the level of artisan, at which solutions to problems fall more within one's personal control. In "Raymond's Run" Squeaky becomes Bambara's metaphor for an aggressive approach to life that involves problem solving within a communal context. Squeaky's devotion to running as "that which I am all about" (28), and her loyalty to her retarded brother, Raymond, provide the occasion for personal growth.

Squeaky grows beyond the destructive need to defeat Gretchen, the only girl who can outrun her, as together they plan to help Raymond learn to run. When Gretchen and Squeaky smile hesitantly at each other, Squeaky realizes that they have not learned how to express such trust, because "there's probably no one to teach us how, cause grown-up girls don't know either" (26). They come to trust each other as each sees that they both value running and that each acknowledges the achievements of the other. Competition gives way to cooperation, with the community, represented by Raymond, standing to benefit.

As an artisan, Squeaky begins to solve problems decisive to her development. Her growth into accepting the people around her emerges from a developing sense of self-acceptance. She can share her expertise with Raymond with an attitude free of condescension. She can acknowledge Gretchen's accomplishments without fearing some implied diminishment on her own. These themes appear as developmental problems in her young life, and she moves toward resolution. The community gives its support and encouragement through her family and school, without which Squeaky could not have matured as she did. The community that nurtured her is now nurtured by her in return.

The level of expert represents years of progress within the four levels, reached through intense experience in a shorter period. Maggie, in "Maggie of the Green Bottles," becomes a quirky expert, but expert nonetheless. She lives with her daughter and son-in-law and their children. Because the son-in-law dislikes her, Maggie first has to learn to handle his insults, discovering how far she can insult him before he completely loses face.

Maggie must content with a negative impression of herself. "They called her crazy" (153). Peaches, one of the children, adores Maggie precisely because she knows how to handle her world. "It is to Maggie's guts that I bow forehead to the floor and kiss her hand, because she'd tackle the lot of them right there in the yard, blood kin or by marriage, and neighbors or no" (153). With her little green bottles of indeterminate contents, Maggie assumes the identity of Obeah woman, who copes with the "hard-core Protestant" world (151). She profoundly desires to pass on what she knows to Peaches, so that learning will continue.

Peaches comes to understand the significance of retaining Maggie's lore. She also knows that her family disapproves of her interest. Maggie keeps notes for Peaches in a book originally intended for good wishes upon christening.

Maggie's book contains drawings of "the fearsome machinery which turned the planets and coursed the stars " (152). The book informs Peaches that "as an Aries babe I was obligated to carry on the work of other Aries greats from Alexander right on down to anyone you care to mention" (152). In short, Maggie's book expands into a collection of folklore, of astral signs and tea-leaf readings. Maggie's room, into which no one expects Peaches may enter, represents "the sanctuary of heaven charts and incense pots and dream books and magic stuffs" (155).

Maggie's lore symbolizes the ancient teachings that the community has to offer, that the youth must learn for the sake of survival. Peaches's father "put magic down with nothing to replace it" (154). Peaches would not make that same mistake. Maggie becomes her guide to the unknown, initiating her into the community of ancient wisdom of Peaches's birthright. Contemptuous of Maggie for being old and poor, Peaches's father, representing modern pressures for material gain, tries to divert her from the traditional values inculcated by these sources of wisdom.

The expert operates without consciously adverting to rules, having achieved the highest level of intuitive understanding. As Maggie feels her end approaching, she sends Peaches into the house to get her special green bottle, which Maggie then hides under her skirts. At her death her family discovers the bottle there, "proof of her heathen character" (159). When family members distribute her belongings, Peaches's father asks her to choose what she wants, since Peaches had seen "her special" (159). Peaches selects the green bottle.

Some adherents of voodoo believe that at death a skilled Obeah woman can send her soul into inanimate objects for safekeeping. Such an idea, therefore, shows the significance of Maggie's green bottles, symbolizing a futile attempt to continue as Peaches's guide after Maggie's death. Maggie's work with Peaches remains incomplete; there are many green bottles left unopened, many secrets left to tell.

The attempt for continuance goes awry as Peaches does not receive those green bottles. At some point there can be no guides, and the learner must venture out on her own.

The emergence of self in community, the development of a personal identity within the boundaries of a communal structure, occurs through the types of knowing with which Bambara confronts her characters. Ideas developed in Michael Polanyi's *Knowing and Being*[4] are helpful at this point for further analysis of learning and identity.

Polanyi indicates that perceptions gained through the use of properly trained sensory organs form the basis for learning. The student correctly ascertains the constitutive elements in a situation, perceiving the working relationship between these parts, specifically how change to one part can alter another. All further action evolves from such perceptions. Developed skills function within given settings. Such skills must become automatic means rather than belabored ends. The learner selects elements in her environment that can impinge on what she knows in order to bring about a discovery of additional knowledge, leading to further personal empowerment.

This learning process as movement roughly corresponds to the levels of learning developed earlier. Bambara's characters pass through this process in order to mature, to gain control of themselves and their surroundings. The community helps or hinders the maturational process but is never merely a neutral background. Bambara delineates community and its effects on character as if it were itself a character.

The basic movement of learning self-identity in Bambara's writing occurs on a continuum between observing and indwelling. The observer spends most of her time simply watching her world, trying to establish meaningful connections between its various parts. The young girl in "Basement" is just starting to weave together the diverse threads where she lives, comprehending their connection. Bambara establishes the girl's childlike lack of understanding of the dangers of going into the basement alone.

As the story progresses, basement dangers reveal themselves as actual—the presence of a potentially perverted janitor, its darkness and isolation, its availability as a site for childhood sexual exploration. Patsy's troublesome lies about the janitor's conduct force the speaker to acknowledge the inherent dangers, if not in that basement then in all such "basements" for women. She begins to comprehend Patsy's wickedness, telling her, "I'm not gonna be your friend any more" (147). But such understanding only takes into account how Patsy's ways affect their individual relationship, not its potential for communal harm. Along the continuum between observing and knowledge as indwelling, the child has yet to move. The process of growth, as Bambara describes it, however, does not adhere to a strict linearity. Rather than a straight-line continuum, learning occurs as perhaps a more spherical movement with lessons learned and deepened as the learning situation reoccurs in other settings.

The speaker in "Basement" exhibits a level of focal awareness, wherein she can identify some of the particulars of her environment, but has trouble integrating them in order to see connections. Basements present danger because of a woman's resemblance to Anna Mae Wong, yet later the speaker herself articulates the actual perils that the basement represents. As the character moves into subsidiary awareness, these connections become accessible to her perception and, therefore, can be taken into account. She then moves from simply observing as a source of knowledge to developing indwelling awareness, intuitive perceptions that she can trust.

Virginia, "The Organizer's Wife," came by such knowledge painfully, as indeed occurs to many of Bambara's women. After police jail Graham, her husband, in order to frustrate his organizing activities, Virginia must come to grips with what loss his imprisonment means to the community and to herself. Graham's positive outlook—"The point is always the same—the courage of the youth, the hope of the future" (5) initially attracts Virginia to Graham. But her hope springs from a narrow, individualistic focus on her personal needs, the means to an education, a ticket out of a small, poverty-stricken town.

However, as she recalls what changes had come about in her life, what her children's lives could be like in a community where the people's roots sink deeply, she moves from a narrow focal awareness of her familial needs, her desire to escape, adopting Graham's wholistic vision of what could be, his community-centered concern for the welfare and empowerment of the people. The enemies of the people can be defeated through "discipline, consciousness, and unity" (13). Binding together, the people draw strength and comfort from each other, realizing that "we ain't nowhere's licked yet, though" (22). The community and its needs become central as Virginia progresses from a focal awareness of individual needs to a subsidiary awareness of communal needs.

Self-awareness within the community setting allows the individual to move beyond a concentration on exterior knowing of disconnected particulars to an interior awareness, knowledge as indwelling. Bambara locates her female characters in settings where such learning must occur. All the women in "The Johnson Girls" are at different places in their self-knowledge, but by uniting to help Inez in her relationship with Roy, they all experience a deepening awareness of themselves.

Roy has gone to Knoxville, leaving simply a "crumpled note" (164). The women help Inez prepare for her trip to Knoxville, at first concentrating on what clothes she should take. Great Ma Drew represents the ancient learning that the younger women lack in this story. Knowing that seductive clothes do not define the issue, she tells Inez, "Love charms are temporary things if your mojo ain't total" (164). Inez comes to understand her "mojo," here the total experience of herself as a woman. The younger girl seems fascinated with divining the future with the aid of cards and incense, a focal awareness of the individual parts without seeing the larger picture. Great Ma Drew gradually shepherds the younger women to a subsidiary awareness. She shows them that deeper understanding might evolve from a consideration of what Inez and Roy could be for each other, by focusing on communal wisdom rather than simply on signs. She remembers the old days when girls learned how to handle men through "charms and things" (165) within the context of community needs, not as isolated customs that she asserts is present practice.

The young women continue to talk about men, their strengths and weaknesses, the difficulty of finding good men. These discussions illustrate the way the women interact. Each, from the most experienced to the least, contributes and is taken seriously. Each brings to the discussion her level of maturity, as the group encourages its members. Without forcing someone to grow faster than she can, the group nurtures such growth through risk.

Through such discussion the community of women brings Inez to where she can acknowledge the need to see the situation as Roy might, that a relationship with "no demands, no pressure, no games, no jumpin up and down with ultimatums" (176), in short, with no boundaries or expectations, might be selfish, producing "the heaviest damn pressure of all" (176). Inez finally admits that she wants to catch Roy being unfaithful, although she insists that there be no formal ties. Her first concession, and big step in growth, is to agree to let him know she is coming to Knoxville to see him. The issue is to recover a broken relationship, as Gail points out. "I know you are not about the heavy drama and intrigue" (176). The issue is trust, the reestablishment of community.

Inez struggles to understand Roy, to transcend her focal awareness centering on herself, and to achieve a subsidiary awareness of herself-in-community, aware of how her behavior may affect others. As the narrator, the youngest understands the source of Inez's problems, a lack of empathy, as "Inez just don't care what's goin on in other people's heads, her program's internal" (174). Bambara's characters grow in community because of the ability to empathize. By anticipating each other's needs, whether physical or emotional, people in community provide an environment that nurtures growth. Trust develops, which allows for risktaking at deeper and deeper levels.

Toni Cada Bambara's stories do more than paint a picture of black life in contemporary black settings. Many writers have done that, more or less successfully. Her stories portray women who struggle with issues and learn from them. Sometimes the lessons taste bitter and the women must accumulate more experience in order to gain perspective. By centering community in her stories, Bambara displays both the supportive and the destructive aspects of communal interaction. Her stories do not describe a predictable, linear plot line; rather, the cyclic enfolding of characters and community produces the kind of tension missing in stories with a more episodic emphasis.

Her characters achieve a personal identity as a result of their participation in the human quest for knowledge, which brings power. Bambara's skill as a writer saves her characters from being stereotypic cutouts. Although her themes are universal, communities that Bambara describes rise above the generic. More fully delineated than her male characters, the women come across as specific people living in specific places. Bambara's best stories show her characters interacting within a political framework wherein the personal becomes political.

NOTES

1. Paulo Friere, *Pedagogy of the Oppressed* (New York: Herder and Herder, 1972), 58.
2. Ibid., 66.
3. In this essay short stories from two collections are mentioned, and page numbers are given in parentheses in the text. *Gorilla, My Love* contains the following: "My Man Bovanne," "Gorilla, My Love," "Raymond's Run," "The Lesson," "Sweet Town," "Basement," "Maggie of the Green Bottles," "The Johnson Girls," and "Happy Birthday." *The Sea Birds Are Still Alive: Collected Stories* contains "The Organizer's Wife."
4. Michael Polanyi, *Knowing and Being*, edited by Marjorie Grene (Chicago: Univ. of Chicago Press, 1969).

A Bibliography of Writings by
TONI CADE BAMBARA

Martha M. Vertreace

BOOKS

The Black Woman: An Anthology. Edited by Toni Cade. New York: New American Library/Signet, 1970.

Tales and Stories for Black Folks. Edited by Toni Cade Bambara. Garden City, N.Y.: Doubleday/Zenith Books, 1971.

Gorilla, My Love (short stories). New York: Random House, 1972; Pocket Books, 1973; Vintage Books, 1981.

[With Leah Wise], ed. *Southern Black Utterances Today.* Institute for Southern Studies, 1975.

The Sea Birds Are Still Alive: Collected Stories. New York: Random House, 1977; Vintage, 1982.

The Salt Eaters. New York: Random House, 1980; Vintage, 1981.

Till Blessing Comes. New York: Random House, 1987; Vintage, 1987.

SCRIPTS AND RECORDINGS

"Zora! " WGBN, 1971.

"The Johnson Girls." The Soul Show, WNET, 1972.

"Victory Gardens." Producer/Director/Script, Martin Luther King Jr. Community School, Chicago, 1977.

"Transactions." Producer/Director/Script. Atlanta Univ. School of Social Work Skills Lab, 1979.
"The Long Night." ABC, 1981.
"Epitaph for Willie." K. Herman Productions, Inc., 1982.
"Tar Baby" (based on Toni Morrison's novel). Sanger/Brooks Film Productions, 1984.
"Raymond's Run." For Learning in Focus/American Short Story Series, PBS, 1985.
"The Bombing of Osage." WHYY-TV, 1986.
"Cecil B. Moore, Master Tactician of Direct Action." WHYY-TV, 1987.

ARTICLES, REVIEWS, STORIES

[Toni Cade] "Mississippi Ham Rider" (story). *Massachusetts Review,* Summer 1960. Also in *Black and White in American Culture,* edited by Jules Chametsky. Amherst: Univ. of Massachusetts Press, 1970.
"Thinking about the Play *The Great White Hope.*" *Obsidian,* Oct. 1968. Reprinted in *The Black Woman,* edited by Toni Cade [Bambara], 237–43. New York: New American Library, 1970.
"Black Theater." In *Black Expressions: Essays by and about Black Americans in the Creative Arts,* edited by Addison Gayle, Jr., 134–43. New York: Weybright and Talley, 1969.
"The Pill: Genocide or Liberation?" *Onyx,* Aug. 1969. Reprinted in *The Black Woman,* edited by Toni Cade [Bambara], New York: New American Library, 1970.
"The Scattered Sopranos." Lecture delivered to the Livingston College Black Woman's Seminar, Dec. 1969.
"On the Issue of Roles." In *The Black Woman,* edited by Toni Cade [Bambara], 101–12. New York: New American Library, 1970.
"I Ain't Playin, I'm Hurtin" (story). *Redbook,* Nov. 1971, 90–91.
"Raymond's Run" (story). *Redbook,* June 1971, 82–83. Also in *Tales and Stories for Black Folks.* Reprinted in *Women Working,* edited by N. Hoffmann and Florence Howe. New York: Feminist Press, 1982.
"Blues Ain't No Mocking Bird" (story). *Redbook,* April 1972, 86–87.
"Black Christmas in New Milford." *Redbook,* Dec. 1972, 78 +.
"Lesson" (story), excerpt from *Gorilla, My Love. Redbook,* Jan. 1973, 79.
"Report from Part One." *New York Times Book Review,* Jan. 7, 1973, 1.
[Toni Cade] "Sweet Town" (story). *Vendome Magazine,* Jan. 1959. Also in *Gorilla, My Love* and *Redbook,* Aug. 1973, 74–76.
"Thinking about My Mother." *Redbook,* Sept. 1973, 73 +. Also in *On Essays: A Reader for Writers,* edited by Paul H. Connolly. New York: Harper and Row, 1981.
"How Black Women Educate Each Other." In *Aging Black Women,* edited by Jacqueline Jackson, 221–22. National Caucus on the Black Aged, 1975. Also in *Sexual Behavior,* 2, 12–13.

Guest editor. *Southern Exposure,* Spring/Summer, 1976. Issue devoted to new southern black writers and visual artists.

"Theater." *Ms.* 5 (Sept. 1976): 36+.

"Mama Load" (story). *Redbook,* Nov. 1979, 33.

Preface for *Cracks,* by Cecilia Smith. Atlanta: Select Press, 1980.

"Luther on Sweet Auburn" (story). *First World,* 1980, 54–55.

"Baby's Breath" (story). *Essence,* Sept. 1980, 90–91.

"What Is It I Think I'm Doing Anyhow." In *The Writer on Her Work,* edited by Janet Sternburg, 153–58. New York: W.W. Norton, 1980.

"Medley" and "Witchbird" (stories). In *Midnight Birds and Black-Eyed Susans,* edited by Mary Helen Washington, 255–74, 173–91. Garden City, N.Y.: Anchor/Doubleday, 1980.

"Beauty is Just Care . . . Like Ugly Is Carelessness." In *On Essays: A Reader for Writers,* edited by Paul H. Connolly. New York: Harper and Row, 1981.

"Foreward" for *This Bridge Called My Back: Radical Women of Color,* edited by Cherríe Moraga and Gloria Anzaldúa. Watertown, Mass.: Persephone Press, 1981.

Foreward for *The Sanctified Church: Collected Essays by Zora Neale Hurston.* Berkeley: Turtle Island, 1982.

"Salvation Is the Issue." In *Black Women Writers (1950–1980): A Critical Evaluation,* edited by Marie Evans, 41–71. Garden City, N.Y.: Anchor/Doubleday, 1984.

A Bibliography of Writings about
TONI CADE BAMBARA

Martha M. Vertreace

"A Selection of Noteworthy Titles." *New York Times Book Review,* Dec. 3, 1972, 76.

Bell, Roseann, Bettye S. Parker, and Beverly Guy-Sheftall, eds., *Sturdy Black Bridges.* Garden City, N.Y.: Anchor Press/Doubleday, 1979.

Bonetti, Kay. "The Organizer's Wife: A Reading by and Interview with Toni Cade Bambara." American Prose Library, Columbia, Mo., 1982.

"Books of the Times." *New York Times,* June 3, 1980, 243.

Broyard, Anatole. Review of *Gorilla, My Love. New York Times,* Oct. 11, 1972, 41.

Bryan, C.D.B. Review of *Gorilla, My Love. New York Times Book Review* Oct. 15, 1972, 31–33.

Burks, Ruth Elizabeth. "From Baptism to Resurrection: Toni Cade Bambara and the Incongruity of Language." In Mari Evans, ed., *Black Women Writers (1950–1980): A Critical Evaluation*, 48–57. Garden City, N.Y.: Anchor/Doubleday, 1984.

Byerman, Keith E. *Fingering the Jagged Grain: Tradition and Form in Recent Black Fiction*. Athens: Univ. of Georgia Press, 1986.

Chevigny, Bell Gale. "Stories of Solidarity and Selfhood" (review of *Gorilla, My Love*). *Village Voice*, April 12, 1973, 39–40.

Chute, Sherree. Review of *The Salt Eaters*. *Ms.*, July 1980, 28–29.

Deck, Alice A. "Toni Cade Bambara." In *Dictionary of Literary Biography 38: Afro-American Writers after 1955*, 12–22. Detroit: Gale Research Co., 1985.

Dybek, Caren. "Black Literature for Adolescents.: *English Journal* 63 (Jan. 1974): 64–67.

Fisher, Jerilyn. "From Under the Yoke of Race and Sex: Black and Chicano Women's Fiction of the Seventies." *Minority Voices: An Interdisciplinary Journal of Literature and the Arts* 2 (1978): 1–14.

Geringer, Laura. "Books in Brief: *The Salt Eaters*." *Saturday Review*, April 12, 1980, 40–41.

Giddings, Paula. "Call to Wholeness from a Gifted Storyteller." *Encore*, June 1980, 48–49.

"*Gorilla, My Love*" (review). *New York Times Book Review*, Dec. 3, 1972, 76.

Guy-Sheftall, Beverly. "Commitment: Toni Cade Bambara Speaks." In *Sturdy Black Bridges: Visions of Black Women in Literature*, edited by Roseann Bell, Bettye S. Parker, and Beverly Guy-Sheftall. Garden City: Doubleday/Anchor, 1979.

Hargrove, Nancy D. "Youth in Toni Cade Bambara's *Gorilla, My Love*." *Southern Quarterly* 22 (1983): 81–99. Also in *Women Writers of the Contemporary South*, edited by Peggy Whitman Prenshaw, 215–32. Jackson: Univ. Press of Mississippi, 1984.

Harris, N. *Obsidian*, Spring 1981, 101.

Harrison, Paul Carter. *The Drama of Nommo*, 159. New York: Grove Press, 1972.

Hogue, W. Lawrence. *Discourse and the Other: The Production of the Afro-American Text*, 55. Durham, N.C.: Duke Univ. Press, 1986.

Hull, Gloria. " 'What It Is I Think She's Doing Anyhow': A Reading of Toni Cade Bambara's *The Salt Eaters*." In *Conjuring: Black Women, Fiction, and Literary Tradition*, edited by Marjorie Pryse and Hortense J. Spillers, 216–32. Bloomington: Indiana Univ. Press, 1985.

Jackson, Angela. "Music in the Silence." *Black Scholar* 12 (March 1981): 90.

———. "*The Salt Eaters*" (review). *Black Scholar* 13 (Fall 1982): 52.

Jackson, Deborah. "An Interview with Toni Cade Bambara." *Drum Magazine*, Spring 1982.

Jefferson, Margo. "Blue Notes." *Newsweek*, May 2, 1977, 76.

Jordan, June. "*Gorilla, My Love*" (review). *Black World* 22 (July 1973): 80.

Lardner, Susan. "Books: Third Eye Open." *New Yorker,* May 5, 1980, 169–73.

Leonard, John. Review of *The Salt Eaters. New York Times Book Review,* April 4, 1980, 1.

Macauley, Robie. *"The Sea Birds Are Still Alive"* (review). *New York Times Book Review,* March 27, 1977, 7.

Marcus, L. "New Feminine Talents, New Feminine Concerns." *Times Literary Supplement,* Sept. 27, 1985, 1070.

McRobbie, Angela. "Fiction: Soundings." *New Statesman* 107 (April 27, 1984): 22.

Morrison, Toni. *"Tales and Stories for Black Folks"* (review). *New York Times Book Review,* May 2, 1971, 43.

Punch, May 2, 1984, 60.

Reed, Ishmael. "Books by Afro-American Writers Which I Enjoyed during the 1970s." *Black Scholar* 12 (March 1981): 87.

Review of *The Sea Birds Are Still Alive. National Observer,* May 9, 1977, 23.

Review of *The Salt Eaters. New York Times Book Review,* Nov. 1, 1981, 47.

Rosenberg, Ruth. " 'You Took a Name That Made You Amiable to the Music': Toni Cade Bambara's *The Salt Eaters." Literary Onomastics Studies* 12 (1985): 165–94.

Rumens, C. *Times Literary Supplement,* June 18, 1982, 676.

Russell, Michele. *"The Sea Birds Are Still Alive"* (review). *New American Movement* (Summer 1977).

Salaam, Kalamu ya. "An Interview: Searching for the Mother Tongue." *First World* 2 (1980): 48–53.

Shipley, W. Maurice. *CLA Journal* 26 (Sept. 1982): 125–27.

Shockley, Ann Allen, and Sue P. Chandler. *Living Black American Authors: A Biographical Directory,* 9. New York: Bowker, 1973.

"Shorter Reviews: *Gorilla, My Love." Saturday Review* 55 (Dec. 1972): 97–98.

Spillers, Hortense J. "A Hateful Passion, a Lost Love." In *Feminist Issues in Literary Scholarship,* edited by Shari Benstock, 185. Bloomington: Indiana Univ. Press, 1987.

Tate, Claudia. "Toni Cade Bambara." In *Black Women Writers at Work,* edited by Claudia Tate, 12–38. New York: Continuum, 1983.

Traylor, Eleanor W. *"The Salt Eaters:* My Soul Looks Back in Wonder." *First World* 2 (Summer 1981): 44–47, 64.

———. "Music as Theme: The Jazz Mode in the Works of Toni Cade Bambara." In *Black Women Writers (1950–1980): A Critical Evaluation,* edited by Mari Evans, 58–70. Garden City, N.Y.: Anchor/Doubleday, 1984.

Tyler, Anne. "Farewell to the Story as Imperiled Species." *National Observer,* May 9, 1977, 23.

———. "At the Still Center of a Dream." *Book World—Washington Post,* March 30, 1980, 1–2.

Wade-Gayles, Gloria. *No Crystal Stair: Vision of Race and Sex in Black Women's Fiction,* 185. New York: Pilgrim Press, 1984.

Ward, J.W. *New Orleans Review* 18 (Summer 1981): 207–8.
Washington, Mary Helen. "Blues Women of the Seventies." *Ms.*, July 1977, 36–38.
Book World—Washington Post, Oct. 8, 1972, 15.
Book World—Washington Post, Nov. 18, 1973, 5.
Wideman, John. "The Healing of Velma Henry" (review of *The Salt Eaters*). *New York Times Book Review*, June 1, 1980, 14.
Willis, Susan. Problematizing the Individual: Toni Cade Bambara's Stories for the Revolution." In *Specifying: Black Women Writing the American Experience*, 129–58. Madison: Univ. of Wisconsin Press, 1987.

GAIL GODWIN

The Odd Woman
and Literary Feminism

Rachel M. Brownstein

At the age of four or five, Jane Clifford, the protagonist of Gail Godwin's *The Odd Woman*, was already concerned with the representation of women in fiction. She asked her mother, Kitty, a college teacher who wrote love stories on weekends:

"Why don't you write a story about a woman who teaches school at the college and writes love stories on the weekend and has a little girl like me?"

"It wouldn't sell, that's why." replied Kitty.
"Oh, I think it would be very interesting to read," said Jane.
"It would be interesting to people like you and me," Kitty said, "but I can assure you, *Love Short Stories* wouldn't buy it." [26–27]

In an article about writing fiction, the author of *The Odd Woman* recalled that her own mother, like Jane's, wrote on week-ends for magazines called something like *Love Short Stories*. Her "specialty was the representative heroine, not the singular, the 'passing strange,' " Godwin explained; she edited "the most interesting parts of herself out of the heroines she sent to New York. . . . For practical reasons, for reasons of sanity as well."[2] Grown-up daughters of romance-writing mothers, having been raised on the profits from *Love Short Stories*, and not on the stories themselves, are shrewd about the lure and the lie of romantic fiction. And they remain preoccupied by it. How fictions and stereotypes of the romantic heroine function in complex real women's minds and lives is a theme of all Gail Godwin's novels. It is articulated most pointedly in *The Odd Woman* (1974). The heroine, Jane Clifford, is defined to begin with as odd first of all— as not representative, singular, "passing strange." In this, Godwin persuasively shows, she is, precisely, representative—of "people like you and me," that is, women who see themselves as more interesting than standard representations of women in fiction. *The Odd Woman* suggests that real, interesting women must imagine and construct their identities in the terms of traditional fiction, so as to revise them.

Like her mother, Jane Clifford thinks about heroines and love stories in the way of business. A thirty-two-year-old single (unmatched, odd) professor of English, she reflects on commercial romances like the ones her mother used to write and also on the kind written by Jane Austen and George Eliot that educated women read; she measures herself against both novel heroines and their female creators. Her own life feels like a fiction. So much, and so literally, does Jane think about the love writ large in novels that she suspects herself of having dreamed her current affair with a married man, the remote, too perfectly named Gabriel Weeks, a comically parodic version of an angel (as opposed to a Romantic demon?) lover. He is a professor, too, of (for a slight change) art history. The love of Jane's mother's life was an English professor; with the exception of her dashing oldest friend, Gerda Mulvaney, the publisher of a radical feminist newspaper, all of Jane's best friends are academics. Pedantic Gabriel aims to catalog the kinds of love—according to him, there are just six—while the women professors tend to think about it novelistically, as story. For them the boundaries between fiction and daily life are transparent and permeable. When her colleague Sonia Marks tells Jane she's trying to imagine the man who'd be just right for her, she means she's trying to decide between Heathcliff and Mr. Knightley. For Jane the twenty-five years George Eliot spent with G.H. Lewes are as personally significant as the twenty-five years of her mother's second marriage to coarse Ray Sparks (Kitty's former student, who courted her by calling her his "Belle Dame Sans Merci" at the end of an exam paper). Nearly as significant as the twenty-five years Gabriel Weeks has been married to Ann, whom he has no plans to leave. Jane is a literary academic to the core: in her fantasy about being attacked by a pervert, she talks the man out of his vile intention and then suggests, hilariously, "Perhaps you ought to apply for a Guggenheim" (30). A pretentious piece of pornographic fiction by one of her colleagues infuriates her because it records its author's passage through a fashionable life stage and also because it fails to give its readers credit for identifying its literary analogue. It is called *The Country Husband;* discreetly, we are told we recognize Wycherley, the Restoration precedent. (Is there also a shy misjudged poke here at John Cheever?) The line between comradely familiarity with academics and satirical contempt of them is very fine.

Godwin's own title echoes the title of a novel by George Gissing (another G.G.), *The Odd Women,* which Jane Clifford is planning to teach (we get her reading notes) in a course called Women in Literature. Jane the professor, like Godwin the novelist, is preoccupied with women's lives, their differences and samenesses, and inevitabilities, the apparently urgent necessity to choose one kind from a finite, already published list. It is her habit to contrast the fullness and pointedness of words, the clarity of roles, and the conclusiveness of finished plots, with the mixed motives, multiple selves, and meaningless accidents and impulses that govern actual selves and experiences. As she fantasizes and thinks and talks and reads about literature and women, a.k.a. art and love, Jane is working at critically understanding and artistically shaping her own character and destiny as if they were in a novel. The personal, for her, is the professional. When she thinks about the taken-for-granted "romantic" pattern of love-then-marriage women's lives are expected to conform to, it is important to her that serious English fiction—by Jane Austen and George Eliot—has given this pattern moral and aesthetic weight: the authority of fiction makes the pattern weigh heavily on her.

The thoroughgoing literariness of its protagonist is a clue to *The Odd Woman*'s historical moment. In the mid-seventies real and fictional literary women like Jane Clifford were fascinating to themselves and others as never before—or perhaps since. One early result of the feminist movement, which was criticizing the accepted images of women as fictions, was to make women writers, of and about fiction, oddly glamorous figures. Bluestockings had been forbidding and schoolteachers notoriously sexless, but the new literary women were something else. Ellen Moer's phrase, the title of her 1976 book, was itself inspiriting; it put women professors and readers in the same category as Jane Austen and George Eliot—and their heroines. Reading and writing, readers and writers, were sexy. A conspicuous literary legacy of the women's movement in the second half of the twentieth century is fiction about English majors by English majors, who set about deliberately to revise the standard heroine's character and life story. Margaret Drabble's novels and Godwin's are the obvious examples, but the protagonist of *Fear of Flying* (1973) is also, remember, a graduate student of literature.

Even when they remained chastely professional, in print, what women professors had to say was in the mid-seventies interesting to an unprecedentedly wide public. They themselves seemed attractive role models, professional women who thought professionally about love and its images and stories, achieving, as they did so, an enviable integration of love and work. In *The Odd Woman* Jane Clifford feels a familiar old-fashioned pang when a New York City cab driver, hearing she's a teacher, says, "That explains it," meaning her frumpy unmarriedness (224); but Jane's classy friend Sonia Marks, with her children, the already-married lover she got to marry her, her intellectual intensity, her charismatic classroom style, her long list of publications, and her tendency to blush endearingly to the roots of her beautiful hair, is a bright female college student's ego ideal. Jane and Sonia share passionate conversations about literature; taking off from fiction, they enter an empyrean where desire, speculation, and imagination come together, as they, together, commune with a third person, the writer. Jane tells a student that literature is valuable for allowing us to share someone else's consciousness; Godwin shows that it also, importantly, provides an occasion for sharing intimate thoughts with an equally literary friend. As they chew the fat frontier between literature and life, Jane and Sonia embark on an ecstatic shared flight into a heady realm where forgetfulness of the small, confining self becomes a sense that that self has been enlarged to include sister selves, of women writers and of women who have been written about. The postcoital talk Jane ekes out of her lover, Gabriel, is careful and dull, in dramatic comparison. The literary women's talk is a model for the reader's response.

The *Odd Woman* is a novel of an odd moment—one that was perhaps not so decisive as the moment when the literate women of England picked up Samuel Richardson's *Pamela* (1742), but that is now as interesting to reflect on. When it first appeared, the new wave of feminist literary criticism was just cresting: Mary Ellman's *Thinking about Women* (1968), Kate Millett's *Sexual Politics* (1969), and Elaine Showalter's *A Literature of Their Own* (1973) had already been published, along with several influential essays on women and art; Patricia Spacks's *The Female Imagination* (1975—the year of *Time*'s "Women of the Year" cover), Ellen Moers's *Literary Women* (1976), and Sandra M. Gilbert and Susan Gubar's *The Madwoman in the Attic* (1979) would round out the decade. Like these books Godwin's addresses the question of how literature and the values a woman reader derives from it reflect and determine women's lives. Although *The Odd Woman* takes pains to distinguish its protagonist (and itself?) from the excesses of man-hating feminists, Gerda Mulvaney and her basement-full of unattractive staff members of *Feme Sole*, it is hard not to read the novel today as an expression of the feminism of the seventies. The conclusion Jane Clifford comes to, about going with or through one's own oddnesses so as to transcend them, asserts the importance of personal liberation rather than the liberation of a group; still, the problems and specificities of women as a group are what the novel most closely attends to.

Reviewing it in 1974 in *The New York Times Book Review,* Lore Dickstein compared *The Odd Woman* to "the best of Doris Lessing and Margaret Drabble" and went on to identify them parenthetically as "two writers who have vociferously rejected the feminist categorization of their work."[3] By now others have joined them and Godwin in insisting not only that they were not feminist writers but also that as they are writers first and only incidentally women they dislike being called "women writers." The question of "feminist categorization" is problematic; there are nearly as many ways of being a feminist as there are of being a Jew. As the South African Lessing and the English Drabble were doing in the seventies, Godwin was writing primarily about women who counted the ways they were like and unlike other women, in fact and in fiction. She would continue to do so, in *Violet Clay* (1978), *A Mother and Two Daughters* (1982), *The Finishing School* (1984), and *A Southern Family* (1987). Godwin's women are not feminist rebels any more than they are a romance writer's stereotyped creatures; they no more attack the establishment than they fall in love with sexy men, period, or concern themselves only with the women's-magazine work of childbearing, child rearing, cooking, and homemaking. But they do share a characteristic which is imagined as distinctively womanly. Women as Godwin sees them (along with Drabble and perhaps Lessing, too) are distinct from men in the kind of self-consciousness they have and in the way images of women compulsively inform their identity. To discover who they are, Godwin's heroines measure themselves against one another and against conceptions of "woman"; they experience other women's characters and destinies (or stories) as eerily mirroring, prefiguring, determining their own. Even when they are artists and actresses, Godwin's protagonists have the souls of novelists. They are literary women who think of themselves as burdened by women's stories, by female character and destiny as it has been imagined; a literary conception of character and destiny compels them to contemplate the selves and lives of other women as if they were reading them. Violet Clay, a painter, earns her living by painting covers for gothic novels, whose heroines suffer agonies that grotesquely parallel her own; Justin, the young protagonist of *The Finishing School*, becomes an actress after making her first connection to art and performance through an older woman she loves as the living image of culture and fine feeling. The author of *A Mother and Two Daughters* confesses that she was interested in the ways each of three women in a family "had shaped and been shaped by the other two heroines";[4] in *The Finishing School*, Godwin went on to explore a girl's formative relationship with a fascinating older woman who seems to represent what she wants to be. Showing her heroine rejecting her own mother and aunt, suggesting how the young girl's unspoken fantasy about her reflects and reinforces the older woman's fantasy image of herself, Godwin writes evocatively and tactfully there about a familiar element of women's lives that feminist discourses about mother-daughter bonds and lesbian relationships do not quite get at.

The life realistically portrayed in *The Odd Woman* is dense with details especially familiar to literary women: less educated women need to muster more imagination to identify with the heroines of gothics. But now that it is nearly fifteen years after its publication, the feminist critic—a professionalized category that has replaced "literary woman"—will be (depending on her age) startled or made nostalgic by aspects of the action. One is awed by the evidence of the women's movement's intensest moment, when it seemed plausible for an exhausted professor, accidentally trapped in a hotel room with another woman and longing to be alone, to launch indefatigably into a discussion of literary prototypes for women's lives, as Jane Clifford does. It is hard to believe that in 1974 it was credible that two women faculty members in their early thirties would exchange notes like these:

Tomorrow in class I'm doing a pop woman's fiction book published in the 1860s, and the thought of the soap opera is much on my mind. *Jane Eyre* is a great soap opera! Too many women's lives conform to its pattern. Do you think the soap opera follows life or do we pattern our lives with their innumerable crises and catastrophes and shifting casts of characters after this model? Have a good week. Sonia.

Dear Sonia: Today when we were talking about Hawthorne again, you said that for him the women represented all the qualities which the man has self-destructively despised in himself and thus projected onto, or "stored" in the woman for safekeeping. You said that (according to Hawthorne) the man needs union with her to restore into himself the sundered parts which would make him a whole human being. Now I can't get out of my mind the possibility that over the centuries we may have abandoned certain human qualities, too; "left them to the men," so to speak, as we leave the garbage and the storm windows to men. I wonder what are these qualities we have given up? Have you any ideas? [53]

Ah, even if they did write in jargon, there were giantesses on the earth, in those days; bliss was it in that dawn to be alive!

The literary feminism of the seventies, personal, passionate, and unmediated by schisms or outside alliances, was perhaps naive but enviably enlivening. Godwin's 1974 portrait of academic literary women enjoying scholarly/personal sympathy contrasts sharply with her 1985 row with a number of them, provoked by her review, in *The New York Times Book Review,* of *The Norton Anthology of Literature by Women: The Tradition in English,* edited by Sandra M. Gilbert and Susan Gubar. For all that she had created a successful novel about a woman who was excitedly rereading literature from a woman's point of view, teaching a course in Women in Literature, and delighting in the covers of novels of Gissing and Wharton reissued in the enthusiasm of the literary feminist moment, Godwin came out strongly against "feminist categorization," in theory and, especially, in these anthologists' practice. And by attacking Gilbert and Gubar's anthology, she brought down upon herself the wrath of the best-placed feminist literary critics, sisterhood being by 1985 a literary power to reckon with. Because it involves the question of canons—what students should read, what values are represented by traditional as compared with revisionist syllabi—, the controversy has unfortunately been interpreted as an argument about reading literature for "narrow" feminist ideological purposes vs. reading for more "purely" "literary" values. But Godwin's novels, which imagine women's lives in terms of their reading and writing, make it clear that such an opposition is less than useful.

Although Jane Clifford would probably have found an anthology of women's writing helpful, however flawed, she might have been annoyed, as Godwin was, by the Norton. Godwin quibbled, as any critic of an anthology can hardly help doing, with the choice and range of the selections; she quarreled, more significantly, with the very idea of an anthology based on Gilbert and Gubar's feminist theory of women's literature. It resulted, she wrote, in a "leveling of artists and their art, . . . forcing the individual female talent to lie on the Procrustean fainting-couch of a 'dis-eased' tradition."[5] Her most serious criticisms of Gilbert and Gubar are (1) that their anthology "is organized to bear out Virginia Woolf's opinion that women's books 'continue each other,' " and (2) that it is dominated by the thesis they set forth in *The Madwoman in the Attic*, that women writers are preoccupied with gender and afflicted by an "anxiety of authorship." In the first instance, as Nancy K. Miller has observed, Godwin makes a symptomatic mistake: Virginia Woolf in fact wrote simply that books, not women's books, "continue each other."[6] With this statement Godwin surely would agree: *The Odd Woman*, like its protagonist, is haunted by intertextuality or literary ancestor-regard, recollections of books about women, and of women writers. The quarrel with Gilbert and Gubar here is a minor one which depends on a definition of terms: "women's books," as Godwin's reference to Gissing dramatically makes clear, are, for her, books written for women to read, books about women's lives—which may have been written by men. Defining the term is something about which reasonable feminists may easily disagree.

Godwin's second objection to Gilbert and Gubar's anthology is more serious, and it is persuasive. The authors of *The Madwoman in the Attic*, eager to establish the legitimacy of feminist literary criticism and theory, accepted a theory of writing as assuming and discoursing with authority. Women, they argued, have traditionally been deprived of authority and therefore suffer anxiety about undertaking authorship. Understandably, Godwin disagrees. Writing in a tradition of literature dominated by women, she rejects the idea that "an anxiety of authorship" besets and cripples writers of her sex. If one is haunted by the example of George Eliot, if one's own mother was a writer, one naturally believes that, on the contrary, women and literature have a special connection—that women have a stake in literature, that it is their birthright to be writers.

The Odd Woman suggests that as Godwin sees it the authority of women writers is both burdensome and real. Godwin's example would serve to support Gilbert and Gubar's thesis that women writers have made peculiar and significant contributions to the discourse on gender, and that their having written—as women or not—has affected the lives of women in general. *The Odd Woman* is about women who imagine their lives as fictions, and about fictions women live by; its heroine sees her life as a plot. Jane Clifford's Great-aunt Cleva, who ran away with a villain (or was it a hero?) of a melodrama, was as moved by literary example as Jane the professor is; and the influences on Jane, for whom Cleva's life is story, are also a mix of real and imaginary people. Desperately seeking idyllic romantic love on which to base a life as perfectly shaped and finished as literary character or literary form, haunted by the contrasting examples of women in her family—her coaxing compliant mother, her delicate lady grandmother, and long-dead Cleva—Jane Clifford is beset by representations of women, that is, by the idea of other women as representations of what a woman's life might be. Her oddness—as opposed to the predictability of her mother's romance heroines—is ultimately ironic; in perceiving other women as images she resembles the heroines of the great tradition of women's fiction in English, Emma Woodhouse, Lucy Snowe, Dorothea Brooke. From a feminist point of view, one might condemn such characters' pride in their superiority to other, simpler women. Or one might, more profitably, study such images beset by images in order to analyze how gender has been constructed in culture, and how it figures in women's subjectivity. Novelists like Godwin, who write in and of the traditional self-reflexive women's novel, are working along lines that run parallel to those of many feminist theorists.

The death of Jane's grandmother provokes the action of *The Odd Woman;* it precipitates the heroine out of the bed in which she has been unable to sleep and into a series of encounters with the significant people in her life. One of those is the dead Edith herself. Looking down at the old lady in her coffin, Jane thinks: "This figure was ageless, queenly, invulnerable. Completed. The expression on the face of this woman who had lived out her life beset with fears about things that never happened was an expression which scorned fears. Fears were for those who had something left to lose. The dead face of Edith . . . was a detached, cool comment on a completed existence. It was a face neither masculine nor feminine, simply regal; a face that had transcended pain, uncertainty, sex. Achieving death, Edith had rid herself at last of troublesome womanhood" (139). Having transcended her womanhood, Edith is, precisely, dead, as a sublimely transcendent "art" unmarked by the particularities of experience would be. As Gilbert and Gubar have argued, identification with ideal transcendent art—the "perfect woman, nobly planned," the "Angel in the House," perhaps, the "Love Goddess," the "ewig Weibliche"—has been projected onto women, to haunt and to cripple them, throughout the centuries. In the nineteenth century—Jane Clifford's specialty—, the idea of woman-as-art became especially complex, especially confining, especially fascinating. As Gilbert and Gubar have shown, woman contained, mirrored, and framed, transformed into a symbol of art, an artifact stripped of desire and vitality, has been a persistent image of transcendence, which has lodged with complex consequences in women's minds. When Jane Clifford looks down at her grandmother's body, she experiences the pull of the image of women as art, which haunts her professional and private life. But she also recognizes that this transcendent, completed Edith is unwomanly and dead—that transcendence as art, for living women, is unacceptable.

For all its regard for nineteenth-century English literature, *The Odd Woman* is inspired by revisionist energy. Its best, most original moments are modern ones: Jane's all-night orgy of self-expression, making pornographic drawings; the half-a-chapter in which she packs her bags, deciding and undeciding to leave Gabriel, in a hotel room filled with cheering, jeering spectral selves. And Jane Clifford's preoccupation with nineteenth-century English novels is distinctively American, the way Henry James in his preoccupation with European culture was American. There is a little absurd snobbishness in this novel about old family noses and heirloom silver, a little too much eagerness to dispatch uncultured close relatives by caricature. One is tempted to venture that Godwin's very earnestness about art as transcendence—like Gilbert and Gubar's—is also oddly American, in the tradition of Edith Wharton and James. (Surprising, in this context, to find some odd infelicities of observation and language: the "tendrils" of an avocado plant get "twined" up grocery string, a "package store" is situated in New York City, and "courtesy phones" are called on without irony.) The most dramatic difference between *The Odd Woman* and the nineteenth-century predecessors that preoccupy it is the vividness with which this novel presents the female body. Created by a novelist concerned with form and frames, Jane Clifford's body is not so much the locus of desire (which seems to be localized in the brain) as a container—not, as traditional imagery has it, for a male organ or a child, but for a distinctive identity.

The female body as Godwin portrays it is not an instrument for pleasure or reproduction but, rather, an enclosure for the self, mortal and vulnerable. The genitalia are less important than other organs. Prominent among these others are the female brain, which keeps Jane up night harboring erotic fantasies and thoughts of insomniac female relatives. But even more important are the viscera. Jane's psychic demons tend to haunt the gut; she suffers constipation for fear of her lover's hearing her shit, and indulges in self-destructive and self-indulgent overeating and drinking, then vomiting. The dark side of both her fantasy life and the town she lives in are menaced by the grotesque and ludicrous Enema Bandit who wears a woman's stocking over his head; she hears about him on the radio and imagines he is just outside her house. When too much pressure to conform to alien standards makes her faint, like her southern grandmother before her and any delicate Victorian heroine, Jane notes her symptoms with a clinician's eye: "She knew the first signs all too well: the cold dampness on the surface of the skin, the queasiness, the rising horror at the prospect of having the self she knew and kept track of dissolve into nothing" (317). Jane's self-consciousness is devoted to keeping track of herself, preventing it from dissolving. She experiences conflicting fluid selves inside her that she seeks to contain; she also wants release from the confines of the body, the family, the limited identity that keep her small and personal. The sense of the body as a fragile, vulnerable container of a self or selves problematically female is what *The Odd Woman* most convincingly conveys. Godwin is good on the body loathsome in dressing rooms and at odds with its digestive tract. Her concern with the containing body neatly parallels Jane's preoccupation with literary role models and also parodies it. The literary idea of the finished, meaningful life, of the self named, shaped, and realized the way a literary character or work is, haunts traditional English novels; novels like Gissing's and Godwin's seek to demystify it. But to grapple with it is, of course, to acknowledge the idea's force, as *The Odd Woman* does, and to testify to its continuing strength. The identification of women and art has lodged persistently in female self-consciousness. It has imprisoned but also enriched and enabled women in a range of ways, by giving Kitty (and Gail Godwin's mother), for instance, a Gothic formula for limited success, by presenting more sophisticated writers like Godwin herself with a complex situation for revision. Perhaps women's real lives are—as Godwin suggests—stranger than women's fiction because the one contains the other, which shapes it.

Godwin continues to explore literary-feminist themes. In her most recent novel, as in *A Mother and Two Daughters*, she writes about a whole family, but as ever she writes best about the writing women in it. The protagonist of *A Southern Family* (1987) is a novelist, alliteratively named Clare Campion; pointing to her autobiographical model, she reflects that she has achieved "an enviable combination of artistic and popular success" (16) through her work. It is not only of biographical interest that Godwin's best characters are women engaged in writing their lives: Clare, who wrote a novel based on the family life of her best friend, Julia; Julia, who writes doggerel to express herself in secret; Clare's sadly unfulfilled mother, the author of an unfinished novel that would have blown the lid off her town; and the lower-class Snow Mullins, who reveals a startlingly high level of literacy and insight in her letters. As the novelist-protagonist, who turned her best friend into fiction, ponders the question of how to avoid the novelist's lie of making too tidy sense of real people and real life, Godwin, behind her, confronts her theme, women's literary self-imaging.

Self-reflexive traditional fiction like Godwin's continues usefully to map literary-feminist concerns. Although feminism and attitudes toward gender have both changed since the mid-seventies, Jane Clifford's work still remains to be done: sorting out *Jane Eyre*, soap opera, and real women's lives; tracing ways men's and women's ideas of the masculine and feminine shape both the literature and the lives they make. Writing novels is one way to do such work. Identifying women with romantic fictions of perfection and transcendence is an old, seductive trick of patriarchy that thoughtful women novelists have long worked together toward deconstructing. It is false and impoverishing; so is polarizing life and art, feminist and literary values.

NOTES

1. In this essay page numbers from *The Odd Woman* (New York: Alfred A. Knopf, 1974) and *A Southern Family* (New York: William Morrow and Co., 1987) are given in parentheses in the text.

2. Gail Godwin, "Becoming a Writer," in *The Writer on Her Work*, ed. Janet Sternberg (New York: Norton, 1980), 236.

3. Lore Dickstein, "The Odd Woman" (review), *New York Times Book Review,* October 20, 1974, 4.

4. Gail Godwin, "Becoming the Characters in Your Novel," *The Writer,* June 1982, 12.

5. Gail Godwin, "One Woman Leads to Another" (review of *The Norton Anthology of Literature by Women*), *New York Times Book Review,* April 28, 1985, 14.

6. Nancy K. Miller, introduction to *Subject to Change* (forthcoming from Columbia University Press).

A Bibliography of Writings by GAIL GODWIN

Mickey Pearlman

BOOKS

The Perfectionists. New York: Harper and Row, 1970; Penguin, 1985.

Glass People. New York: Knopf, 1972; Penguin, 1979.
The Odd Woman. New York: Knopf, 1974; Penguin, 1985.
Dream Children (short stories). New York: Knopf, 1976; Avon, 1983.
Violet Clay. New York: Knopf, 1978; Penguin, 1986.
A Mother and Two Daughters. New York: Viking, 1982; Avon, 1983.
The Finishing School. New York: Viking, 1985; Avon, 1986.
A Southern Family. New York: William Morrow, 1987.

LIBRETTOS

"The Last Lover." [For a musical work by Robert Starer.] Katonah, N.Y., 1975.
"Journals of a Songmaker." [For a musical work by Robert Starer.] Pittsburgh, 1976.
"Apollonia." [For a musical work by Robert Starer.] Minneapo.' ., 1979.
"Anna Margarita's Will." [For a musical work by Robert Starer.] Recorded by C.R.I., 1980.

ARTICLES, REVIEWS, STORIES

"Sorrowful Woman" (story). *Esquire,* Aug. 1971, 75–76.
"An Oates Scrapbook." *North American Review* 256 (Winter 1971–72): 67–70.
"Interstices" (story). *Harper's,* May 1972, 86–90.
"Towards a Fully Human Heroine: Some Worknotes." *Harvard Advocate,* Winter 1973, 26–28.
"Why Does a Great Man Love?" *Paris Review* 15 (Winter 1974): 176–85.
"If She Hadn't Called Herself George Eliot, Would We Have Heard of Marian Evans?" *Ms.,* Sept. 1974, 72–75, 88.
"False Lights" (story). *Esquire,* Jan. 1975, 68–70.
"Nobody's Home" (story). *Harper's,* Feb. 1975, 91–94.
"The Southern Belle." *Ms.,* July 1975, 51.
"Finding the Right Shape for Your Story." *Writer* 88 (Sept. 1975): 9–11.
"His House." *Triquarterly* 35 (Winter 1976): 32–34.
"Angry Year." *McCall's,* Feb. 1976, 106–7.
"Dream Children" (story). *Ms.,* April 1976, 75–78.
"Discovering the Form for Your Fiction." *Writer* 89 (Dec. 1976): 11–14.
"Southern Men, Southern Lies." *Esquire,* Feb. 1977, 126–29.
"Review of *The Other Woman,* by Philippe Jullian." *New York Times Book Review,* March 20, 1977, 4+.
"Cultural Exchange." *Atlantic,* Feb. 1978, 77–85.
"Fate of Fleeing Maidens." *Mademoiselle,* May 1978, 130.
"Violet Clay" (story). *Viva* 5 (June 1978): 99+.
Review of *Secrets and Surprises,* by Ann Beattie. *New York Times Book Review,* Jan. 14, 1979, 14.
Review of *Chamber Music,* by Doris Grumbach. *New York Times Book Review,* March 25, 1979, 15.
"The Unlikely Family" (story). *Redbook,* Aug. 1979, 163+.

"A Writing Woman." *Atlantic Monthly,* Oct. 1979, 84–92.
"Being on Everybody's Side." *Writer* 92 (Dec. 1979): 12+.
"Becoming a Writer." In *The Writer on Her Work,* edited by Janet Sternburg, 231–55. New York: Norton, 1980.
Review of *The Transit of Venus,* by Shirley Hazzard. *New York Times Book Review,* March 16, 1980, 7+.
[With Shyla Irving, Stanley Elkin, Richard Selzer, Daniel Halpern, William McPherson, Marvin Bell, Ira Sadoff] "Poetic Food License." *Esquire,* May 1980, 55+.
Review of *The Playhouse,* by Elaine Ford. *New York Times Book Review,* Oct. 5, 1980, 14+.
Review of *Jacob Have I Loved,* by Katherine Paterson. *New York Times Book Review,* Dec. 21, 1980, 25.
"A Mother and Two Daughters" (story). *Redbook,* Dec. 1981, 141, 64.
"Keeping Track." In *Ariadne's Thread: A Collection of Contemporary Women's Journals,* edited by Lyn Lifshin, 72–85. New York: Harper and Row, 1982.
"The Effects of Snobbery—on Snobs and Victims." *New York Times,* Jan. 7, 1982, 18.
"Hers (Author Recalls Children She Has Known)" (column). *New York Times,* Jan. 14, 1982, 16 C2.
"How Separate from The Rest of Society Should An Artist Be?" *New York Times,* Jan. 21, 1982, 18, C2.
"Hers (Curious People)" (column). *New York Times,* Jan. 28, 1982, 16.
"Becoming the Characters in Your Novel." *Writer* 95 (June 1982): 11+.
"An Epic of West Virginia" (review of *The Killing Ground,* by Mary Lee Settle). *New Republic* 186 (June 16, 1982): 30+.
"Afternoon Interlude" (story). *Cosmopolitan,* Aug. 1982, 246+.
Review of *Katherine Anne Porter,* by Joan Givner. *New Republic* 187 (Nov. 22, 1982): 30+.
Review of *Code Name 'Mary': Memoirs of an American Woman in the Austrian Underground,* by Muriel Gardiner and Anna Freud. *New Republic* 188 (May 30, 1983): 33+.
"A Sorrowful Woman." In *Great Esquire Fiction: The Finest Stories from the First Fifty Years,* edited by L. Rust Hills. New York: Viking, 1983.
Review of *The Witches of Eastwick* by John Updike. *New Republic,* 190 (June 4, 1984): 28+.
"Over the Mountain." In *The Pushcart Prize IX: Best of the Small Presses,* edited by Bill Henderson. Wainscott, N.Y.: Pushcart Press, 1984.
"A Novelist Sings a Different Tune." *New York Times,* Dec. 15, 1985, 1.
"House Parties and Box Lunches: One Writer's Summer at Yaddo." *New York Times Book Review,* July 10, 1986, 1.
Review of *The Prince of Tides,* by Pat Conroy. *New York Times Book Review,* Oct. 12, 1986, 14.
"The Uses of Autobiography." *Writer* 100 (March 1987): 7.

Review of *The Thanatos Syndrome*, by Walker Percy. *New York Times Book Review*, April 5, 1987, 1.
"A Southern Family" (fiction). *Cosmopolitan*, Sept. 1987, 312+.
"How I Write." *Writer* 100 (Oct. 1987): 17+.

A Bibliography of Writings about GAIL GODWIN

Mickey Pearlman

Allen, Mary. *The Necessary Blankness: Women in Major American Fiction of the Sixties.* Urbana: Univ. of Illinois Press, 1987.
Auerbach, Nina. "Women on Women's Destiny: Maturity as Penance." In *Romantic Imprisonment*, 83–91. New York: Columbia Univ. Press, 1986.
Avant, John Alfred. "*The Odd Woman*" (review). *New Republic*, Jan. 25, 1975.
Baker, J.F. "Publishers Weekly Interviews." *Publishers Weekly*, Jan. 15, 1982, 10.
Bell, P.K. Review of *The Southern Family. New Republic* 198 (Feb. 29, 1988): 38–41.
Betts, Doris. "More Like an Onion Than a Map." *Ms.*, March 1975, 41–43.
"Breaking Out." *Publishers Weekly* 227 (May 31, 1985): 30-34.
Brown, Laurie L. "Interviews with Seven Contemporary Writers." In *Women Writers of the Contemporary South*, edited by P.W. Prenshaw, 3–23. Jackson: Univ. Press of Mississippi, 1984.
Caldwell, Gail. "Living and Dying in Dixie: *A Southern Family*" (review). *Boston Globe*, Sept. 20, 1987.
Carter, Liane Kupferberg. "*The Finishing School*" (review). *New Directions for Women* 14, (July/Aug. 1985): 14.
Contemporary Authors, vols. 49–52. Detroit: Gale Research Co., 1975.
Crain, Jane Larkin. "*The Odd Woman and Dream Children*" (reviews). *New York Times Book Review*, Feb. 22, 1976.
Davenport, Guy, "*The Finishing School*" (review). *Sewanee Review* 94 (Spring 1986): 296–302.
Dickstein, Lore. "A Gallery of Bright Women and Pale Men" (review of *The Odd Woman*). *New York Times Book Review*, Oct. 20, 1974, 4.
"*Dream Children*" (review). *New York Times*, March 6, 1983, 39.
Duffy, Martha. "Women in Love." *New York Review of Books* 25 (June 20, 1978): 46–47.
Durban, Pam. "Private Chronicles of Bewilderment, Grief and Love" (*review of A Southern Family*). *Atlanta Journal*, Oct. 18, 1987.

Edwards, Thomas R. Review of *Dream Children. New York Review of Books,* April 1, 1976.

Ericson, Raymond. "Music Notes: A New Way to Make Operas." *New York Times,* July 1, 1979, D19.

Feinstein, Elaine. Review of *The Odd Woman. New Statesman,* Aug. 15, 1975.

Fox-Genovese, Elizabeth. "The New Female Literary Culture." *Antioch Review* 38 (Spring 1980: 193–217.

Frank, Katherine. "Gail Godwin's *Violet Clay." Iowa Journal of Literary Studies* 3 (1981): 118–22.

Frye, Joanne S. "Narrating the Self: The Autonomous Heroine in Gail Godwin's *Violet Clay." Contemporary Literature* 24, (Spring 1983): 66–85.

"Beyond Teleology: *Violet Clay* and *The Stone Angel."* In *Living Stories, Telling Lives: Women and the Novel in Contemporary Experience,* 109–42. Ann Arbor: Univ. of Michigan Press, 1986.

Fuller, Edmund. *"A Mother and Two Daughters"* (review). *Wall Street Journal,* Jan. 11, 1982, 20, 26.

"Furman, Laura. "Tale of a Southern Family Shattered by a Death" (review of *A Southern Family). Philadelphia Inquirer,* Sept. 27, 1987.

"Gail Godwin Interview." *Contemporary Authors, New Revised Series* 15 (May 23, 1984):157–59

Garrett, George. "Fables and Fabliaux of Our Times." *Sewanee Review* 85 (Winter 1977): 104–10.

Gaston, Karen C. " 'Beauty and the Beast' in Gail Godwin's *Glass People." Critique* 21 (1980): 94–102.

Gies, Judith. *"Mr. Bedford and the Muses"* (review). *New York Times,* Sept. 18, 1983, 14, 37.

Gimbel, Wendy. "Romance in the Ruins" (review of *A Southern Family). Savvy Magazine,* Nov. 1987.

Graeber, Laurel. "Sticking to the Insoluble" (interview). *New York Times Book Review,* Oct. 11, 1987, 28.

Graff, Gerald. "Tradition versus Theory." In *Professing Literature: An Institutional History,* 259–63. Chicago: Univ. of Chicago Press, 1987.

Gray, P. "Polite Forms of Aggression" (review of *A Southern Family). Time,* Oct. 5, 1987, 82.

Hendin, Josephine. "Renovated Lives" (review of *A Mother and Two Daughters). New York Times Book Review,* Jan. 10, 1982, 3 +.

Jamal, Zahir. "Pressed Men." *New Statesman* 96 (Aug. 18, 1978): 219–20.

Kearns, K. *"Mr. Bedford and the Muses"* (review). *New Republic* 189 (Dec. 19, 1983): 38–39.

———. "Godwin's Novel of the Truths That Don't Resolve Neatly." *News and Observer,* Oct. 4, 1987.

Krystal, Arthur. *"Mr. Bedford and the Muses"* (review). *New York Times,* Sept. 6, 1983, 3.

———. "The Best American Short Stories, 1985." *New York Times*, Sept. 29, 1985, 46.

———. "*The Finishing School*" (review). *New York Times*, Jan. 24, 1985, 23.

Lehmann-Haupt, Christopher. "*A Mother and Two Daughters*" (review). *New York Times*, Dec. 22, 1981, 22.

———. "*A Southern Family*" (review). *New York Times*, Sept. 21, 1987, 17.

"Letters." *New York Times Book Review*, May 26, 1985, 13–14. [Letters responding to Godwin's review of the *Norton Anthology of Literature by Women*].

Leverich, Kathleen. "*Mr. Bedford and the Muses*" (review). *Christian Science Monitor*, Sept. 2, 1983, B2.

Levine, Paul. "Recent Women's Fiction and the Theme of Personality". In *The Origins and Originality of American Culture*, edited by Tibor Frank. Budapest: Akademiai Kiado, 1984.

Levy, Barbara. "A Sentimental Education." *Women's Review of Books* 2 (Aug. 11, 1985): 17–18.

Lorsch, Susan E. "Gail Godwin's *The Odd Woman*: Literature and the Retreat from Life." *Critique* 20 (Winter 1978): 21–32.

Lowry, Beverly. "Back Home in Carolina" (review of *A Southern Family*). *New York Times Book Review*, Oct. 11, 1987, 1.

Lyons, G. "*Mr. Bedford and the Muses*" (review). *Newsweek* 102 (Sept. 12, 1983): 80+.

"Magnolia Leaves and Family Ruins" (review of *A Southern Family*). *Glamour Magazine*, Oct. 1987.

Malone, Michael. "The Sorrows and Squabbles of Going Back Home" (review of *A Southern Family*). *Newsday*, Oct. 4, 1987.

Mickelson, Anne Z. "Gail Godwin: Order and Accommodation." In *Reaching Out: Sensitivity and Order in Recent American Fiction by Women*, edited by A. Z. Mickelson, 68–86. Metuchen, N.J.: Scarecrow Press, 1979.

Milton, Edith. "Books Considered: *Violet Clay*." *New Republic*, July 8–15, 1979, 40–41.

Miner, Valerie. "*Mr. Bedford and the Muses*" (review). *Los Angeles Times*, Sept. 11, 1983, 14.

Mitchell, Lisa. "*The Finishing School*" (review). *Los Angeles Times*, Feb. 24, 1985, 2.

Mitgang, Herbert. "Gail Godwin Talks of Her Fiction and Her Muses." *New York Times*, Oct. 4, 1983, 2.

Monaghan, Charles. "*The Finishing School*" (review). *Wall Street Journal*, Feb. 13, 1985, 26–28.

"*A Mother and Two Daughters*" (review). *New York Times*, Dec. 5, 1982.

"*A Mother and Two Daughters*" (review). *New York Times*, Jan. 2, 1983.

Nance, Guin A. "Gail Godwin." *American Women Writers: A Critical Reference Guide from Colonial Times to the Present*, edited by Lina Mainiero, 2: 148–50. New York: Ungar, 1979.

Oates, Joyce Carol. *"The Perfectionists"* (review). *New York Times Book Review*, June 7, 1970, 5+.

———. "Transparent Creatures Caught in Myths." *Book World—Washington Post*, Oct. 1, 1972, 8, 10.

O'Conner, Patricia T. *"The Finishing School"* (review). *Publishers Weekly* 228 (Dec. 20, 1985): 64.

———. *"Glass People"* (review). *New York Times Book Review*, March 2, 1986, 34.

———. *"Violet Clay"* (review). *New York Times Book Review*, March 2, 1986, 34.

———. *"The Finishing School"* (review). *New York Times Book Review*, Dec. 7, 1986, 82.

"The Odd Woman" (review). *Book World—Washington Post*, Oct. 27, 1985, BW 16.

"The Perfectionists" (review). *New York Times*, Oct. 14, 1979, 55.

"The Perfectionists" (review). *Book World—Washington Post*, Oct. 27, 1985, BW 16.

Piercy, Marge. *"A Mother and Two Daughters"* (review). *Chicago Tribune Book World*, Jan. 10, 1982, 3.

Pinsker, Sanford. *"Dream Children"* (review). *Studies in Short Fiction*, Fall 1977, 408–9.

Pollitt, Katha. "Her Own Woman." *New York Times Book Review*, May 21, 1978, 10–11.

Pritchard, William H. "Novel Sex and Violence." *Hudson Review* 28 (Spring 1976): 147–60.

———. *"Violet Clay"* (review). *Hudson Review* 31 (Autumn 1978): 517–29.

Reed, J.D. "Postfeminism: Playing for Keeps." *Time*, Jan. 1983, 46–47.

Renwick, J. "An Interview with Gail Godwin." *Writer*, 1983, 15–17.

Rhodes, Carolyn. "Gail Godwin and the Ideal of Southern Womanhood." *Southern Quarterly* 21, (Summer 1983): 55–66. Also in *Women Writers of the Contemporary South*, edited by Peggy Whitman Prenshaw, 54–66. Jackson: Univ. Press of Mississippi, 1984.

Rowen, S. (review of *A Southern Family*). *Commonweal* 115 (March 25, 1988): 187–89.

Rubenstein, Roberta. "Adventures in Self-Discovery." *Progressive* 42 (Oct. 1978): 56–57.

Sadoff, Dianne F. *"The Odd Woman"* (review). *Antioch Review* 33 (1975).

Sage, Lorna. *"Violet Clay"* (review). *Times Literary Supplement*, Sept. 15, 1978, 1011.

Scholes, Robert. *"The Perfectionists"* (review). *Saturday Review*, Aug. 8, 1970, 37–38.

Scott, Anne Firor. *The Southern Lady: From Pedestal to Politics, 1830–1930*. Chicago: Univ. of Chicago Press, 1970.

Smith, Marilyn J. "The Role of the South in the Novels of Gail Godwin." *Critique* 21 (1979): 103–10.

Steinberg, Sybil. "A Truce with Time." *Publishers Weekly* 231 (May 15, 1987): 267.

Sweeney, Louise. "Gail Godwin: Collecting People's Stories like Seashells at the Beach." *Christian Science Monitor,* July 21, 1983, B1.

Taliaferro, Frances. "*The Finishing School*" (review). *New York Times,* Jan. 27, 1985, 7.

Totton, Nick. "Dream Children" (review). *Spectator,* Jan. 15, 1977.

Tyler, Anne. "Stretching the Short Story." *National Observer,* March 13, 1976, 21.

———. "All in the Family." *New Republic,* Feb. 17, 1982, 39–40.

"Uncle Wiggily's Karma and Other Childhood Memories." *New York Times Book Review* (Christmas Book Issue), Dec. 7, 1986, 46.

Weeks, Brigitte. "*A Mother and Two Daughters*" (review). *Ms.,* Jan. 1982, 40–41.

———. "*The Finishing School*" (review). *Ms.,* Feb. 1985; 75+.

Weeks, Carl Solana. *Dictionary of Literary Biography, vol. 6: American Novelists since World War II,* 105–9. Detroit: Gale Research Co., 1980.

Welch, Kathleen. "An Interview with Gail Godwin." *Iowa Journal of Literary Studies* 3, (1981): 77–86.

Wood, Susan. "*The Finishing School*" (review). *Book World—Washington Post,* Feb. 3, 1985, 1.

Yardley, Jonathan. "Writing about Our Real Lives: Godwin's Novel Breaks the Best Seller Rule: *A Mother and Two Daughters*." *Washington Post,* Feb. 7, 1983, C1.

———. "Gail Godwin: Reflection and Renewal: *A Southern Family*" (review). *Book World—Washington Post,* Sept. 13, 1987.

Zimmerman, P.D. "*Dream Children*" (review). *Newsweek* 87 (Feb. 23, 1976): 86.

JAYNE ANNE PHILLIPS

Women's Narrative and the Recreation of History

Phyllis Lassner

At the conclusion of "Rayme," a story in Jayne Anne Phillips's new collection called *Fast Lanes*, the narrator recalls her experiences with a group of drifting students in the early seventies. She names specific addresses and dates, as well as the objects her friends use, destroy, or just throw away—their drugs, their food, their ramshackle furniture. Yet what fixes their identities and stories in the reader's mind are not these details but our experience of following the narrator as she transforms her memory of these characters' chaotic lives into a pattern of continuity and connection. In her narrative each person becomes part of a cycle of connection and disruption "to continue the same story in even more fragmented fashion. . . . Our destinations appeared to be interchangeable pauses in some long, lyric transit. This time that was nearly over, these years, seemed as close to family as most of us would ever get" (32-33).[1]

Machine Dreams, Phillips's widely acclaimed first novel, takes her image of "lyric transit" and expands it into an epic of a West Virginia family between the years of World War II and the Vietnam War. The novel shapes the fragmented, acutely individual memories and dreams of Mitch, Jean, Billy, and Danner into a story of connection and disruption. As isolated as each character often feels from the others, from their pasts and from imagining their futures, they make connections as their voices create a web of family and social activity made up of similarities and repetitions in their experiences. They may not speak directly to each other, but through the narration of their dreams and memories, the voices of Jean and her daughter, Danner, the letters of Jean's husband, Mitch, and their son, Billy, and the involved yet detached voice of Phillips's narrator speak to us, to themselves, and to each other. The separate sections of the novel in which these narrative events take place come to overlap in the reader's experience. As we recognize images repeating themselves again and again—snow, cars, the dead being dug up or in—we create connections in the characters' experiences amid their inexorable separation.

Phillips has talked about the book in terms of the tragedy that traditional male-female roles wreak on people when those roles no longer exist in society. Indeed, as each section unfolds, misunderstandings, misperceptions, or the elusiveness of others show the disintegration of traditional middle-class expectations about family and community steadfastness. To be sure, the voices of Phillips's narrators and their individual histories convey a sense of ongoing community in their specific regional and social activities. Yet as Jean contemplates divorce, as Danner cannot stay in one place once Billy is killed, their voices also guide us to read their stories as both a recognition of discontinuity and an equally strong plea for continuity and relatedness. Only the women narrators, however, can achieve this dual expression and in terms radically different from traditional expectations. Unlike Mitch, who rails against the breakup of the family, despite its inability to sustain him, Jean and Danner restructure its meaning for themselves. Going beneath the surface of their differences that they feel unable to express openly, they tap into each other's dreams and memories to create a narrative tapestry out of their deepest feelings about their intransigent separateness and yearning for connection.

The urgency of the narrator's pleas is revealed immediately in the novel's title. *Machine Dreams* conflates words usually associated with two separate and distinct spheres—machine as concrete object and dreams as a combination of elusive images reconstructed by memory, fear, and desire. Conflated, the materiality of the one lends substance to the other, making dreams as much a palpable reality as machines. In *Black Tickets*, Phillips's first collection of short stories, objects reflect human senses and feeling and seem to enact significant emotional realities of their own. The cars, bulldozers, trains, and houses of *Machine Dreams* become the stuff of dreams and only then reveal their significance to characters and readers alike. Dreams, in fact, take center stage in *Machine Dreams*. On the one hand, reading the events of the characters' lives is like experiencing a dream; they seem to take place in slow motion, their movements momentarily suspended in time and space, their ordinariness heightened by the emotion in a narrator's voice. In contrast, dreams are narrated as though they are the dramatic center of life, their compressed events given the weight of a determining plot.

Phillips's method of conflation expresses vision of acute ambivalence about selfhood in the American family. The very desire for relatedness and continuity produces rage at the failure to be recognized as individual and autonomous. Dependency leads not to mutual respect for individual differences but to aggressive playing out of one's needs. What happens in war begins in the family, and the family replays the aggressions and hostilities of war. Phillips's highly individualized characters are at odds with themselves and with each other in their equally and simultaneously creative and destructive urges, expressing desires for responsibility and regression, for civilization and anarchy. Mitch dreams of feeling both disgust at the violence of war and of his own aggressive urge as he bulldozes the war dead. Jean dreams about a community watching bodies being dug up in the aftermath of a family murder. The images of "reasonless suffering" and mass voyeurism in Jean's dream are relieved by her vision of her mother expressing hope for those people who "come together and want to understand." The connection between dreams of war and those of family and community life is not oxymoronic. As an old man tells the child Jean in her adult dream, "Not a pretty sight, little girl, but history is made here today" (100).

In Phillips's creative imagination, there are compelling differences between how we participate in events and how and why we write stories about them. We write stories in order to make sense of the nonrational events and dreams that comprise our ambivalent and idiosyncratic histories. That is, we create fictional narratives that take us out of the private fears and wishes that accompany our sleeping and waking actions by making connections between our story and those of other people, times, and places. Our fictional narratives are proof to us that if we cannot create "a pretty sight," there is meaning in continuity because between our story and others, we have "made history."

Phillips's novel, which is structured as a series of dreams and memories of different people, creates connections among those who remain isolated.[2] Whatever alienation her characters experience, their dreams and memories reveal the emotional fusions they feel. The narrative strategy of dreams condenses all characters and contexts into aspects of one's identification with other people, places, and even times. But dreams also isolate the self while charading as a drama of self and other. In Mitch's dream of Katie's funeral, he and Katie become interchangeable as though "all the numbers changed around and Katie had come out wearing his. All the time had caught up with him, all the floating around since he was a kid" (89). His fear of death in the war and his wish for family continuity become intertwined with a vision of Katie's death. The psychological logic of the dream centers on the image of "floating," which connects Mitch's experience of homelessness and lack of family with death. Mitch's fear strikes at the very heart of his ability to figure out what or who he really is as it fuses his memories. Refusing to sort out fear from external realities, to translate emotional history into narrative history, leaves him confused about his past, his present, and his future. Allowing his memories to be overtaken by a dream ensures that he belongs nowhere and is disconnected.

Jean and Danner experience dream and memory differently. As they recognize themselves in each other, the past in the present, and the present as a foretelling of the future, they feel a need to sort out their fears from their hopes, to decode the language of dreams and memory. As Jean recalls for her daughter, "Later you look back and see one thing foretold by another. But when you're young, these connections are secrets" (4). Stated so early in the novel, Jean's pronouncement serves to foretell the purpose of narrative for Phillips. Narrative as the history of people's interdependence establishes continuity as an ideology in an age of discontinuity. With each section of the novel about a different character in different times and places, Phillips demonstrates the importance of telling "the same story" in order to answer a question she poses in two works, *Machine Dreams* and *Fast Lanes*: "Where were we all really going, and when would we ever arrive?" (FL, 33). "What journey was this, and where were we all going?" (MD, 307).

The continuity of the characters' identities depends on their being able to internalize the memories and dreams of other characters; only as they are able to become conscious of this process do they enact their own stabilizing continuity. Only the women, however, turn out to be capable. The sense of continuity between Phillips's various works and among parts of each work depends on mothers and daughters transmitting their identities to each other as they transform their memories and dreams into narratives, as they become storytellers. Although several of Phillips's first-person narrators are men—for example, Mitch and Billy and Mickey in "How Mickey Made It"—each one merely lives out his dreams and memories. Narrative for them is a translation of events into the mystery stories that make up their lives; as in Mitch's recollection of Reb and Marthella driving into the river, these events occur "like something in a dream" (41), to be experienced in feeling but to remain unfathomable. Such a translation process cannot produce self-consciousness, only the conversion of one kind of emotional energy into another. Perhaps this is why Mitch and Billy identify so strongly with machines. As cars, bulldozers, trains, and planes become images in dreams, they begin to reflect the kind of self-enclosed production of energy suggested by the image of a cement-mixer going round and round: a kind of circular sublimation, if we translate the image back into Mitch's consciousness, of drive and energy into drive and energy. Without the creation of self-conscious narrative histories, even the letters of Mitch and Billy require explication by female narrators. Their dreams acquire meaning through the women's reflections upon their own dreams. In the story "Blue Moon," comprised of characters from *Machine Dreams*, Danner, as witness-turned-storyteller, assumes the responsibility of ensuring continuity even in the face of a suicide attempt by her brother's girlfriend. "And I was witness, connected to her; the boundary I'd imagined between myself and anything I saw or touched, was gone" (FL, 121). As in her mother's dream, witnessing becomes an act of connection. Following that, making up a story about what one sees erases emotional, temporal, and spatial boundaries between self and other while ensuring the self's individuality. Narration mitigates the sense of total loss men experience but cannot transform.

Characters in all of Phillips's fiction experience losses of loved ones, of family homes, of a sense of the past, or of options for the future. That men cannot transform their losses into narrative fictions leads to their becoming weak or even disappearing. The letters that Mitch and Billy write from the war front reflect their lack of attempts to make sense of events that therefore must remain inexplicable to them. Mitch's observation about dropping the atom bomb on Japan is the hallmark of his reflections. "No one really understood what had happened at first" (44). Similarly, despite or perhaps because of the nature of the narrative Mitch creates, the story of the Chinese leper remains "a secret" to him (45). Mitch comes home from the war to look for normality; he marries Jean, goes into business, fathers two children. But these experiences remain secrets to him as well. Burying his wartime memorabilia in a trunk in the attic signals how he buries his ability to achieve continuity. By the time Jean divorces him, Mitch has retired early, drawing a disability pension and selling "a doubtful brand of life insurance from a makeshift office in the basement of the[ir] house" (298).

His narrative, called "The Secret Country," is punctuated by spaces without writing: information "no one ever told me" and questions he never asks (25). Mitch cannot fill in the blanks because he is complicit in the maintenance of secrecy. He refuses to sift through his memories or make meaning of them; instead he reports hearsay and describes only the objects that seem to him to be the sum total of reality. Thus, he does not remember what his father looked like, "except from pictures," and never questions who his real mother is and what happened to her (25). He dismisses all evidence except material facts, answering the question "what's the difference" with "it don't matter" (28).

Mitch's failure to use memory to answer questions forces him to relive the inexplicable in his dreams. His dreams, however, are no comfort, for they expose the terror that secrets contain by dramatizing it. The conflation in Phillips's title becomes the logical method to show how this terror works in Mitch's dream of Katie's funeral. Here we see his dreaming mechanism conflate two acts of violence from his past that remain undeciphered in his memory: seeing his father fire on a pet raccoon and firing "again and again" at a Japanese soldier in New Guinea during the war. In the dream he hears rifle shots that "kept on as though in celebration or ceremony" (89). We are not told of any associations Mitch makes between these events, his memories, and his dream; they gain meaning only through the narrator and the structure of Phillips's novel. The narrative structure tells us that the dream occurs after an incident in which Mitch takes Katie to the movies to see *Peter and the Wolf*. "On the bright screen the cartoon kid led a band of animals through snow, deep snow, holding his worthless popgun and menaced by thick blue trees" (83). The popgun triggers a memory of firing compulsively at the Japanese soldier, which, in turn, was brought on by his spontaneous vision of "the fields behind the farm at home" (85). Immediately following the war memory, there is a fire alarm in the theater, and Mitch carries Katie out and takes her home. It is while resting after this ordeal that he has his dream.

Working parallel to the structure of dreams, the narrative constructs associations between all the instances of "firing" in Mitch's experience. Unlike Mitch's consciousness, however, the narrative self-consciously explores the implications of the word *firing* as event and as trope. The process of discovering similarities intensifies the experience of fear and highlights the location of home as the source of violence and its resulting terror. For the reader this process makes meaning of the narrative strategies of memory and dream. Because Mitch cannot or will not sort out the images his unconscious acts out, he remains victimized by the terrible violence he continues to feel. Under the weight of repressed explanations, his memories are enacted in dreams where despite his efforts to gain control, to contain violence, he persistently loses. His dream of bulldozing the war dead creates an experience of the "horrible and terrible [smell] of death" associated with "some gigantic fetid woman sick to death between her legs" (59). The antidote to this terror in the dream is Mitch's control over his machine—his bulldozer. Lowering the dozer blade without realizing it, he feels "the give of the earth" as he pushes his bulldozer into action (60). But the crying of the dead overwhelms the comforting sound of the machine. His memory of the bulldozing reveals the source of the smell to be Warrenholtz's body out of control, besieged by cramps. Their jeep and Mitch's gun provide no antidote to the violence they feel compelled to enact and that over-takes them.

The title *Machine Dreams* works as a metaphor for the way memory persists against those who would resist its potency. By appearing in an even more terrifying form as dreams, memories become impossible to resist. Machines, which are supposed to be instruments of control, become, in dreams, the tools of the repressed, undermining control. Thus, those who rely on machines to save them from the terrors and losses of the past find that machines appear in dreams as grim reapers of the past. The train that dropped off the leper is like all the machines in Mitch's experience. They are vehicles in which he invests his hopes for mastery but which invariably, in his dreams, he drives out of control.

The inability to make meaning out of memory drives it under-ground into the world of nightmares. Here consciousness yields to the purely emotional impact of past experience; in the world of dreams, all external realities are translated back into the fears and desires that underlie the events of one's life. The conflations of past and present experience and the interchangeability of character in Mitch's dreams do not imply that he enjoys this as an experience of continuity or connection but rather that he fears losing himself in an easy exchange. In all of Mitch's narrative, in his letters, in his story of his early life and background, or in his dreams, he both fears separation as a loss of self and emphasizes it as a defense against such loss. The fear of isolation is enacted in his story of the Chinese leper, a man in exile with no hope of returning to his homeland or to his family. The leper is an isolate whose death, according to Mitch, is the logical conclusion to not being "sure anymore who he was" (45). Like Mitch the leper has no story of his own; he cannot communicate, not only because of language differences, but because his disease prevents anyone from getting close. The leper illustrates Mitch's belief that memory "don't matter"; it doesn't make any difference because it can't restore one's identity based on connection with a family home. Memory only reminds one of the continued and endless separation from a past that remains as mysterious as the way in which it is taken away from us.

Mitch is complicit in the destruction of his past and of his continuity. The story of his background and childhood is bulldozed not only in history but in his dreams and in his failure to translate memory into meaning. To be sure, the farm that nourished an extended family is ultimately parceled out and sold to the mines that excavate it away, but losing the place of his home leaves Mitch feeling "like I'd lost my memory and might be anyone" (45). Interchangeability thus results from a sense of loss that leads to a feeling that his identity is diffused without a family place to ground it in. Because he cannot create a narrative fiction that assuages these losses, he not only loses his sense of individuality but never sees that all through his history his individuality was sacrificed to a fiction that wasn't working. For Mitch's memories show us, if not him, that his family was always fragmented and never sustaining. The aunt who raises him may be his mother, according to the gloss provided by her narrative in the short story "Bess," in which case his story of his mother is a wish-fulfillment fantasy. There is no sustaining family structure in his or in anyone else's experience in Phillips's fiction, only the connections made by working out a pattern of empathetically leaving one person alone to sort out what sustains him or her.

The culmination of Mitch's loss occurs when his son bails out of a machine—a helicopter in Vietnam—and is missing in action forever. The hereditary links to this tragic but inevitable conclusion are clear. Like Mitch in World War II and on the home front, Billy has counted on the palpable strength of machines to carry him over and beyond the violence he can neither understand nor explain. Billy has felt his father's awe of machines. In two powerfully resonant scenes, the fascination with machines is shown to be childlike and frought with fantasy. Billy dreams of his father holding him to look into the drum of a cement truck. Although his father's big hands seem in control, they disappear. In this image and in one of his Uncle Clayton sitting in a desk chair, the dream foretells the mortality of both older men. For shortly thereafter, Clayton dies in his desk chair, and of course, after a postwar career of operating and then selling machinery, Mitch's primary occupation by the end of the novel is sitting at his desk in the basement. In another scene Billy wakes Danner early one morning to ride their bikes out to the airfield to see the planes before an air show begins. They climb into the plane, exploring its cockpit. Like Mitch, Billy endows the machine with the ability to provide power. As in Billy's earlier dream of peering into the cement truck, this belief derives from the father's demonstration that machines are powerful and useful because they can be explored and understood; unlike memories and dreams, machines yield their secrets without risk to the self. Despite this connection between father and son, however, machines provide no pathway to continuity, only an illusion of power. The helicopter Billy believes in must be abandoned in battle as Billy and his friend Luke bail out, never to be seen again.

Billy's final appearance, however, in Danner's recollection of his letters, contrasts the futile reliance on machines, on material facts, with a plea for a more fluid meaning of connection as the key to continuity. Danner's explication of the letter provides a key to the meaning of connection in both narrative and human terms. Danner's only solace at losing Billy is to remember his reference in a letter to "the Luke is my shepherd," a play on a prayer that confirms that although he is lost, he was not alone (317). Danner's reading provides the gloss to her mother's assertion that "family was more than blood relation" (19), that connection is experienced metaphorically, because to rely on the literalness of words is to keep past and present, self and other, discrete but also isolated and unconnected. Mitch remains alone and lost in not finding meaning in the "official" government language of Billy's disappearance. While Danner finds meaning in a letter from Billy's friend, Robert Taylor, Mitch only accepts it as "hearsay," an untrustworthy personal document requiring official truth. Stories, or the language of personal experience, contain no intrinsic truth for Mitch, and he will not endow them with meaning. The appearance of hearsay in his own narrative early in the novel and now at the end shows that whatever truths they contain, stories need interpretation to bear meaning. But his need for meaning to be denotative, inherent in the literalness of an officially sanctioned language, for language to be as palpable as machines, is as much a dead end as the initial telegram announcing Billy as missing.

As Danner recognizes, when the army representative comes to offer the government's regrets along with the news of Billy's missing status, to literalize language is to destroy the possibility of making meaning. The army's words are unsatisfactory precisely because they yield no connotations; its language is as dead as its subject, but as in its insistence on Billy being missing, the real meaning of its words is missing: dead. Mitch's pursuit of dead language will ensure that he will be alone. He will isolate himself from the connections made possible only through expansive interpretation. Danner and her mother will make Billy part of their identities by fusing their memories and dreams of him; therefore, they will never really lose him. Meaning for them is generated by the relationship between story and audience; for them there are no official keys to meaning that can be consulted as Cliff Notes to understanding. The only path to understanding is through piecing together emotional associations they make between memories and dreams and then creating an organizing principle that gives shape to their associations. Meaning derives from constructing a narrative out of what one feels about the past experiences that, in turn, lend their images to memories and dreams. Billy dies of an inherited disease: reliance on the machinery of unreflective living. But in his war experiences, unlike those of his father, he senses the meaning to his narrative as he writes to Danner, "These guys are the only country I know of and they're what I'm defending" (291). Identity and continuity are achieved only through human connection expressed in figurative, emotionally charged language.

The gift of recognizing that the key to meaning lies in the figurative language of narrative is given to the women in Phillips's fiction.[3] Each generation of women achieves continuity by incorporating her mother's capacity for creating and reading stories, dreams, and memories as an interpretive process. Upon her mother's death, Rayme, in the short story in *Fast Lanes*, wears her mother's expression to say she hadn't lost her. In another story from the same collection, a pregnant woman narrates a series of impressions to her unborn child. Similarly, the story "Something That Happened" is about a daughter becoming her mother as she mothers her mother who lives alone after her divorce. To mother or to be a daughter and become one's mother is equivalent to narrative acts in Phillips's fiction—sequential, patterned, and causal. In "Blue Moon," where the characters of *Machine Dreams* reappear, Danner articulates what she enacts in the novel. "I had plans. Maybe I was in training to become my mother, become that kind of supremely competent, unfulfilled woman, vigilant and damaged" (101). The vigilance of

Phillips's women lies in their need to keep "structures intact by attending to surfaces, trying to conceal the fact that [they] belonged nowhere" (FL, 91-92). These surfaces trigger memories that become the repository of meaning and the foundations of identity. Like Mitch, Danner "didn't want to be the one who would remember everything." Doing so gives her what she calls "déjà vu," a sensation in which a pattern of meaning is formed as one experiences the "surfaces" of past and present as images of feelings about the places and people those surfaces represent (FL, 93). Danner and her mother, Bess, and the various women narrators of the short stories bear the responsibility of transforming these patterns of memory into stories. As they are always about family, these narratives become the instruments of continuous identity in a time of belonging nowhere.

The dreams of Danner and Jean differ from those of Mitch in several important ways. Jean's dream of watching dead bodies being dug up is triggered by her effort to connect with the past, to interpret memory. She purposely drives to the cemetery where her mother is buried, falls asleep in the car, and dreams. Her dream thus appears to result from her need to understand the meaning of loss, not only in death, but in living relationships. On the way to the cemetery, she reflects on the meaning of anniversaries of the deaths of loved ones and associates them with wedding anniversaries. She connects her mother's marriage with her own as she wonders whether her mother loved her father in the beginning of their marriage. Reaching the cemetery on a road just beyond Mitch's concrete yard, she suddenly feels depressed. The gravestones she sees, now linked to the *concreteness* of Mitch's efforts to build continuity, become markers of discontinuity, signifying his misperception of what ties families together. Weeping loudly, she feels the presence of Mitch's new car and falls asleep and dreams. This machine dream, however, does not leave her perplexed and lost, for unlike Mitch, Jean later ruminates upon the dream. She remembers the incident that triggered the events of her dream, an isolated event in her memory, "a sort of myth" (111). But Jean demystifies the dream by connecting its images to her past and present and by asking, "Didn't people have to do more than just endure? Didn't they have to be smart, as well, and know what things meant?" (112). Jean feels she inherits this capacity from her mother, a strength she "loved most and what she hated" (112).

A significant part of the connection Jean feels with her mother derives from the sense Danner describes as déjà vu, that she had journeyed "to some lost place still existing alongside this one." This place is now defined by the fluid emotional boundaries experienced between mother and daughter and interpreted through the patterns established in their figurative language, in their talk and in their narratives.[4] For Jean her mother's death was traumatic because it was a time when "there was no more talking . . . no one whose past she knew, who knew her" (101). Nevertheless, the connection between mother and daughter is so strong that during her mother's last days Jean recalls feeling a sense that her mother's consciousness now floated "forward and backward, witness to all that happened" (102). Like the narrator of the story "Fast Lanes" whose wanderings she describes as "floating" (FL, 52) and Danner who narrates "Blue Moon" and calls herself "witness," such sensations remove the "boundary between myself and anything I saw or touched" (FL, 121). Unlike Mitch's experience of "floating," however, the women feel no loss of self, only gain. Thus, at the time of her mother's dying, Jean feels that "she dreamed her mother's dreams, not hers" (102). Such sensations elide historic time and lead to a kind of thinking that conflates and compresses sequential time. To translate such thinking into comprehensive narrative requires the creation of a pattern that shows inevitable continuity between generations of women. The sympathetic identification between mother and daughter leads each to recognize the need to achieve continuity, "a long lyric transit" through creating and interpreting stories.

The spool of thread Jean hides in order to find an excuse to go out to the cemetery suggests connection to her mother and daughter. Such connection is impossible between Jean and Mitch because he remains silent, a state of entropy that recalls the death of Jean's mother, but worse because he keeps his consciousness all to himself. The shock of recognition that Jean feels at the cemetery leads her to recognize that the failure of her marriage originates in Mitch's silence, in his inability to recall and transmit the past as an act of interconnection. Continuity is not possible between husband and wife, as it was not between Jean's mother and father. "A long, lyric transit" is only conceived, born and interpreted through mother and daughter. Jean keeps her relationship to her mother alive by first "talk[ing] to her in my mind, and answer[ing] myself with memories of things she'd said" and then "when I knew I had a daughter, I was so thankful—like my own mother had come back to me" (17, 22). In naming her daughter Danner after her mother's family, Jean conceives of her as a living and linguistic sign of continuity; Danner will generate meaning both in human and in narrative relationships. She will be threaded to her own mother and her mother's mother. A woman who "held her own," Jean's mother personifies the aim of the women's narrative: it endows autonomy within connection, giving them a place to belong.[5]

In *Machine Dreams* the women create a succession of lives as mothers and daughters transmit their perspectives of family history. While this interchange of identity and resemblance may suggest a lack of individuality and autonomy, all characters are given distinct voices in the narrator's process of creating meaning. Thus, Danner's name, the hallmark of her identity and significance, is the linguistic sign that ensures both her distinction and her continuity. *Danner* becomes a crucial element in a sequential, patterned story that endows everyone with an autonomy they can't have as long as they interpret family relationships only in literal terms—as long as language is a material reality and not figurative.

Unlike Mitch, who tries to create identity, family life, and continuity by literalizing the meaning of family home—building a house for his family—the women find meaning in the human connections that reside in homes and give them life. For them meaningful space is created in the relationships that are translated into narrative structures, where each discovers the other in herself but her difference as well. Discovery of these interconnections and differences leads inevitably to the creation of home and family as metaphors for each other. Thus, although Danner responds to Billy's death with hate for her country, she can't leave. Equating her divided country with her family, she explains: "But my parents are my country, my divided country. By going to California, I'd made it to the far frontiers, but I'd never leave my country. I never will" (324).

Although boundaries between self and other, between sequential time and personal association become fused in memory and in dream, they form a complex definition of space as home, the place from which all the women wish to escape but which nevertheless holds the key to identity. The women narrators in Phillips's work define narrative space as a place where family space can be experienced figuratively so that both autonomy and interrelatedness become possible—"a zone free of interference and boundaries" (326). Here neither is threatened by seeing oneself only as part of a solid, literally defined unit: the family. In their stories the women interpret and go on, stretching boundaries between events and people through the metaphoric connections they recognize and create between themselves and others. They thus weave an intersubjective space that overcomes the divisions created by war and divorce, death and silence.[6]

NOTES

1. In this essay, Jayne Anne Phillips's books are identified in the following way, and page numbers are given in parentheses in the text: *Fast Lanes* (FL); *Machine Dreams* (MD).

2. The relationship between memory and dream is explored by Mary Jacobus in her essay "Freud's Mnemonics: Women, Screen Memories, and Feminist Nostalgia," where she points out that "memory is like dreaming not only in its distortions and displacements, but in its paradoxical relation to a forgetting that is always, though unconscious, deliberate and purposive" (*Michigan Quarterly Review* 26 [Winter 1987]: 119).

3. Margaret Homans brings together the French and American psychoanalytic perspectives on women's writing in her discussion of women writers' uses of figurative and literalized language in the nineteenth century. *Bearing the Word: Language and Female Experience in Nineteenth-Century Writing* (Chicago: Univ. of Chicago Press, 1986).

4. For discussion of how women's early childhood development leads to their management of fluid ego boundaries, see Nancy Chodorow, *The Reproduction of Mothering: Psychoanalysis and the Sociology of Gender* (Berkeley: Univ. of California Press, 1978); Carol Gilligan, *In a Different Voice: Psychological Theory and Women's Development* (Cambridge: Harvard Univ. Press, 1982); Marianne Hirsch, "Mothers and Daughters," *Signs* 7 (Autumn 1981): 200–222.

5. See Susan Rubin Suleiman for a discussion of questions related to motherhood, daughterhood, and writing. "Writing and Motherhood," *The (M)other Tongue: Essays in Feminist Psychoanalytic Interpretation*, ed. Shirley Nelson Garner, Claire Kahane, and Madelon Sprengnether. (Ithaca: Cornell Univ. Press, 1986).

6. The idea of intersubjective space derives from Jessica Benjamin's discussion of how women develop a creative sense of their relationship to external realities. See "A Desire of One's Own: Psychoanalytic Feminism and Intersubjective Space," *University of Wisconsin-Milwaukee Center for Twentieth-Century Studies Working Paper No. 2* (Fall 1985).

A Bibliography of Writings by JAYNE ANNE PHILLIPS

Phyllis Lassner

BOOKS

Sweethearts. Short Beach, Conn.: Truck Press, 1976. [Limited ed.]
Counting. New York: Vehicle Editions, 1978. [Limited ed.]
How Mickey Made It. St. Paul: Bookslinger Press, 1981. [Limited ed.]

The Secret Country. Winston-Salem, N.C.: Palaemon, 1982. [Limited ed.]
Black Tickets. New York: Delacorte, 1979.
Machine Dreams. New York: E.P. Dutton/Seymour Lawrence, 1985.
Fast Lanes. Short Beach, Conn.: Truck Press, 1984; New York: E.P. Dutton/
    Seymour Lawrence, 1987.

ARTICLES, REVIEWS, STORIES

"Souvenir" (excerpt from *Black Tickets*). *Redbook,* Nov. 1979, 41.
"How Mickey Made It." *Rolling Stone,* Feb. 5, 1981, 28–30.
"Reminiscence to a Daughter." *Atlantic,* Nov. 1981, 32–40.
"Rayme—A Memoir of the Seventies." *Granta: Dirty Realism-New Writing
    from America* 8 (Winter 1983): 33–42.
"Danner, 1965." *Granta: The True Adventures of the Rolling Stones* 12
    (Winter 1984): 147–66.
"Reply to Letter to Editor." *Granta: The True Adventures of the Rolling
    Stones* 12 (Winter 1984): 255.
"Bess." *Esquire,* Aug. 1984, 58–60.
Introduction to *The Pushcart Prize IX: Best of the Small Presses,* edited by
    Bill Henderson. Wainscott, New York: Pushcart Press, 1984.
Review of *White Noise,* by Don DeLillo. *New York Times Book Review,* Jan.
    13, 1985, 1.
"Fast Lanes." *Granta: More Dirt: The New American Fiction* 19 (Fall 1986):
    47–71.
Review of *Persian Nights,* by Diane Jackson. *New York Times Book Review,*
    April 5, 1987, 8.
Introduction to *Maggie: A Girl of the Streets and Other Short Fiction,* by
    Stephen Crane. New York: Bantam Classics, 1988.

A Bibliography of Writings about
JAYNE ANNE PHILLIPS

Phyllis Lassner

Adams, Michael. "Jayne Anne Phillips." *Dictionary of Literary Biography,*
    1980, 297–300. Detroit: Gale Research Co., 1981.
Allen, Bruce. "*Machine Dreams*" (review). *Christian Science Monitor,* Nov.
    5, 1984, 21.
Baker, James N. "Being Left by a Whisper." *Newsweek,* Oct. 22, 1979, 116,
    118.

Benet, Mary Kathleen. "*Machine Dreams*" (review). *Times Literary Supplement*, Nov. 23, 1984, 1359.

"Boston's Best Writer: Jayne Anne Phillips." *Boston Magazine*, Aug. 1985, 148.

Browne, Joseph. "*Black Tickets*" (review). *America* 141 (Dec. 8, 1979): 376.

Burke, Jeffrey. "Ineffable Pleasures" (review of *Black Tickets*). *Harper's*, Sept. 1979, 99–100.

Carter, Liane Kupferberg. "*Machine Dreams*" (review). *New Directions for Women* 13 (Nov./Dec. 1984):23.

Clemens, Walter. "*Machine Dreams*" (review). *Newsweek*, July 16, 1984, 7 +.

Cushman, Keith. "*Black Tickets*" (review). *Studies in Short Fiction* 18 (Winter 1981): 92–94.

Dillard, Annie. "Critics' Christmas Choices." *Commonweal* 106 (1979): 693–94.

Edelstein, D. "The Short Story of Jayne Anne Phillips: She Transforms Isolation and Dark Obsession into Exquisite Prose." *Esquire*, Dec. 1985, 106–8.

Edwards, T.R. "*Black Tickets*" (review). *New York Review of Books* 27 (March 6, 1980): 43–45.

"*Fast Lanes*" (review). *Kirkus Reviews*, Feb. 15, 1987, 251.

"*Fast Lanes*" (review). *Publishers Weekly*, Feb. 27, 1987, 152.

"*Fast Lanes*" (review). *Library Journal*, March 15, 1987, 91.

"*Fast Lanes*" (review). *Tribune Books*, April 19, 1987, 6.

"*Fast Lanes*" (review). *Book World—Washington Post*, April 26, 1987, 9.

"*Fast Lanes*" (review). *Boston Review* 12 (June 1987): 25.

"*Fast Lanes*" (review). *Ms.*, June 1987, 18.

"*Fast Lanes*" (review). *Time*, June 1, 1987, 70.

"*Fast Lanes*" (review). *Observer*, Sept. 6, 1987, 25.

Gies, J. "*Machine Dreams*" (review). *Ms.*, June 1984, 33–34.

Gilbert, Celia. Interview with Jayne Anne Phillips. *Publishers Weekly* 225 (June 8, 1984): 65–67.

Gilbert, Harriett. "*Machine Dreams*" (review). *New Statesman* (Nov. 9, 1984): 32.

Gorra, Michael. "*Machine Dreams*" (review). *Boston Review* 9 (Aug. 1984): 27.

Greenwood, Gillian. "How It Happens." *Spectator* 253 (Nov. 3, 1984): 28.

Grumbach, Doris. "Stories Caged in Glass." *Books and Arts* 1 (Nov. 23, 1979): 8–9.

Hulbert, Ann. "*Machine Dreams*" (review). *New Republic*, Dec. 24, 1984, 36.

———. "Jayne Anne Phillips." *New Republic*, Sept. 2, 1985, 25.

Hutchison, Paul E. "*Machine Dreams*" (review). *Library Journal*, July 1984, 1348.

Irving, John. "Stories with Voiceprints." *New York Times Book Review*, Sept. 30, 1979, 13, 28.

Iyer, P. "*Fast Lanes*" (review). *Time*, June 1, 1987, 70.

"Jayne Anne Phillips." *Harper's Bazaar* Oct. 1984, 213 + .

"Jayne Anne Phillips's *Fast Lanes*." Booklist, Feb. 1, 1987, 809.

"Jayne Anne Phillips's *Fast Lanes*." *New York Times Book Review*, April 11, 1987, 11.

Jenks, Tom. "How Writers Live Today." *Esquire*, Aug. 1985, 123.

Kakutani, Michiko. "*Machine Dreams*" (review). *New York Times*, June 12, 1984, C17.

————. "Escape and Memory." *New York Times*, April 11, 1987.

Lasdun, James. "*Machine Dreams*" (review). *Encounter*, Feb. 1985, 42.

Lee, Hermione. "Long Lost America." *Observer*, Oct. 28, 1984, 25.

"*Machine Dreams*" (review). *Book World—Washington Post*, Dec. 21, 1979.

Maguire, Gregory. "*Machine Dreams*" (review). *Horn Book*, Nov./Dec. 1984, 793.

"Major Authors in Minor Presses." *New York Times Book Review*, Dec. 23, 1984, 4.

"Making It Big at 30." *Harper's Bazaar*, Oct. 1984, 206.

McGowan, W. "*Machine Dreams*: Retooling Fiction." *Washington Month*, March 17, 1985, 42 + .

McInerney, Jay. "Lost on the Open Road" (review of *Fast Lanes*). *New York Times Book Review*, May 3, 1987, 7.

Merkin, Daphne. "Mastering the Short Story." *New Leader* 62 (Dec. 3, 1979): 18–19.

Moyer, L.L. "*Machine Dreams*" (review). *Christianity and Crisis* 46 (July 14, 1986): 253–54.

Nelson, Peter. "An Interview with Jayne Anne Phillips." *Vis a Vis*, May 1987, 80.

Norris, Gloria, ed. *New American Short Stories: The Writers Select Their Own Favorites*. New York: NAL Books/Plume, 1987.

Overland, Janneken, and Moi, Toril. "Du er det su Ser: Samtale med Jayne Anne Phillips." *Venduet* 37 (1983): 23–33.

Peterson, Mary. "Earned Praise." *North American Review* 264 (Winter 1979): 77–78.

Phillips, Robert. "Recurring Battle Scars" (review of *Machine Dreams*). *Commonweal* 111 (Oct. 19, 1984): 567–68.

Pooley, E. "Jayne Anne Phillips' American Dream." *New York*, July 23, 1984, 14.

"Portrait of Jayne Anne Phillips." *Harper's Bazaar*, Oct. 1984, 213.

Prescott, P.S. *Newsweek*, Oct. 22, 1979, 116.

"Publishing's New Starlets" (women writers). *U.S. News and World Report* 101 (Dec. 1, 1986): 61–63.

"Showbound with Jayne Anne Phillips." *Art and Antiques*, Feb. 1985, 52.

Simpson, Mona. "An American Beauty" (interview). *Vogue*, July 1984, 117–18.

Skow, John. "*Machine Dreams*" (review). *Time*, July 16, 1984, 69.

Stanton, David M. "An Interview with Jayne Anne Phillips." *Croton Review* 9 (Spring-Summer 1986): 41 + .

Tyler, Anne. "The Wounds of War" (review of *Machine Dreams*). *New York Times Book Review*, July 1, 1984, 3.

"Writing the Second Novel—a Symposium." *New York Times Book Review*, March 17, 1985, 1.

Yardley, Jonathan. "Jayne Anne Phillips: West Virginia Breakdown." *Book World—Washington Post*, June 24, 1984, 3.

MARY LEE SETTLE

"Ambiguity of Steel"

Jane Gentry Vance

Mary Lee Settle's claim to be a major contemporary novelist rests
on *The Beulah Quintet* (*Prisons*, 1973; *O Beulah Land*, 1956; *Know
Nothing*, 1960; *The Scapegoat*, 1980; and *The Killing Ground*, 1982),
the epic story of Beulah Valley in West Virginia. Subtract that work
from her ten novels and those remaining (*The Love Eaters*, 1954; *The
Kiss of Kin*, 1955; *The Clam Shell*, 1971; *Blood Tie*, 1977; and *Celebration*, 1986) are narratively accomplished, thematically wise, but still
not remarkably cohesive or substantial as a body of work. In the
quintet the destinies of several pioneer families of divergent backgrounds (indentured servants from London, illegitimate and/or
younger sons of gentry, the Scotch-Irish, Irish, German, and, later,
Italian) meet, and their lives inextricably intertwine to form a microcosm of American experience.

The quintet traces the forces that bring Beulah into being, sustain
its brief flowering, and dissipate quickly as old manners and values
catch up with the frontier and take root in new ground. Conjuring
images that carry the reader back through 350 years of lived experience, the novels recreate the passions, actions, and ideas that under-
gird the ideology of America. Beginning in 1649 in *Prisons*, with the
ideals of social, political, and religious liberty of Johnny Church, a
twenty-year-old Leveler in Cromwell's New Model Army during the
English Civil Wars, Settle discovers in his rhetoric the formative
American vision of freedom. She follows as his illegitimate son by his
aunt migrates to Virginia and as his descendant, Capt. Jonathan
Lacey, in *O Beulah Land*, settles at Beulah, where he briefly realizes
Church's dreams of social equality and freedom. She picks up Lacey's

descendants, intermarried now with the families of other settlers at Beulah, in *Know Nothing*, as they shape Beulah into a large plantation blighted by slavery and as Johnny Catlett, master of Beulah Plantation, bows to family pressure and fights for the Confederacy. The descendants of the original families, mixed still further in *The Scapegoat*, participate in the preliminary conflicts of the Mine Wars at the Laceys' Seven Stars Coal Mine. Finally, in *The Killing Ground*, the families, now thoroughly intermingled after almost 200 years, attempt to come to terms with the technological age and struggle to recover a sense of identity and liberty in post-industrial West Virginia.

Chronologically, the narrative comes forward from seventeenth-century England through the five books to present-day Canona (a city much like Charleston), near Beulah. However, the impetus of emotion and of suspense, both for writer (by her own account) and for reader, runs backward in time rather than forward. In *The Killing Ground*, novelist Hannah McKarkle comes home in 1980 to speak about her work to a group of old friends. She intends also to investigate the death of her brother, Johnny McKarkle, in 1960 in the drunk tank of the Canona jail, where he was struck by his distant cousin, Jake Catlett. According to Settle, her fantasy in 1954 of that blow bloomed into the great flower of the quintet (RPF, 36).[1] Obsessed with the vision of this scene, Settle felt compelled to discover the forces that brought the two men together in the cell and made them enemies in their ignorance of themselves and of each other. She set out to correct the failures of collective memory that kept Jake and Johnny from knowing that, literally, they spring from the same seed. For in the quintet, as in *Oedipus Rex*, the real drama lies in the step-by-step acquisition of the truth of a lost past. Hannah McKarkle's recovery of her family's story creates the energy and the movement of the whole quintet. And its mystery is the Oedipal mystery: the heroes turn out to be the culprits, and the "solutions" lie in the heroes' discovery of their own true identity.

Essentially, then, the quintet takes the prototypical American consciousness back through time, uncovering layer after layer of willfully forgotten experience until the reader arrives at Johnny Church, who, at the point of his execution by Cromwell, realizes his identity as it is formed by his past as the son of his particular father and mother. The various later protagonists carry the remnant of Church's epiphany as it waxes again briefly at Beulah before the Revolutionary War and then wanes gradually until, in the eighties, it is finally grasped again by Hannah McKarkle who, in the story of the quintet, writes the novels. But Church's reality as a character and the persuasiveness of his vision of his own wholeness and of the ideal of liberty are enhanced greatly by the reader's previous knowledge of Hannah McKarkle, his twentieth-century incarnation. Actually, she is his daughter many times removed, and more important, she is his sister, his Antigone, in rebellion against the social and spiritual constraints that kill. "Of all the volumes," Settle says (RPF, 37), "the most truly autobiographical, the most urged on me by present circumstances, was *Prisons.* . . . Out of fear, and a hope that blasted hopes survive the hopeful, I found *Prisons* and Johnny Church. I am Johnny Church." Hannah McKarkle and Mary Lee Settle both find their identities as novelists, as recoverers of lost histories.

The quintet is best read backward, beginning with *The Killing Ground* and concluding with *Prisons.* One reason the quintet has not been widely appreciated is that most readers naturally start with *Prisons,* which seems fragmentary, difficult to get into, without benefit of the context of the other four novels. But read last, *Prisons* discovers in fitting crescendo the family situations, the personalities, the emotional, economic, and political forces that are the seeds of Hannah and the story she is to write within the story, that of Jake Catlett and Johnny McKarkle. Settle unearths the taproot of American ideas of liberty in Church's voice, which she makes so audible to the reader's ear through her imaginative absorption of the extensive research she did in the actual pamphlets written by soldiers during the Civil War. Each of the other novels, too, gains emotional and intellectual impact from being read in the context of the books that succeed it in actual historical time, for that is the direction of the development of Settle's vision.

Because Settle works, then, from the particular to the general, from the present to the past, and not the other way around as is often the case with historical novelists, the psychological immediacy of her characters is the hallmark of her fiction. In digging for the sources of American experience, the richest vein she mines is her characters' voices. She calls herself "an archaeologist of language";[2] she probes in newspapers, letters, pamphlets, and popular drama of all the periods she treats to get to the bone of individual character, the voices and gestures that will bring back to the present the lived ideas and emotions. She begins with the gesture of Jake Catlett's blow to Johnny McKarkle in the Canona jail, that "carried within it abandoned hopes, old hates and a residue of prejudices. To trace them," she says, "I knew that I was going to have to travel back to when the hates were new, the hopes alive, the prejudices merely contemporary fears" (RPF, 36).

Settle explains her own theory of historical fiction better than any critic. Like Georg Lukacs she believes that "historical fidelity" and inclusiveness arise most often out of the dramatization of "the outwardly insignificant events, the smaller (from without) relationships."[3] Thus, the Beulah novels are set mainly in the periods preceding the great turning points of history: *Prisons*, before Cromwell's eleven-year dictatorship; *O Beulah Land*, in the thirty years before the Revolutionary War; *Know Nothing*, mainly in the decades before the American Civil War; and *The Scapegoat*, in 1912 just before the labor movement became a dominant force in American life.

Settle quotes Nicola Chiaromonte to explain why she writes fiction to "learn something real about individual experience. Any other approach is bound to be general and abstract" (RPF, 1). And fiction, to function as recreated experience, must be predominantly specific and concrete. "Both time and space are distances, and they work for historians and novelists in the same way—not as a gulf, but as a psychic focus. Hindsight—which revises, tears down, discovers trends and explains by concept—has little place in fiction. To try to see, to hear, to share a passion, to become contemporary, is its task" (RPF, 36). She aims, then, to dramatize "what people thought was happening during the times they lived in, rather than what historians tell us was really happening. I never read a single secondary source, or any book published after 1649, when I was working on the first volume (*Prisons*)."[4] Only the imagery of fiction can recover these obscure beginnings. She writes, "By its nature, history is bound in time; fiction is timeless when it reaches the reality of a person, an act or a scene that transcends the words conveying it" (RPF, 1). She cites Homer, Shakespeare, Defoe, Tolstoy, George Garrett (*The Succession*), and Norman Mailer (*Ancient Evenings*) as writers who open to their readers the lived human experience, the genesis of historical events.

Most reviewers of *Prisons* objected to Settle's abdication of what William J. Schafer calls "the large interpretive role of the historical novelist."[5] But she writes:

I think there is an urge that cannot be satisfied by the more disciplined and defined study of history. It is deeper than the surface urge to find our roots. It hears an echo more profound and more elusive than that. So we try to conjure out of the rescued fragments of forgotten time the historic memory that haunts us in dreams, in the residue of language, gesture and prejudice, traced to its genesis. There is a generation whose taproot was cut somewhere in each American past, whether by poverty, diaspora or land enclosure. It is the generation that had to leave home. We inherited from it a sense of loss. . . . We seek a personal identity, and sometimes, with more luck than perseverance, when the memory has been truly evoked, we find it, a historic déjà vu. We have been there somehow and we are there again. It is a way of facing the old, cold passions, the fears, the notions that seemed once to be fact—things that can form nodules deep within the present as black as manganese. (RPF, 1)

The dramatic evocation of these "nodules" is the pulsing heart of Settle's Beulah books. "The fictional process," she writes, "is a mixture of nonchalance, memory, choice, subjective and sensuous vision, formed in the unconscious and raised into reality" (RPF, 36).

One of the purest of these realizations comes to Johnny Church in the crystalline moment when he stands before Cromwell's firing squad. Now he knows why he cannot doff his hat as his father had demanded and as Cromwell now demands. He sees why he must be able to say, "I am freeborn and bow to no man nowhere" (P, 228). When he defies his father and joins the army, he chooses disinheritance, as all Settle's visionary characters must, as Hannah McKarkle does 300 years later in order to be able to rediscover the history that connects her to Johnny Church and tells her who she is. At the end of *The Killing Ground*, Hannah asks, "How far back could the unknown scars go? How deep was the anger behind Jake Catlett's fist?" (KG, 355). Recovering her beginnings in Johnny Church empowers Hannah McKarkle to live freely as an authentic self, as the artist who can write the quintet.

Other characters, who fail to undertake or to complete this quest for identity (Johnny Catlett, in *Know Nothing*, who bows to family pressure and fights for slavery; Beverly Lacey, in *The Scapegoat*, who clings to outmoded paternalistic attitudes toward labor in the family coal mines; and Johnny McKarkle, in *The Killing Ground*, who cannot wrest himself away from his mother), make "the sad incestuous choice" (KG, 340) of conformity to procrustean family expectations and social pressures. Even Hannah strongly feels "the seduction of duty and comfort and compliance, the deep training of a place I had not asked for, earned or prepared." The opposite extreme poses equal danger: she must withstand the "impotent seduction of the rebels, the wild boys like Doggo Cutwright, the Indian killer, Peregrine Lacey [both in *O Beulah Land*], and the one moment of Jake Catlett's fury, the feral edge of what has made us." But Hannah does manage "to grasp as hallowed the choice of disinheritance," exactly as Johnny Church, Johnny Lacey, and Lily Lacey (the latter in *The Scapegoat*) have before her. She carries "that itch for balance between the two extremes, a quality that quarrels with itself, poised between democrat and slaveowner, a dilemma all the way to our founding, that seemed so often to have no place in the pragmatic surviving days of living, but yet had had a place, had built a country, fused dreams into cities seeking always the elusive balance" (KG, 340). This balance, Hannah says, is "the ambiguity of steel, on which I have built my book."

This understanding is the bedrock of Hannah's identity, and of Johnny's and Jake's had they not been cut off from the community of memory. Memory saves; in the possession of history lies the only possibility for a future. "Know thyself," the Beulah books say, seeing the same destruction outside that knowledge as did the Delphic Oracle. Not to know who you are, like Oedipus, to have lost your history, places you in jeopardy of destroying yourself and those whose lives you touch. In Settle's vision the original ideal of America offered the opportunity to establish a political and social context in which the individual would be free to develop toward full realization of self.

Settle's characters struggle both personally and publicly and psychologically and politically. Understanding this, Settle has Cromwell play upon Johnny's gut-deep need for the loving father. As Johnny stands before the frantic, sorrowful Cromwell awaiting judgment, he thinks: "I know he is still there, but I cannot keep track of his raving. No matter, for it is old words, and he is already an old man, usurping in our hearts our father's place. I need you not, Oliver, as metaphor for my father, but there's your danger, for father's a fathom's deeper need than lover, and the war with you is ever-lasting, for it is against the slavery within and the easy fall of the knees" (P, 224). Johnny escapes the "slavery within" by understanding his own father, who pulls himself up from chandler to great landowner, then joins Cromwell as he turns from champion of freedom to protector of a new order of fathers, a new privileged class, very like James I and his nobles.

But like Jesus (whose initials he carries and to whom Settle draws explicit parallels at the end of *Prisons*) and like Socrates, Johnny chooses to die rather than to compromise his conviction of the psychological and political necessity of freedom. Cromwell, manipulating through both his psychological and his political power, identifies himself with God. "I have a warrant from God to do my duty to make this land of England a place fit for the Saint. I promise you, I promise you . . . as our God has promised me . . . 'Thou shalt not be termed Forsaken; neither shall thy land any more be termed Desolate: but thou shalt be called Hephzibah, and thy land Beulah" (P, 225).[6] Quoting Isaiah 62:5, Cromwell betrays this ultimate illusion of power and ironically gives name to the vision that Johnny's descendants will live out.

In *Prisons* Johnny dies victorious, as Jesus and Socrates do, and his vision generates the energy of the development of Beulah, which is to follow. He sees in a dream that "all that sets men apart from the beasts is the act without hope of reward" (P, 206). He chooses death because he understands that life without freedom to grow and to be is not life. Although people will forget the impassioned words of freedom he has written in pamphlets and letters and spoken in assemblies, he says that "at least they can remember that my legs did not buckle, and I did not befoul the way we came together by weeping and howling and begging God's forgiveness for using the heart he gave me and my sight to see" (P, 230). Understanding the previous naïveté of his belief in Cromwell and seeing that "freedom's a costly thing and rare," he still knows that Cromwell "will murder a free heart" (P, 229) when he kills him.

The American amnesia sets in several generations after Church's death, when the English sense of class rears its head in the new world, as the various families begin to want to forget their origins, to shed their own true history. In Beulah Valley, Settle's microcosm of the American experience, the corruption of Church's vision can be exactly dated to 1765, the year Johnny Lacey brings Sally Mason, his aristocratic wife, to the frontier station, where before her arrival all the settlers of various backgrounds (German, Scotch-Irish, English; rich and poor) work together harmoniously for their survival in the wilderness and to create a new order in which they will all be better off than under European manners. But when Sal introduces her silly corruptions of traditional gentility, the snake slithers into Eden. On her first day at Beulah, Sal sees from her window a scene that sets the tone for her frustrating few years on the frontier.

Around one of [her] spreadout quilts the women and children had settled like great birds, the children naked, the women stripped to the waist from their work in the field. None of them said a word, but from time to time one would pass a worn square hand out over the silk that had come from Polly's petticoat, or the piece of scarlet that had been Sal's father's sash. . . .

Sal saw the heavy fingers moving over the scraps of her whole life, laid out like a map for anyone to read, and she ran across the grass and snatched the guilt up into her arms.

"Get away!" she called, as she would have at birds. "Don't ye touch my only fine quilt with your dirty fingers!" (BL, 219)

The bird image recalls the solitary bird woman, raped by Cromwell's soldiers, shrieking and dripping blood, in *Prisons* (114-15), in whom Johnny Church sees all quenched human lives, those unable to claim their freedom. Johnny redeems Sal's rudeness by talking to the women as equals and by compelling Sal to invite them into the house to look at her treasures.

This house, lovingly built by Jonathan in preparation for Sal's coming, deeply disappoints her pretensions. Her dismay at its lack of finish hardens Johnny's happy pride into foreboding.

"Green, green. 'Tis all green—all green like something growed and not built at all," was all he could get her to say, her mouth square under her handblinded eyes. "I never knowed before how poor we was.'"

In her moment of despair and of coming face to face with some vision of herself . . . as in the empty room, Sal neither heard the children nor realized Jonathan was watching her, his face gone blank as an Indian's. She was completely alone in a limbo of poverty, her foot still, of its own accord, testing the rough floor that would never, never be smooth. (BL, 217-18)

In the form of this house, Sal sees the hopelessness of her position as a wife on the frontier, where traditional ideas of breeding and manners, her only real values, are unimportant. Within hours the disheartened Jonathan understands her limitations for the first time and senses that they are ruinous to his dreams for Beulah. God cannot "marry the land in blessedness" if Sal's divisive values have any place there. She stays at Beulah for nine years (1765-1774) until she is unhinged by its challenge to her reality. Later Johnny asks of Jarcey Pentacost, second in command and schoolmaster at Beulah, "What can we become out here? We may have brought the English virtues, but we've brought a cancer, too" (BL, 233).

This, then, is the source of the dangerous forgetting: these beginnings of class consciousness in theoretically classless America. In the quintet the new social mobility distorts the various families' sense of historical continuity, preventing the evolution of truthful community tradition. As the families leave behind humble origins and poverty for status, wealth, and political power, they wish to erase the memory of hard times, of powerlessness, and, sometimes, of criminality. In the *Contemporary Authors* interview, Settle says that her idea was "to set forth the sort of social and political impulses that formed America— the reasons many of our forebears came here. Out of any given 100,000 settlers who came to Virginia from 1675 to 1775 . . . 80,000 would probably be felons. It's extraordinary that no Virginian ever seems to have been descended from any of them—they must all have been sterile."⁷ This all too typical amnesia both springs from and feeds family pride. The resulting sense of aristocracy, misplaced and ludicrous on the frontier, today remains repressive to less privileged family groups in American society. In *The Killing Ground,* Hannah McKarkle, highborn but having grown in awareness, describes the destructiveness of this snobbery. "I saw what we stood for. We, more Anglo than the angels, were models of decorum, we strutted before the apers; we, apers and aped in turn, destroying not by force but by something more evasive, a turning away, in indifference. . . . There was not a voice raised, not a blow struck in the death we dealt and suffered" (KG, 146).

Beginning in *O Beulah Land* and on down through *Know Nothing, The Scapegoat,* and *The Killing Ground,* Settle's characters are to various degrees vulnerable to the ill effects of these manners and this willful forgetting of a past that nevertheless keeps intruding. The nonrebellious, conventional women in Settle's vision guard and perpetuate treacherous family myths. Their motherly and wifely voices urge their kin to procrustean beds of pretentious attitudes and country club manners. In *Know Nothing* old Mrs. Catlett, a Lacey from Virginia, descendant of Johnny Lacey and grandmother of Confederate officer Johnny Catlett, derives her identity from a farfetched family history. "The Catletts now . . . were French. Norman French knights. Their name was really de Chatelet, which means castle. They laid claim to Beulah with a ruby ring and a silver riding crop. It shows what fine folks they were to have such things" (KN, 73). Partly she lies out of her own need to prettify, and partly she merely passes on the distortions of previous family suppressions.

Actually, Jeremiah, the first Catlett at Beulah, was a backwoods Ranter, deported from England, and a squatter on Johnny Lacey's land grant. With his hog, Hagar, he lived in a dirt-floored cabin, a far-cry from the castle of Mrs. Catlett's dream. The silver crop he stole from a land shark, whom he shot point-blank. The shark, in his turn, had stolen the whip from the corpse of a well-to-do English cousin of Johnny Lacey's. The "ruby" in the heirloom ring is found by Hannah Bridewell, a thief and later a conscripted whore for Braddock's army, in a creek on her flight back east across the Endless Mountains after Braddock's defeat at Fort Duquesne in 1755.

Settle sees establishment women, like Mrs. Catlett, as destructive to psychic growth and creative being. They, in collusion with the men, transmit inaccurate stories of who they are and how they came to be. In *The Scapegoat* a rebel Lacey, Althea, distant cousin and eventually sister-in-law of Sally Brandon (later McKarkle, and Hannah's and Johnny's smothering mother in *The Killing Ground*) describes Sally's snobbery and its background. "Sally Brandon, the stuck-up skinny-necked bitch . . . whatever needle she wants to stick in me. You don't wear this with that and you don't eat that with this and you don't use them with those and these with they, to which my answer to my beloved sister-in-law is Fuck you Miss Sally, if you'll pardon my French. They make me downright sick. All of their Senator Daniel Neill this and Senator Daniel Neill that. Senator Neill was a war profiteering son of a bitch and they all know it" (S, 161). Senator Neill, who left office in disgrace, founds their petty sense of propriety. His granddaughter Sally, namesake of Sally Lacey of Beulah, culminates in the quintet the role of women as guardians of the mythos of false culture.

From *O Beulah Land* on through the remaining three novels, this repressive sense of position, based on false history and corrupted memory, dominates increasingly, until in *The Killing Ground*, it destroys Johnny McKarkle, whose existence is choked by his mother's sense of class and the restrictions it lays on his life. He is struck and killed in the Canona jail by his poor relation, Jake Catlett, who knows him, but whom he does not know since Jake is socially inferior. Jake strikes out at the unearned privilege he hears in Johnny's voice, against all that has been denied to the resentful cousin by chances of death, marriage, and inheritance. Ultimately, Johnny is rich and Jake is poor because one's ancestor inherited bottomland at Beulah where coal was discovered and the other inherited higher ground where it was not.

While the repressive social forces eviscerate the men in the last two novels of the quintet, the women's voices take on strength and promise anew the freedom for which the earlier men like Johnny Church and Johnny Lacey have fought. One of the strongest voices in the novels belongs to Mother Jones, the real-life union organizer, who comes to the Beulah coalfields in 1912, looking like "somebody's grandmother" (S, 21). "Old woman looked like the queen of England, and called herself Mother Jones like she borned them all. Cussed like a section foreman. . . . Her and her lace jabot" (S, 55). Mother Jones's voice is one of Settle's most significant archaeological finds and most imaginative creations. No records of any speeches of hers were extant until Settle unearthed a deposition that included a transcript of one. Her voice, as Settle extrapolates it, carries the vision of freedom that began with Johnny Church and that the Beulah men have lost. Settle makes immediate the reality of Mother Jones's personality and the power of her voice to inspire.

At the end of *The Killing Ground*, Hannah McKarkle, heir of the voice of Johnny Church, finds her power in having recovered the memory of who she is. The voice she discovers, the true voice of her families' history, becomes the narrative of *The Beulah Quintet*. Hannah becomes the novelist who resurrects Johnny Church and late in the twentieth century recovers his idea of freedom from the buried past that determines the present they all live. The search carries her back 350 years. "How the past goads us! We move toward tomorrow but the past informs us" (P, 139), thinks Johnny Church as he begins to know what fate awaits him as Cromwell surrounds Burford village in the Cotswolds. Without memory there is no real identity, personal or communal. Without identity there is no self. Without self there is no being. In *The Beulah Quintet*, the process of fiction is lifesaving.

As history inspires and shapes the Beulah novels, so myth inspires and shapes *Blood Tie* and *Celebration*. Although *Blood Tie* dramatizes the relation between the ancient mythic world and the modern workaday one and *Celebration* deftly interweaves the stories of its four middle-aged main characters struggling toward lives and minds of their own, still these two best of Settle's other five novels lack the vision and insight of the Beulah epic. But the two pose the same questions as the quintet and are well crafted and wise.

Blood Tie takes place in the early seventies in Turkey, in what was ancient Greek Ionia. The symbolism of the novels centers on Mt. Latmos where the grave of Endymion and a temple to the fertility moon goddess, Artemis, are somewhere hidden. The characters, caught in webs of power that reach back into that mythic past, know themselves and these forces only superficially, and several are destroyed by their lack of awareness. Like the quintet, *Blood Tie* asks, "How far back did the accident that had taken her [a character who drowns] go?" (BT, 104). Since no event in Settle's world is accidental, she traces the causes back through the lives of the characters to the end of the Caliphate in 1923 and ultimately into the prehistorical era of the origins of the Endymion myth. The characters who learn from suffering and who come to know, as Ataturk said, that earth, "this hell, this heaven is ours" (BT, 381) know what Settle calls "the ambiguity of steel." Ariadne, the pivotal figure in the story, says this knowledge "costs too much" (BT, 320), this rare and most worthwhile human achievement.

Celebration, too, celebrates the power of the Great Goddess, the moon in all her phases, ageless symbol of "the power and beauty and indifference of God" (C, 277). A less successful novel than *Blood Tie*, *Celebration*'s four separate stories share backgrounds of myth:

Greek, African, Middle Eastern, and Chinese. Settle pulls tricks out of the old bag of narrative devices to get all these stories told, relying too heavily on flashbacks and hallucination. Because of these mechanisms, Teresa, the earth character, the center of the story, does not come alive convincingly, and the magnetism that Settle claims for her remains an attribution. Similarly, the perspective on issues of social class, so central to Settle's focus, is not clear as it is in the quintet and in *Blood Tie*, where upper-class manners and arrogance are unambiguously oppressive and divisive. While Settle attributes to Teresa the rejection of upper-class values, she undercuts this claim by the extent to which Teresa's life is shaped and guarded by these values. In the end the Goddess, the moon, dropping her light on murdered and murderers alike, embodies the knowledge of both death and the simultaneous immortality we can experience through the living whole in which we are individual dying parts. This ambiguity dominates this novel as well. And the voices of the characters, reaching back into their own experience and into the mythic past, struggle to articulate this hard-won understanding.

Mary Lee Settle is a writer who believes in words, in language, in voice: the power of words to name, the power of language to teach, and the power of voice to create freedom, articulate memory, and express identity. She sees history and its telling as essential for the health (i.e., the wholeness) of the self and the community. She is a novelist whose phrases ring unabashedly, who knows she is doing well, whose vision bravely confronts the fundamental ambiguity of the human condition, its lack of any comforting absolutes. Understanding is Settle's primary value—understanding of the oneness of all individuals; of the fluidity of past, present, and future; and of the necessity for freedom to become oneself within the limits of the ambiguities. She sums up her aims best at the end of "Recapturing the Past in Fiction." "In our bewildered time, when we feel powerless, perhaps we need to recognize through looking at the past that doubt is timeless, change the only norm and accepted 'facts' too often passing notions. We can learn to trust to understanding instead of the frozen certainties we yearn for, and for which we might surrender the birthright earned by nameless people through the 300 years of our becoming" (RPF, 37).

NOTES

1. In this essay Mary Lee Settle's books and one article are identified in the following way, and page numbers are given in parentheses: "Recapturing the Past in Fiction" (RPF); *Prisons* (P); *The Killing Ground* (KG); *O Beulah*

Land (BL); *Know Nothing* (KN); *The Scapegoat* (S); *Blood Tie* (BT); *Celebration* (C).

2. Mary Lee Settle, reading and commentary at Kentucky State University, Frankfort, Nov. 18, 1982.

3. Georg Lukacs, *The Historical Novel*, trans. Hannah and Stanley Mitchell (Boston: Beacon Press, 1962), 42. See Joyce Coyne Dyer's "Mary Lee Settle's *Prisons:* Taproots History," *Southern Literary Journal* 17, no. 1 (Fall 1984) for a helpful discussion of Settle's theory of historical fiction as it relates to *Prisons*.

4. John F. Baker, interview, *Contemporary Authors*, 89, ed. Frances C. Locher (Detroit: Gale Research Co., 1980), 467.

5. William J. Schafer, "Mary Lee Settle's *Beulah Quintet:* History Darkly, through a Single-Lens Reflex," *Appalachian Journal* 10 (Autumn 1982): 80.

6. Dyer, *"Prisons,"* 35. Her explanation of the Beulah passage from *Isaiah* is comprehensive.

7. Baker interview, *Contemporary Authors*, 467.

A Selected Bibliography of Writings by
MARY LEE SETTLE

Jane Gentry Vance and Mickey Pearlman

BOOKS

The Love Eaters. London: Heinemann, 1954; New York: Harper, 1954; Scribner, 1986.

The Kiss of Kin. New York: Harper, 1955; Scribner, 1986.

O Beulah Land. New York: Viking, 1956; Scribner, 1986.

Know Nothing. New York: Viking, 1960. Reprinted as *Pride's Promise*. New York: Pinnacle, 1976; Ballantine, 1981.

Fight Night on a Sweet Saturday. New York: Viking, 1964.

All the Brave Promises. New York: Delacorte/Seymour Lawrence, 1966; Ballantine, 1980.

The Story of Flight. (juvenile) New York: Random House, 1967.

The Clam Shell. New York: Delacorte/Seymour Lawrence, 1971; Scribner, 1987.

The Scopes Trial: The State of Tennessee versus John Thomas Scopes. New York: Franklin Watts, 1972.

Prisons. New York: Putnam's, 1973. Republished as *The Long Road to Paradise*. London: Constable, 1974; Ballantine, 1981.

Blood Tie. Boston: Houghton Mifflin, 1977; Scribner, 1986.
The Scapegoat. New York: Random House, 1980; Ballantine, 1982.
The Killing Ground. New York: Farrar, Straus & Giroux, 1982; Bantam, 1983.
Water World.: New York: Lodestar, 1984.
Celebration. New York: Farrar, Straus & Giroux, 1986.

ARTICLES, REVIEWS, STORIES

"Senator Burney's American Dream." *Paris Review* 2 (Fall/Winter 1954/55): 114–29.
"The Old Wives' Tale." *Harper's* 211 (Sept. 1955): 73–78. Reprinted in *Prize Stories 1957: The O. Henry Awards,* edited by Paul Engle, 241–61. Garden City, N.Y.: Doubleday, 1957.
"Paragraph Eleven." In *The Girl in the Black Raincoat: Variations on a Theme,* edited by George Garrett, 103–8. New York: Duell, Sloan and Pearce, 1966.
"Excerpt from Novel-in-Progress." *Blue Ridge Review* 1 (1978): 26–31.
Review of *Woody Guthrie: A Life,* by J. Klein. *New York Times Book Review,* Dec. 7, 1980, 3 + .
"Work of Art or Power Tools (Crisis in Publishing)." *Virginia Quarterly Review* 57 (1981): 1–14.
Review of *The Sea Runners,* by I. Doig. *New York Times Book Review,* Oct. 3, 1982, 9 + .
Review of *The Barefoot Brigade,* by D.C. Jones. *New York Times Book Review,* Oct. 3, 1982, 9 + .
"The Story of a Company Man." *Nation,* Dec. 3, 1983, 559–62.
"Recapturing the Past in Fiction." *New York Times Book Review,* Feb. 12, 1984, 1 + .
"Book Awards." *America* 151 (Sept. 1–8, 1984): 110–14.
Review of *The Weaker Vessel,* by Antonia Fraser. *New York Times Book Review,* Nov. 18, 1984, 40.
"How Pleasant to Meet Mr. Eliot." *New York Times Book Review,* Dec. 16, 1984, 10–12.
"Atlas of a Writer's World." *New York Times Magazine,* Oct. 6, 1985; 28–30.
[With others] "The Writer in Our World: A Symposium." *Triquarterly* 65 (1986): 154–68, 235–43, 260–65, 266–73, 277–309.
" 'London—1944.' " *Virginia Quarterly Review* 63 (1987): 565–86.
"Somerset Maugham." *Yale Review* 76 (Spring, 1987): 428–39.
"If I Had Five Minutes with the Pope." *America* 157 (Sept. 12, 1987): 126–35.
"Legendary Cities." *New York Times Magazine,* Oct. 4, 1987, S16.
"The 30's and the 40's." *Woman's Day,* Oct. 27, 1987, 66 + .
"Introduction" to *The Prodigal Women,* by Nancy Hale. New York: NAL Plume, 1988.

A Selected Bibliography of Writings about MARY LEE SETTLE

Jane Gentry Vance and Mickey Pearlman

Amorese, Cynthia. "Interview with Mary Lee Settle." *Commonwealth: The Magazine of Virginia,* Jan. 1981.

Bach, Peggy. "The Searching Voice and Vision of Mary Lee Settle." *Southern Review* 20 (Autumn 1984): 842–50.

Baer, Elizabeth. "Retrospective on Mary Lee Settle." *Belles Lettres* 3 (May/June 1988): 12.

Bain, Robert, Joseph M. Flora, and Louis D. Rubin, Jr., eds. *Southern Writers: A Biographical Dictionary,* 404. Baton Rouge: Louisiana State Univ. Press, 1979.

Baker, John F. "Interview with Mary Lee Settle." In *Contemporary Authors* 89:467. Detroit: Gale Research Co., 1980.

Betts, Doris. Review of *Celebration. America* 156 (Oct. 18, 1986): 211–12.

Blackford, S.D. "All the Brave Promises." *Sewanee Review* 90 (1982): 305–13.

———. "Women at War (New Books of Memoirs)." *Sewanee Review* 90 (1982): 305-13.

"Blood Tie" (review). *New York Times Book Review,* May 4, 1986, 43.

"Blood Tie" (review). *New York Times Book Review,* Dec. 7, 1986, 82.

Boyd, William. *"Celebration"* (review). *New York Times Book Review,* Oct. 26, 1986, 14.

Brown, Laurie L. "Interviews with Seven Contemporary Writers." In *Women Writers of the Contemporary South,* edited by P.W. Prenshaw, 3–22. Jackson: Univ. Press of Mississippi, 1984. Also in *Southern Quarterly* 21 (1983): 3–22.

Brown, R. *"The Scapegoat"* (review). *New Republic* 183 (Dec. 27, 1980): 37–39.

Broyard, Anatole. Review of *The Scapegoat. New York Times,* Oct. 22, 1980, 2.

"Celebration" (review). *Publishers Weekly* 230 (Aug. 22, 1986): 79.

"Celebration" (review). *Library Journal* 111 (Sept. 1, 1986): 216.

Contemporary Authors 89: 466–68. Detroit: Gale Research Co., 1980.

Doctorow, E.L. "Mother Jones Had Some Advice" (review of *The Scapegoat*). *New York Times Book Review,* Oct. 26, 1980, 1 + .

Dong S. "P.E.N. Establishes New Award for Fiction." *Publishers Weekly* 217 (June 20, 1980):19–20.

Dyer, Joyce Coyne. "Mary Lee Settle's *Prisons:* Taproots History." *Southern Literary Journal* 17 (Fall 1984): 26–39.

———. "Embracing the Common: Mary Lee Settle in World War II." *Appalachian Journal* 12 (Winter 1985): 127–34.

————. "*The Clam Shell:* Mary Lee Settle on East Coast Gentility." *Appalachian Journal* 13 (Winter 1986): 171–83.

Garrett, George. "Mary Lee Settle's *Beulah Land Triology.*" In *Rediscoveries,* edited by David Madden, 171–78. New York: Crown, 1971.

————. "An Invitation to the Dance: A Few Words on the Art of Mary Lee Settle." *Blue Ridge Review* 1 (1978): 18–24.

————. *Dictionary of Literary Biography: American Novelists since World War II,* 2nd ser., 6: 28–89. Detroit: Gale Research Co., 1978–1980.

————. *Understanding Mary Lee Settle.* Columbia, S.C.: Univ. of South Carolina Press, 1988.

Godwin, Gail. "An Epic of West Virginia" (review of *The Killing Ground*). *New Republic,* June 16, 1982, 30–32.

Gunton, Sharon R., ed. *Contemporary Literary Criticism* 19: 408–12. Detroit: Gale Research Co., 1981.

Hagel, Margaret M. "*Water World*" (review). *School Library Journal* 31 (Sept. 1984): 133–35.

"Hard Road to a Boxed Edition." *Publishers Weekly* 233 (Feb. 12, 1988): 65.

Hicks, Granville. Foreword to *O Beulah Land,* xiii-xvii. New York: Ballantine, 1965.

Houston, R. "*The Scapegoat*" (review). *Nation* 231 (Nov. 8, 1980): 469–71.

Jenks, Tom. "How Writers Live Today." *Esquire,* Aug. 1985, 123–28.

Joyner, Nancy Carol. "Mary Lee Settle's Connections: Class and Clothes in the Beulah Quintet." *Southern Quarterly,* 22 (Fall 1983): 33–45.

————. "Mary Lee Settle's Connections." In *Women Writers of the Contemporary South,* edited by P.W. Prenshaw, 166–78. Jackson: Univ. Press of Mississippi, 1984.

"Key West Dialogue." *New York Times Magazine,* March 18, 1984; 592–96.

"*The Kiss of Kin*" (review). *New York Times Book Review,* Sept. 28, 1986, 42.

Latham, Aaron. "The End of the Beulah Quintet" (review of *The Killing Ground*). *New York Times Book Review,* July 11, 1982, 1+.

Neal, G. Dale. "Filling an Empty Room—The Art of Mary Lee Settle." *Wake Forest University Student,* Spring 1980, 18–22.

O'Conner, Patricia T. "New and Noteworthy" (review of *The Love Eaters*). *New York Times Book Review,* Sept. 28, 1986, 42.

O'Hara, J.D. "Reflections on Recent Prose." *New England Review* 3 (1981): 450–64.

Prenshaw, Peggy Whitman. "Introduction." In *Women Writers of the Contemporary South,* edited by P.W. Prenshaw, vii-xii. Jackson: Univ. Press of Mississippi, 1984.

Rosenberg, B. "Mary Lee Settle and the Tradition of Historical Fiction." *South Atlantic Quarterly* 86 (Summer 1987): 229–43.

Rosenfelt, Deborah S. "Getting into the Game—American-Women Writers and the Radical Tradition." *Women's Studies International Forum* 9 (1986): 363–72.

Sanoff, Alvin P. "Life Is Really a Dance" (interview). *U.S. News and World Report,* Dec. 22, 1986, 64.

Schafer, William J. "Mary Lee Settle's *Beulah Quintet:* History Darkly, through a Single-Lens Reflex." *Appalachian Journal* (Autumn 1982): 77–86.

"Settle May Write 'Gone with Wind" Sequel." *Charleston Gazette,* Jan. 24, 1981, 11.

Shattuck, Roger "A Talk with Mary Lee Settle." *New York Times Book Review,* Oct. 26, 1980, 43–46.

———. Introduction to *Beulah Trilogy.* New York: Ballantine, 1981.

Smith, Wendy. "*Publishers Weekly* Interviews." *Publishers Weekly* 230 (Oct. 10, 1986): 73–75.

Steel, Edward M., Jr. "Review Essay: Fact or Fiction" (review of *The Scapegoat*). *West Virginia History* 42 (Spring-Summer 1981): 314–15.

Swaim, K.M. "A Fictional Gloss on the History of the 1640's (Milton in Mary Lee Settle's *Prisons*)." *Milton Quarterly* 15 (1981): 97–98.

Taormina, C.A. "On Time with Mary Lee Settle." *Blue Ridge Review* 1 (1978): 8–17.

Tyler, Anne. "Mary Lee Settle: Mining a Rich Vein." *Book World—Washington Post,* Sept. 28, 1980, 1 +.

Vance, Jane Gentry. "Mary Lee Settle's *The Beulah Quintet:* History Inherited, History Created." *Southern Literary Journal* 17 (Fall 1984): 40–53.

———. "Historical Voices in Mary Lee Settle's *Prisons:* 'Too Far in Freedom.' " *Mississippi Quarterly* 38 (Fall 1985): 391–413.

Zieger, R.H. "The Labor Novel Strikes Again—Two Books of the 70's." *Journal of American Culture* 4 (1981): 37–47.

Notes on the Writers

TONI CADE BAMBARA was born March 25, 1939, in New York. She received a B.A. from Queens College in 1959 (in Theatre Arts) and an M.A. from City College of New York in 1963. She taught in the SEEK Program at City College and was an assistant professor at Rutgers, a visiting professor of African American Studies at Duke, Atlanta University, and Emory, and an artist-in-residence at Spelman and Stephens colleges and at the Neighborhood Art Center of Atlanta. Bambara won the Zora Neale Hurston Society Award, an NEH Literary Grant, and the Langston Hughes Medallion. She is currently a filmmaker and videomaker in Philadelphia and has recently completed *Till Blessing Comes*, based on the Atlanta missing and murdered children. It will be published by Random House/Vintage in 1988.

JOAN DIDION was born December 5, 1934, to a fifth-generation California family. She received her B.A. from the University of California at Berkeley in 1956 and won *Vogue* Magazine's Prix de Paris and worked in Paris as an editor until 1963. She won the Bread Loaf Fellowship in Fiction and, after marrying John Gregory Dunne in January 1964, returned to Los Angeles. She lives near the beach with Dunne; they have a daughter, Quintana. *Play It As It Lays* (1970) won an award from the National Institute of Arts and Letters; *A Book of Common Prayer*, her 1977 novel, was a best-seller; *The White Album* was nominated for the American Book Award in nonfiction; and *Democracy* (1984) was nominated for the Los Angeles Times Book Prize in fiction.

LOUISE ERDRICH was born July 6, 1954, in Little Falls, Minnesota, and now lives in Cornish, New Hampshire, with her husband, Michael Dorris, author of *A Yellow Raft in Blue Water* (1987), and their five children. She grew up near the Turtle Mountain Reservation in North Dakota, where her German-born father and Chippewa mother both worked for the Bureau of Indian Affairs. *Love Medicine*, her first novel, won the National Book Critics Circle Award for the best work of fiction published in 1984. *The Beet Queen* (1986) is the second novel in an expected trilogy about her mixed European and Chippewa heritage. She considers herself a survivor, one of 1 million living Native Americans who must tell the stories of the 12 to 20 million Native Americans who lived here long ago.

GAIL GODWIN was born June 18, 1937, in Birmingham, Alabama. She received her B.A. (1959) in journalism from the University of North Carolina and an M.A. (1960) and Ph.D. (1971) in English from the University of Iowa. Although she is a transplanted southerner who lives in Woodstock, New York, her rebellious female protagonists are usually southern-born and southern-bred. Godwin was awarded a National Endowment for the Arts grant (1974-75) and a Guggenheim Fellowship (1975-76) and has been a fellow of the Center for Advanced Studies at the University of Illinois (1971-72). Among her novels, *Violet Clay* (1978), *A Mother and Two Daughters* (1982), and *The Finishing School* were Book-of-the-Month Club alternate selections.

MARY GORDON was born December 8, 1949, on Long Island, New York, and now lives in New Paltz, New York. She received a B.A. in 1971 at Barnard College and an M.A. in 1973 from Syracuse. *Final Payments* (1978), her first novel, was a Literary Guild selection. The book's critical and popular success won her a paperback contract with Ballantine Books. Her first collection of stories, *Temporary Shelter*, is, in part, about poor, immigrant Irish Catholics from New York City and the Long Island rich.

ALISON LURIE, who was born September 3, 1926, in Chicago, writes about articulate, educated, and sophisticated members of the upper middle class. She received an A.B. from Radcliffe College in 1947 and has been teaching at Cornell since 1969. She was a Yaddo Foundation Fellow in 1963, 1964, and 1966 and won a Guggenheim grant (1965-66) and a Rockefeller Foundation grant (1967-68), among others. Lurie's novel *Foreign Affairs* (1984) won the American Academy of Arts and Letters Award in literature (1978), the American Book Award nomination in fiction (1984), the National Book Critics Circle Award nomination for best work of fiction (1984), and the Pulitzer Prize in fiction for 1985.

JOYCE CAROL OATES was born June 16, 1938, in the small town of Lockport, New York, in Erie County, which she often calls Eden County in her short stories and novels. She earned her B.A. and graduated Phi Beta Kappa in 1960 from Syracuse University and received an M.A. from the University of Wisconsin in 1961. She is one of America's most prolific writers and since 1978 has published more than fifteen books with trade and smaller presses and has been elected to the National Academy and Institute of Arts and Letters. Oates is now a writer-in-residence at Princeton where she and her husband, Raymond Smith, publish *Ontario Review*. Three of her plays, *Ontological Proof of My Existence* (1972), *Miracle Play* (1973), and *Triumph of the Spider Monkey* (1979), were produced Off-Broadway in the seventies.

JAYNE ANNE PHILLIPS was born July 19, 1952, in Buckhannon, West Virginia, and now lives in Cambridge, Massachusetts. She received a B.A. from West Virginia University in 1974 and an M.A. from the University of Iowa in 1978. Phillips won the Pushcart Prize in 1977 and 1979, a National Endowment for the Arts Fellowship (1978), and the Sue Kaufman Award for First Fiction from the American Academy and Institute of Arts and Letters (1980) for *Black Tickets* (1979). She received a Bunting Institute Fellowship from Radcliffe College. Her first novel, *Machine Dreams* (1984), was highly acclaimed. *Fast Lanes* (1987), her latest collection of short stories, is about life in the ghettos and on her native soil of West Virginia.

SUSAN FROMBERG SCHAEFFER was born March 25, 1941, in Brooklyn where she still lives. She received her B.A. (1961), M.A. (with honors) (1963), and Ph.D. (with honors) (1966) from the University of Chicago and holds the Broeklundian Chair of English at Brooklyn College, where she has been teaching since 1966. Schaeffer has given readings of her poetry at Yale, the University of Massachusetts, the University of Texas, and elsewhere. *Anya* (1974) won the Edward Lewis Wallant Award and the Friends of Literature Award. *Granite Lady* was nominated for the National Book Award (1974), and *Time in Its Flight* and *Love* were Book-of-the-Month-Club selections. She has published five volumes of poetry and two children's novels.

MARY LEE SETTLE was born July 29, 1918, in Charleston, West Virginia, and now lives in Charlottesville, Virginia. She attended Sweet Briar College (1936-38), served with the Women's Auxiliary Air Force (1942-44), and was associated with the Office of War Information in England (1944-45). Settle won Guggenheim fellowships (1957-58, 1959-60) and a National Book Award for *Blood Ties* (1977), her ninth book and her eighth novel. Most of her work has been published by distinguished publishers in Great Britain, including the volumes of her "Beulah Land Trilogy"—*O Beulah Land* (1956), *Know Nothing* (1960), and *Fight Night on a Sweet Saturday* (1964). Settle was a model for Powers and Harry Conover in the late thirties; she has been "discovered" several times by critics but has never been neglected by other writers.

Notes on the Contributors

RACHEL M. BROWNSTEIN, professor of English at Brooklyn College and the Graduate School of the City University of New York, is the author of *Becoming a Heroine: Reading about Women in Novels.*

FRANK R. CUNNINGHAM, formerly Senior Fulbright Lecturer at the University of Cracow, is professor of English at the University of South Dakota, where he teaches modern American literature, criticism, and literature/film. Author of fifty articles and essay-reviews in such books and journals as *American Writers, Critical Essays on Eugene O'Neill, Sewanee Review,* and *American Literature,* he has recently completed a book, *The Literary Vision of Sidney Lumet's Major Films.*

KATHERINE USHER HENDERSON, professor of English at the College of New Rochelle, is the author of *Joan Didion* (1981) and coauthor of *Half Humankind: Contexts and Texts of the Controversy about Women in England, 1540-1640,* as well as articles on contemporary American fiction.

ANNE HIEMSTRA is a doctoral candidate at Columbia University.

PHYLLIS LASSNER teaches women's studies and composition at the University of Michigan. She has written about the psychodynamics of teaching writing and about modern women writers, including a study of the World War II novels of Elizabeth Bowen and Rose Macaulay. Her feminist analysis of Bowen's fiction will be published in England.

MARVIN MAGALANER is the author of several books on James Joyce, and of *Katherine Mansfield,* and is coeditor of *A Reader's Guide to Great Twentieth-Century English Novels.* He now teaches literature at New York University.

JOHN W. MAHON, associate professor of English at Iona College, recently completed a two-year term as director of Institutional Planning. He has edited a Festschrift in honor of the Shakespearean scholar Harold Jenkins, and has published on Shakespeare, Evelyn Waugh, and Paul Theroux. He teaches sixteenth-century and modern British/Irish, American, and world literature.

MICKEY PEARLMAN (Ph.D. CUNY) is the author of *Re-Inventing Reality: Patterns and Characters in the Novels of Muriel Spark* (forthcoming), *Tillie Olsen* (forthcoming), and many critical/biographical articles on women authors. She is also editor of the forthcoming *Mother Puzzles: The Theme of Mothers and Daughters in Contemporary American Literature.* She taught at Iona College for eight years.

KATHARINE M. ROGERS, professor of English at Brooklyn College and the Graduate School of the City University of New York, has published *The Troublesome Helpmate: A History of Misogyny in Literature, William Wycherley,* and *Feminism in Eighteenth-Century England,* as well as numerous articles. Her latest work, coedited with William McCarthy, is *The Meridian Anthology of Early Women Writers: British Literary Women from Aphra Behn to Maria Edgeworth.*

JANE GENTRY VANCE is a poet whose work appears in recent issues of *Harvard Magazine* and *Journal of Kentucky Studies.* An associate professor in the Honors Program at the University of Kentucky, her articles on contemporary novelists have appeared in *Southern Literary Journal, Mississippi Quarterly,* and *Kentucky Review.*

MARTHA M. VERTREACE, poet-in-residence at Kennedy-King College, Chicago, is the author of *Second House from the Corner* (Kennedy-King College Press, 1986). Her poetry has appeared in *College English, Midwest Quarterly,* and *Images.* She received the 1986 Illinois Association of Teachers/Harcourt Brace Jovanovich Award for excellence in professional writing. In 1987 the Illinois Arts Council granted her a literary award for her poem "Trade Secrets." Her chapbooks *Artist Proof* and *Entering the Dream* will be published in 1988.

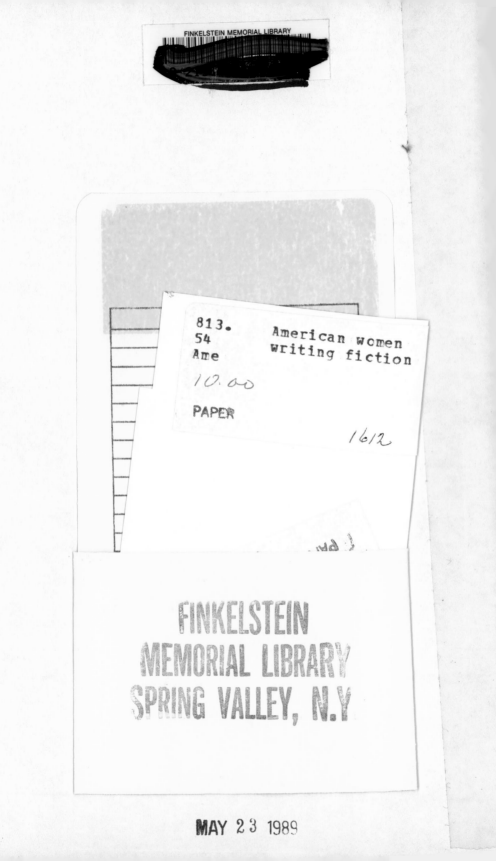